THE YESHUA PROTOCOL

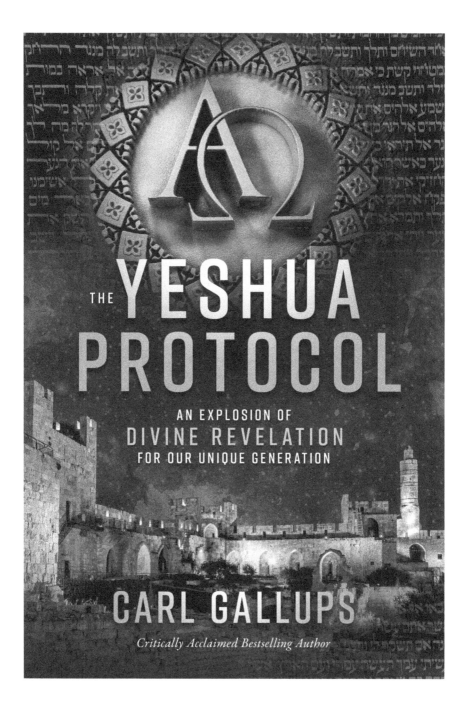

THE YESHUA PROTOCOL

AN EXPLOSION OF DIVINE REVELATION
FOR OUR UNIQUE GENERATION

CARL GALLUPS

Critically Acclaimed Bestselling Author

DEFENDER

CRANE, MO

The Yeshua Protocol
By Carl Gallups

Defender Publishing
Crane, MO 65633
© 2022 Thomas Horn
All Rights Reserved. Published 2022.

Printed in the United States of America.

ISBN: 978-1-948014-60-1
A CIP catalog record of this book is available from the Library of Congress.

Cover design by Jeffrey Mardis.

Dedicated to the eternal praise of Yeshua Ha Mashiach—
Jesus the Messiah.
The name above all names.

✧

Let them praise the name of the LORD: for His name alone is excellent;
His glory above the earth and heaven.
PSALM 148:13, KJV

Other Bestselling Books by Carl Gallups
From Defender Publishing

Glimpses of Glory
(March 2022)

The Summoning
(January 2021)

Masquerade
(March 2020)

The Rabbi, the Secret Message, and the Identity of Messiah
(February 2019)

Gods of the Final Kingdom
(July 2019)

Gods of Ground Zero
(October 2018)

Gods and Thrones
(October 2017)

Acknowledgements

To my precious wife, Pam. Always by my side.

To all the amazing staff at Defender Publishing, especially CEO Dr. Tom Horn. I cannot thank you enough for your kindness, tenacity, and encouragement through the years. Without you, a huge part of my overall ministry endeavors would be sorely lacking. You are a genuine blessing from the Lord.

Along these lines, I must once again give a very special thanks to Defender's editor, Angie Peters. Your patient and incisive editing is truly a thing to behold! You are a joy to work with. I am deeply grateful to you.

To Jeffrey Mardis, cover designer. I am always stunned not only by the sheer beauty of your designs, but by how you so adeptly capture the essence of my books on the very first visual the readers see. Thank you for yet another home run!

And to my long-time brother in the Lord, dear friend, and associate in the Kingdom work, Messianic Rabbi Zev Porat of Tel Aviv, Israel. Thank you so much for your priceless and insightful additions to this book.

A Word from the Author

I've been prayerfully contemplating the idea for this book for the last several years. I'm grateful the Lord has enabled me to finally bring it to life.

If you've read any of my other works, you will recognize my former law-enforcement background as well as my passion for teaching the Word of God in this book's general movement and approach. Due to the combination of those two life callings, I truly enjoy unraveling profound biblical mysteries that might aid the reader in pondering the cavernous depths of God's majesty, as well as His eternal plan for our lives.

So, in the next few chapters, a biblically contextual foundation is set forth that addresses the overall premise of the journey we'll be taking. As we proceed, we'll systematically collect the evidence necessary to back up what we're uncovering. Piece by piece, we'll examine the metaphorical fingerprints, scientific analysis, and DNA evidence, as well as eyewitness testimony, expert testimony, closed-circuit television (CCTV) footage, and so forth.

The book begins and ends with several chapters of immersive narrative, plunging us into the very last days of Jesus' earthly ministry and the lives of some of those around Him. Hopefully, this technique will help us "feel" the thrill of what will eventually be unwrapped throughout our biblical expedition.

So, hang in there with me. Enjoy the ride as you savor even the smallest elements of each surprise, especially as they begin to meld into a startling glimpse of the unspeakable glory of our Savior. The deeper we go, the more stunning the picture will become.

Keep in mind that our journey is heading toward something significant and relevant concerning the days in which we live, as well as your own personal walk with Yeshua.

Thank you for turning to the next page.

C. G.

The name of God is uniformly treated in Scripture as something very different from a mere arrangement of letters or an arbitrary vocal sound. The name of God was not of man, nor from man, but of his own direct revelation.... Like the "word" of God, it cannot be dissociated from God himself. It is in some sense an extension outwards, into the sphere of the created and sensible, of the ineffable virtues of the Godhead itself.[1]

~DR. H. D. M. SPENCE-JONES

From now on I will tell you of new things, of hidden things unknown to you. They are created now, and not long ago; you have not heard of them before today. So you cannot say, "Yes, I knew of them."

~Isaiah 48:6–7

CONTENTS

PART VIII

THE NAME

PART IX

THE CREATION

PART X

THE REVEALING

PART I

THE JOURNEY

Scriptural Background

On the Emmaus Road
> And beginning with Moses and all the Prophets, Jesus explained to them what was said in all the Scriptures concerning himself.
> ~LUKE 24:27

On the Night of the Resurrection
> Jesus said to them, "This is what I told you while I was still with you: Everything must be fulfilled that is written about me in the Law of Moses, the Prophets and the Psalms." **Then he opened their minds so they could understand the Scriptures.**
> ~LUKE 24:44–45, EMPHASIS ADDED

At the Ascension—Forty Days after the Resurrection
> After his suffering, he **presented himself to them** and gave **many convincing proofs** that he was alive. He **appeared to them over a period of forty days** and **spoke about the kingdom of God.**
> ~ACTS 1:3, EMPHASIS ADDED

I

THE ESCAPE

The whole thing was still a jumbled mess of horror.

Cleopas and James were on the run.

The two friends, members of the larger circle of Yeshua's disciples, were putting as much distance as they could between themselves and Jerusalem.

The men scurried along the narrow, rock-paved Roman thoroughfare, trying to conceal themselves by blending in with the other travelers.[2] They were only two among the larger throng of people leaving Jerusalem's Passover festivities. The men knew where they would go first, but had no idea where they would go next...or what kind of life would await them in the days to come.[3]

They were still in a stupor from what had transpired over the last several days. So, they ambled along the best they could, keeping their heads low and their feet moving full speed ahead. They just needed to get some miles under their belts, to try to ease the pain of the travesties they were leaving behind, and they hoped nobody recognized them as they were leaving.

Right now, Cleopas and James[4] were headed to Emmaus. It would be their first stop. Once there, out of relative danger, they would evaluate their options. The village was only about seven miles from Jerusalem.[5] But that was far enough to at least get away from most of the crowds, especially the Jerusalem authorities who would surely be looking for them.

If all went well, they had a little less than a couple more hours to walk.[6] It was still early and quite chilly on this spring morning in the mountainous Jerusalem countryside. Both men had their hoods pulled up, as did a number of other travelers.[7] They had slipped out of the city as soon as they heard the news. The gossip was already spreading among the awakening populace. It seemed the impossible had actually happened—or, most likely, had been the result of a criminal act of theft.

Of course, almost everybody wanted to get the latest details, or to pretend they actually knew something about the affair firsthand. In any case, Cleopas and James had been drawn into the middle of the thing because of their intricate affiliation with the now-infamous group of Yeshua followers. At this point, it appeared the final outcome was shaping up to be a nasty one, regardless of what had happened to the body. Right now, they didn't care where it was. They only knew *they* didn't have it. James pulled his hood lower on his head, covering more of his face.

What a difference a few days could make. Three days ago had been the most dreadful day of their lives. *No.* Actually, it had been infinitely worse than dreadful…it had been horrific…absolutely appalling. *Devastating.*

But today, the body of Yeshua had been reported missing from the heavily guarded tomb. The prevailing powers were currently hunting down those who had been a part of what they were calling the "fanatic" group that was widely "claiming responsibility" for stealing the corpse. Of course, both of those accusations were flatly untrue.

As they made their way toward Emmaus, Cleopas tried to mentally formulate the proper words so that he might be able to reasonably explain the affair, just in case they were asked about it later…either by incessantly nosy people or the Roman authorities investigating the matter. It was a foregone conclusion that, eventually, they would be asked by someone.

Cleopas mulled over the scenario again and again. But each time he flipped through the pages of his memories, the mental picture of the despicable situation only grew worse. The whole thing was still a jumbled mess of horror.

He glanced at James, plodding along the road as if today were to be his last one on the earth. Cleopas truly feared for the poor man. He was concerned this affair might be the onset of his friend's undoing. He watched as James' slogging feet accidently stumbled over a rock in the road. James picked it up, and almost in a rage, slung it into the bushes with a pitiful grunt as though the incident had been the rock's fault. He continued on, but now with clinched fists dangling at his side as though he were looking for a fight.[8]

Cleopas finally conceded that the situation couldn't be properly expressed—not in real words. Not yet, anyway. It was just too soon. In fact, it was still impossible to believe the nightmarish thing had actually happened. And it was obvious that James didn't want to talk about it—not now. *Maybe later.*

Cleopas figured their futures were pretty much ruined anyway. They might even lose their lives in the days ahead—possibly in the hours ahead…or in minutes. Who knew? Right now, their immediate safety was of foremost concern. He grabbed James by the arm and picked up the pace.

James followed, compliant…but still silent, fists still balled up.

2

THE MEMORIES

*Cleopas felt ashamed for the words he had
just spoken, but facts were facts.*

As they walked, neither man could imagine the looming task of verbally hashing back through what they had witnessed, so for the longest time, both traveled in silence. They just kept shuffling along, heads held low.

What barbaric gruesomeness! Cleopas thought. *No mercy has been shown whatsoever. Not an ounce of pity! It simply isn't right. The flogging. The nails. The rivers of blood. The raw suffering. The pitiful screaming and begging from the criminals who were crucified there with Him.*

The friends couldn't get rid of the shadowy images and haunting sounds that filled the grief-darkened hallways of their minds. Every now and then, Cleopas shook his head back and forth, beating his temples with his open hands, trying to make the haunting memories go away. But they wouldn't leave him alone. They lingered like vultures waiting for something to die, tormenting the men with their overshadowing omnipresence.

There had been no justice for Yeshua. Only vile plotting, innuendos, a bevy of corrupted politicians, self-righteous religious elite, and hideously raw jealousy that seemed to seep and ooze from the blackened souls of everyone involved. And, for all of that, Yeshua was now dead. Beaten beyond recognition as a mortal being. Crucified between two common thieves. Cleopas had witnessed more sympathy for a pack of scavenging dogs than he'd seen given to those three poor, crucified souls.

At the end of it all, Yeshua had been roughly torn down from the cross, and the spikes had been pulled out of His hands and feet with about the same level of concern as if the soldiers had been cleaning a fish. His body was collected by two members of the Sanhedrin Council, then whisked away to a nearby tomb. It certainly appeared that Yeshua's enemies had finally won.

For several days after the execution, Roman soldiers had been guarding Yeshua's signet-sealed tomb by order of Judea's governor and the Sanhedrin religious rulers. It was as if this brutally murdered man—for that's what it *really* had been, a murder—was somehow going to escape.

What were they expecting? A ragtag band of fisherman and society's outcasts to overpower Roman authorities and take the body? What would they do with it if they *did* take it? *How ridiculous.* Why in the world had they treated Yeshua as one of the worst enemies Rome had ever encountered? And why were they now transferring that blood-lust hatred of theirs to the dead man's frightened followers?

Neither Cleopas nor James had yet expressed their thoughts aloud. How would one even initiate such a dialogue? What words would one use? The pain was simply too much to bear. But they had to somehow unload the burden from their labored spirits, and they both knew it. It was almost suffocating not to do so. After some time, Cleopas, the older of the two, finally mustered the courage and took the lead.

"James, we've got to talk about what happened…and what we're doing, where we're going, and our own futures."

James didn't acknowledge his words.

"We can't simply ignore this!" Cleopas continued with a tone of exasperation. "The pain won't go away just because we don't acknowledge its presence. Everything has changed—you *know* it has!" He looked over at his friend. Still no response, not even a glance his way. They trudged on.

Cleopas continued his musings, mumbling as he pressed down the road. "I know people are claiming Yeshua has risen from the dead," he muttered, "but I still find that awfully hard to believe. If He had really risen, wouldn't we and all the other disciples have seen Him by now? Surely, the whole city would have seen Him by now! If He has truly come out of the grave alive, then why hasn't He made arrangements to take His throne as the King of all kings? Why is life seemingly going on as before, as if nothing important has happened?

"No, I simply don't believe that He has risen, James. If He had, there would be no hiding it. It would be impossible!"

He paused only a moment or two, then carried on, still seeming to speak aloud only to himself. "Think about it," he said. "The women said the tomb was empty this morning. Peter and John went there and confirmed it. Still…an empty tomb does not mean He's alive. No one could survive what we saw happen at that cross. *No one*! Personally, I think those women are crazy. I'm convinced they only saw what they *wanted* to see. Peter and John, too—same with them. The whole lot has gone mad! They just *want* to believe. They *have* to believe!"

Cleopas felt ashamed for the words he had just spoken, but facts were facts. Someone had to say it. He and James had to come to grips with reality; it was the only way to go on. Perhaps it was the only way to survive, in the end. The end? *If this nightmare would only end!* Cleopas opened the flask strapped over his shoulder and gulped down a swig of cool water. With the back of his sleeve, he wiped the excess off his face. He held the flask out, but, with an uplifted hand, James refused.

James still hadn't uttered a word. So, the two simply carried on, one foot ahead of the other. Cleopas sank deeper into despair as he walked, hunched over, looking like a doddering and confused old man.

3

THE DOUBTS

James' crippling despair had visibly returned.

About a quarter of an hour went by and Cleopas spoke again, as though he had just completed the last words he'd spoken. "As hard as it is to admit, James, it appears the life we were counting on has come crashing down upon our heads." He may as well have said the words to the obviously famished dog that had just stepped into the road, looking for a handout by randomly sniffing the hands of various travelers.

James didn't acknowledge the beast, but he did finally cast a forlorn glance in Cleopas' direction. At least there was that. It *was* something. Maybe James was softening?

So, after a few more minutes, Cleopas spoke again. "Here's my plan," he said. "Let's go on ahead, all the way to Emmaus. We'll get a room at the inn right on the edge of town. It's on this side, so it'll be easy. We can probably slip in unnoticed."

He looked over at James. Still no response.

Cleopas sighed, shaking his head, betraying a hint of disgust as he spoke again. "Tomorrow, maybe we can find some of our friends and stay with them for a while, until we see what happens next," he said. "But we've got to lay low for a few weeks. The authorities will probably still be looking for us, even then…and they'll definitely be looking for the Eleven!

11

They're probably staying back in Jerusalem. If they are, I know exactly where they'll be—at least some of them, anyway. The women might be there, too. And if they don't give up their location, if they're all very careful, they'll be safe there for a good while."

It was as though Cleopas had spoken each of those words into the wind. James seemed wholly detached. He had been looking straight ahead almost the entire time they had been walking…with a painfully apparent sense of defeat swelling in his watery eyes. At Cleopas' weighty words, James hung his head even lower, and with a still-darkening countenance, he continued to shuffle his heavy feet along the road, lightly muttering under his breath as he went.

A steady flow of humanity was still plodding on the narrow roadway with them, myriad travelers in both directions, man and beast. But no one seemed to notice the two men, or their pain…especially their pain. Apparently, even with the ubiquitous talk about the crucifixion of Yeshua, life was casually going on for everyone else…except them. Were their lives really over now? Who knew? Who cared, besides them? *Probably no one.*

"I suppose you're right, Cleopas," James finally spoke, breaking the long silence that had embraced him. Cleopas' eyes widened, but he remained quiet, allowing James to further collect his thoughts.

After a few more moments, James eked out more words. "It's just so difficult," he whimpered. "I'm still astonished by all that has happened, and I'm angry. No—worse than angry; I'm bitter! It's as though it didn't really happen—it *couldn't* have happened! *But it did.* It feels like the most horrible nightmare one could imagine. I just wish I could wake up from it. They murdered our Teacher, Cleopas! They finally got what they wanted. It's just not right. *He's gone!*" James glared at Cleopas with a look that seemed to say, "And what are *you* going to do about it?"

"I know, James. Believe me, I do." James was shocked at the river of words now freely flowing from the mouth of his friend. "But now, we've got to face what has happened. He's gone. You've spoken truth; that's all there is to it. And, because of that missing body, there's an evil wind blowing all about Jerusalem. I've even heard people discussing it along the road this morning. We *have* to decide what we will do in the midst of this horrible turn of events, and in its aftermath as well."

"But," James interjected, "Yeshua *did* tell us that He was going to Jerusalem to die, didn't He?" He looked over at Cleopas. "And that the Jews and the authorities would kill Him? On multiple occasions He told us these things! Don't you remember?"

Before his friend could answer, for it really wasn't a question, James persisted. "Yeshua was clear about it. He even said He would rise three days later. But where is He now? He wouldn't just rise, then simply disappear—would He? I guess none of us took His words that seriously."

James shrugged his shoulders in defeat, satisfied that perhaps he had answered his own questions with his last declaration. He simply continued to amble along.

Nearby, a gaggle of children, joining themselves together from within the masses of the human caravan, suddenly began screeching in delight. They had spotted the interloping dog and rushed toward him, probably just to pet him. But, their mad, mob-like lunge at the animal terrified the poor beast. Like a mangy and hair-matted version of a magician, the stealthy creature vanished into the thick undergrowth lining the roadway. The squealing youngsters chased after him, but their efforts were in vain. He was gone in a flash; only the bushes rattled in the wake of his panicked escape.

Within moments, barely noticing the commotion, James spoke up again. "Maybe we misunderstood what Yeshua truly meant? Maybe His 'rising' was to be viewed in some symbolic way, or perhaps it was supposed to be some kind of 'spiritual' experience? I don't know. But to actually deliver Himself to death on a Roman cross—a very real death, the worst kind of death one could imagine—I still can't feature it! There seemed to be something much more *purposeful* about it. It was as though He *knew* what He was doing! Yet…here we are. We don't have a clue what we're doing, or what we're going to do from this point forward. *He's dead,* the body's missing, and we're running for our lives!"

James' crippling despair had visibly returned. Cleopas offered him a drink of water, and this time James accepted, gulping down several huge swallows. Handing the container back to Cleopas, he faintly smiled at his friend.

Within the next few moments, however, this mournful day would meld into a memory they would talk about for the rest of their lives.

4

THE STRANGER

Did not the Messiah have to suffer these things…
and then enter His glory?

An unknown traveler along the way startled Cleopas and James. He seemed to have appeared out of nowhere. "Men!" the man said. "May I speak to you for a moment?"

Traveling in the same direction they were headed, the man had edged up alongside the two grief-weary nomads. "May I be a little forward?" he asked, "Could I please know your names?"

The man looked friendly enough. Pleasantness exuded from his countenance. Cleopas responded, a note of caution rising in his voice, "I'm Cleopas." Then, nodding in James' direction, he spoke on his friend's behalf. "And he's James. He's not talking very much right now. And when he does talk, he's a bit apprehensive. We've had a rough day, and I fear it's only just begun."

The stranger shook his head in polite acknowledgment.

"Well then," he said. "I hope you don't think poorly of me, but I couldn't help hearing you, especially as I got closer." The man chuckled as he raised his hands in feign surrender. "I really wasn't eavesdropping," he said.

Pointing his finger at Cleopas, the man teased, "But you, sir, *were* a bit loud…and with so many words, too! So, I really couldn't help but hear your laments."

The two friends glanced at each other and shrugged as they resumed walking. James, glancing toward Cleopas, joined the lightness of the moment. "Boy," he said with a smirk, "he's got your number!" Cleopas rolled his eyes, and then continued to address the stranger. "Perhaps our grief and anxiety were coarsely betrayed in the tone of our voices." Cleopas tried to insert at least a bit of polite levity into their broken lives. James said nothing else, but was quietly sizing up the man who had joined them.

The stranger continued walking in step with them, obviously wanting to engage in more conversation. As odd as it might have otherwise seemed in an encounter of this sort, something about the man put them both at ease. His present company, spiced with a little well-meant humor, was a refreshing break. It seemed that someone else along the way actually seemed to *care*.

"What are you discussing, if I might be so bold?" the stranger asked. "It sounds pretty serious."

There was an awkward silence.

The man picked up where he had left off. "Forgive me, but is the problem something I could, perhaps, help you with? I've been told I have a gift for helping others sort through the tough things of life. What has happened that has made the two of you so distraught?"

The man looked somewhat familiar to the friends, but much of his face was covered within the several light folds of his hooded garment, as with many of the other travelers, because the morning air was still chilly along the mountainous pathway. At the moment, Cleopas and James could only see some of the man's forehead, his nose, parts of his cheeks, and his eyes. From time to time, they got a glimpse of his fuller facial features. But it was *those eyes*…there was *something familiar* about those eyes.

At the offer to talk to them about the reason for their gloom, the disciples stopped in the middle of the road. Cleopas grabbed James by the arm again and, with a tone of subdued sarcasm, said, "You've got to be kidding, sir! Are you really asking us *what has happened*? Are you the only one visiting Jerusalem who doesn't know the things that have taken place there in these last few days? Terrible things…unbelievably vile things. We thought you wanted to talk to us *because* of what happened!"

"*My goodness*! Exactly what things are you speaking of?" the stranger asked.

"What do you mean…*what things?*" Cleopas, shocked, let out a breath of exasperation as he asked the question. *How could this man not know what was on the minds, and lips, of practically everyone in Jerusalem?*

"Please, don't keep me in suspense," the man replied. "I'm not sure I know what you're talking about."

"We are talking about Yeshua of Nazareth!" Cleopas answered.

"Yes! We were indeed speaking of Yeshua of Nazareth!" James echoed, the tone of his voice indicating the depth of his incredulity.

"That's interesting," the stranger said. "Tell me about him." A faint, knowing glimmer appeared in those penetrating eyes as he talked.

Cleopas spoke first. "Well, for one thing—he was a prophet. He was powerful in word and deed, before God and all the people. The miracles He worked were astonishing—impossible things. But we *saw* Him perform them! The blind were healed, lepers were cleansed, the deaf were made to hear with just a word, a touch, or a simple command. You wouldn't believe all the things we saw. They were indescribable…miracles from Heaven! I can assure you, there's never been one like Him. Nothing like this has ever been done before."

James broke in. "But the chief priests and our rulers handed Him over to be sentenced to death, and they crucified Him. It was what they had wanted all along. Right before our eyes, we saw it all. He had done nothing illegal. But, you see, we also hoped He was the One who was going to redeem Israel. And what's more, it is now the third day since all this took place."

"Right!" added Cleopas. "And, in addition to all that, some of our women amazed us. They went to the tomb earlier this morning, just as the sun was rising, but didn't find His body. They came back and told us they had seen a vision of angels. They claimed one of the angels told them Yeshua was alive! In fact, Mary Magdalene, one of Yeshua's close disciples, later claimed to have seen Him, and to have spoken with Him!" He paused, trying to steady his trembling voice. The stranger listened intently and nodded at Cleopas' words.

"But," Cleopas still struggled to speak, "we're not so sure we believe He *actually* rose from the dead. We didn't think He meant He would, or even *could*, do that in any sort of physical way. I'm really not certain what the women saw. *Angels,* really? Who knows? A ghost? Perhaps. An imagination gone wild, because of grief? Most likely. Any of those things are conceivable."

"All I know," Cleopas continued, "is that He hasn't appeared to us. We've not laid eyes on Him. We've not spoken to Him. I for one, would want to see His hands and feet, the nail scars—but, I don't know…"

He gulped to catch his breath. His emotions grabbed at his throat. Tears began to trickle from his eyes. He wiped them from his face, appearing agitated as he did.

While Cleopas collected himself, James filled in the rest of the story. "I know it sounds crazy, but Cleopas is correct. Some of our companions went to the tomb and found the state of it just as the women had claimed, but they didn't see Yeshua, even though the tomb was empty. Except for what Mary Magdalene told us. But, I've always wondered about her trustworthiness…after all, she *did* have seven demons driven from her."[9]

After a brief pause, Cleopas added another detail. "And…the men who went to the tomb…they didn't see any angels, nothing of the sort. All they found was that the body was indeed not there!"

James smirked. "He's right," he said. "No angels. No resurrected Yeshua. And the Roman soldiers were not there either. And now we find out the authorities are literally hunting down the disciples. Hunting *us*! They blame us for stealing the body! *Imagine that!* Fishermen and tax collectors defeating the Roman regiment, as well as the Sanhedrin council and their Temple guards, stealing the body of Rome's latest worst criminal—then hiding it so no one could find it. What would we want with a mangled, beaten, bloodied corpse? This is madness! The whole Roman world has lost its mind!"

James hesitated a few seconds, then explained, "That's why we're leaving Jerusalem. We've got to get out of here. It's just not safe for us to be here, at least not right now."

"My friends," the stranger said to them, "I understand your concerns. But how unwise you have been in this matter. And how slow you are to believe all that the prophets have spoken! Did not the Messiah have to suffer these things…and then enter His glory? You should, by now, understand these things…you are a part of something that is spiritually earth-shattering, whether you know it or not!"

Cleopas and James halted in their tracks and stood looking at the man, astonishment dripping from their countenances. *Who is this? How uncaring can he be…to call us "unwise" and "slow to believe." Where has he been these last three years? Who is he to judge us in such matters?*

The man continued. "The world will never be the same because of what has happened here. And those things happened in *your* lifetimes. Indeed, *you* were a part of making them happen—wonderful things! Just wait…be patient. You'll soon see!" The stranger's eyes sparkled as he spoke.

Cleopas was dumbfounded, "So, you *have* heard of Him? And…you *do* know about this?" The stranger shook his head, slightly raising his eyebrows in agreement with what Cleopas had said.

Then, with most of his face still obscured, he winked at them. "Yes, I know," he said. "Believe me. *I know….*"

The two disciples still had no idea who the traveler was. In fact, they had not even thought to ask his name.

5

THE TEACHER

They could scarcely believe what they were hearing. But the more he spoke, the more they understood that what he said was true.

"Come," the mysterious one invited them. "I'm going the same direction as you. Let me explain what those Scriptures say concerning what you've just been through and what lies ahead. Let me see if I can help you. Okay?"

The two disciples looked at each other in disbelief. How did he know so much about the Scriptures—and about *them*? Was he a rabbi? A sage? A Sanhedrin spy? Maybe even an angel? How did he just "happen" upon *them* as they were absconding from Jerusalem? Had they spoken too quickly? Had they told him too much?

Furthermore, where exactly had he come from? It seemed as though he had materialized out of nowhere. But that couldn't be true…could it? Neither could recall seeing the man approaching. However, considering their state of depression, they could have simply missed him. Perhaps he had been near them all along, in the midst of the mass of people. At any rate, at this point, what could it hurt to listen to him?

"Yes, please join us," Cleopas responded. "We would love for you to tell us more. We've got nothing else to do. And we certainly need some cheering up. Our future is not shaping up to be very promising at this point."

Then it hit him. "Please, sir," he asked the stranger, "what is your name? I'm sorry we didn't ask you earlier."

"Think nothing of it!" the man said. "Some just call me 'teacher'—that'll do for now. Many people know me, believe it or not. So, I'm also traveling with the hope that I won't be recognized right now. You understand, don't you?"

Cleopas responded, nodding his head. "Oh, yes. We understand." James managed a faint smile.

While they strolled along, the teacher resumed his lesson, starting with the book of Genesis. He lingered over its first sentence, dissecting the well-known passage as he quoted it word by word. He told of a number of marvelous truths about Messiah, things hidden in that passage since ages past, but were now being revealed by this *knowledgeable one*. The men were flabbergasted by what they were hearing. How had they not seen or known these things before?

In the days to come, they would recall it was at this very moment when they had wondered why God would hide things such as these from His own people until a time far into the future. The sage then turned to them and said, "Why do you wonder to yourselves why Elohim might conceal certain matters, only to reveal them more completely in the future? Have you not read what the Lord said to the people of Isaiah's day?"

The mysterious teacher knew their exact thoughts at the very moment they were thinking them!

Then he quoted the prophet Isaiah:

From now on I will tell you of new things, of hidden things unknown to you. They are created now, and not long ago; you have not heard of them before today. So you cannot say, "Yes, I knew of them."[10]

Before they could respond, the teacher went on. "Or what about the prophet Daniel; surely you remember what he said." Then he quoted:

God gives wisdom to the wise and knowledge to the discerning. He reveals deep and hidden things.[11]

"And *this*…also from the prophet Daniel:"

Roll up and seal the words of the scroll until the time of the end. Many will go here and there to increase knowledge.[12]

"Do you remember these passages?" the teacher asked.

Of course they knew them! The rabbis frequently read them and expounded upon the traditional interpretations of each. But they had never dreamed those words might also have been meant for them…especially in any literal sense. But that understanding was changing rapidly, even as this teacher was instructing them.

As their journey continued, the stranger disclosed a string of intricate details about prophetic fulfillments they had never considered. Now they were finally beginning to recognize their significance! The light of truth slowly but surely illuminated the very core of their beings. The only time they had felt this sensation before had been back when they listened to Yeshua speak of the Scriptures.

They felt as if what they were now hearing was somehow meant to have been decrypted just for them. These were amazing revelations, and they unraveled what the ancient Scriptures had declared—even in their most mysteriously veiled meanings—especially concerning Messiah.

The teacher then spoke again. "I can tell you this, my friends," he said, "here is what you've been discovering today. Until heaven and earth disappears, not the smallest letter, not the least stroke of a pen, will by any means disappear from the Word of God until everything is finally accomplished. There's a message in those words, to be sure—and, in many places, there's even a deeper message as you consider those words more closely, much more closely, and then ponder over their real meaning. Meditate upon them. Write them out, from your memory. You've learned them in your synagogue lessons! Look for the connections. They were meant for you to understand, especially *after* the things you are now experiencing have happened! These mysteries were placed in God's Word *for you*…as well as for the generations yet to come. You'll see!"

Haven't we heard something like this before? "Not a jot or tittle of My Word will pass away." *Yes! We heard that declaration from Yeshua Himself! Had this man been in the crowds while Yeshua was teaching?*

With his powerful words and vivid imagery, the enigmatic stranger unfolded before them additional mysteries of the Scripture's most veiled disclosures. He opened their spirits to the undeniable connections of various fulfillments from all the prophecies. Many of those prophecies had come to fruition throughout the last three years—several even in the last few days!

They could scarcely believe what they were hearing. But the more he spoke, the more they understood that what he was saying was true. There was no denying it.

He continued to teach them in this same manner for the rest of their journey, then, as they were finally approaching the village of Emmaus, its small buildings and houses already in view, the teacher spoke as if he would continue down the road toward another destination. But Cleopas wasn't yet ready to part from his company. "No," he urged, "*please*—stay with us, at least a little longer! It's already afternoon; let's eat together. We really want to know more. Our souls thirst for this kind of knowledge and revelation. Our faith is already being strengthened. You've been such a help. You have spoken truthfully; you have a gift!"

The men pointed to a small inn just ahead where they could get a quick meal. The sage agreed to stay with them a while longer and eat with them. As they entered the diminutive establishment, the teacher thanked them for their hospitality, his cloak still covering a good portion of his face.

6

THE UNVEILING

Weren't our hearts burning within us while
he talked with us on the road?

They had been walking in the brightness of the sun's glare for hours, so as they stepped into the dining room, their eyes had to adjust to the dimly lit interior. So far, they were the only patrons in the place; for now, they would have the communal table to themselves. That fact would probably change within the next thirty minutes or so, but right now they still had a little privacy with their newfound friend and teacher.

After the late-afternoon meal had been laid out before them by the elderly innkeeper, the teacher reached for the bread, hooked his finger in the side of the basket, and pulled it across the table toward him. He took a piece, gave thanks, broke the bread, and began to serve it.

It was at the moment the innkeeper had stepped out of the building to greet a friend when their traveling acquaintance casually pulled back his hood and let it drop to his shoulders. His head was held low. He took a huge bite of bread, raised His head, and, with His cheeks swelled, making Him look like a chipmunk with a mouthful of acorns, He grinned. His full countenance now gleamed before them. In that moment, their eyes were opened and they recognized Him. Sitting before them was the Risen Yeshua! He was serving their meal…and eating with them! *How could this be?*

His presence in front of them, revealed in such dramatic fashion, put both men in a state of terror. Were they looking at a ghost? James shoved his chair back and fell to the floor like a rag doll as he toppled backwards. He was barely able to get himself up, but finally, he stood, gawking, eyes and mouth wide open.

Cleopas had also propelled himself away from the table at the shocking revelation, the legs of his chair screeching across the hard wooden planks of the floor as he did. He dropped to his knees with a dull thud, and cried out, "My Lord and my God! Yeshua, be merciful to us! We didn't know! We weren't expecting…we watched You die! We never dreamed it could be You speaking with us! How can this be?"

James, trembling and weeping almost inconsolably, could be heard muttering, "I'm sorry. I'm sorry. *I'm so very sorry.*"

Yeshua stood to His feet. "Don't be afraid," He comforted them. "It is I!"

He made no attempt to purposely display His hands; they were just there, with the nail scars visible. How had they missed seeing those marks as they had been walking? Had they really been that blind?

"Now do you believe?" Yeshua asked, eyeing them both.

Cleopas opened his mouth to respond—and to apologize yet again. But then, in an instant, without moving from His place, Yeshua dissipated from their sight.

As His visage melted away before them, they had seen His penetrating gaze. Those eyes were full of the deepest love they had ever experienced: Understanding. Kind. Forgiving.

Cleopas, still in shock, whispered under his breath, to no one: "We have been with Him all day long and didn't even know who was talking to us! How foolish we have been!"

After composing themselves enough to at least speak to each other, James blurted out, "Weren't our hearts burning within us while He talked with us on the road and opened the Scriptures to us? That's when we should have known! Only *one* has ever taught us the Word like that! Think of it! We have just spent the better part of the day with the Risen Yeshua!"

Cleopas now had a plan. It seemed he always had a plan, and he was good at formulating the schemes necessary to carry them out. He went over his intentions with James, who agreed without hesitation. Reaching into their coin satchels, the men quickly withdrew the necessary amount and paid the bill to the owner who had just now reentered the building. Then they bolted out the door, setting out on the road again, headed toward Jerusalem.

The innkeeper, thoroughly confused, ran to the door and shouted as they were sprinting away, "Where's that other man—the one who came in with you?"

Cleopas shouted back, "He's risen! Yeshua has risen! We've seen Him!"

As he ran, James was beaming.

The innkeeper shook his head. "Crazy young men," he mumbled. "Probably suffering from too much sun or something." Then, in a quick afterthought, he looked into the empty dining area, which was illuminated only by a few oil lamps. *Where in the world is that man who was with them?* he thought. *I know fully well that I didn't see Him leave with the other two! Oh well, at least they paid for His meal.*

The old proprietor ambled over to the dining area to collect the bowls and clean off the table. Sitting there, in the middle of the table, was a basket larger than the one he had brought out to them. It was brimming over with bread…and fish.[13]

THE ARRIVAL

"Just wait until we tell you what He told us!"

W hat they had to tell couldn't wait.

It was imperative that they get to the other disciples—especially the ones from within Yeshua's inner circle. They needed to know; they needed to hear. *They must hear!*

Cleopas and James had been with the Risen Lord, and the men and women in hiding deserved to know every detail of what they had seen, heard, and learned. The two friends were no longer afraid of anything, of anyone. What they experienced in that inn had changed all that, and more.

On the way back to Jerusalem, they were eventually able to catch a ride on the rickety cart of a merchant who was headed to market with his goods. The man barely had enough room for them—and for a price, of course, as was customary along the Roman roadways. A couple of can-tankerous, talkative mules pulled the creaking contraption. However, the current travel arrangement certainly beat walking—or running—and it gave them time, along with some relative comfort, to go back over all that had happened on this day.

It was in the early evening when they finally arrived back in Jerusalem. They leapt from the back of the cart, waving and thanking its owner as they hurried to find the other disciples. Cleopas had a good idea where they would most likely be.[14]

He was not mistaken. When Cleopas and James arrived at the door of the house Cleopas had sought, they knocked, looking over their shoulders, scanning for spies or government officials who might have seen them arrive. When Matthew eased the door open and peeked outside, James and Cleopas found the room filled with almost all the disciples!

"Come in…James! Cleopas!" Matthew turned to the others in the room. "Look who's here!" He quickly shut the door behind them and eased the heavy wooden lock-bar into its cradle. They were safe—for a while longer, anyway.

"My brothers!" Peter yelped as he stood from the table. "It's so good to see you! You have no idea how good it is to have you with us. Join us at the table—have something to eat. Refresh yourselves!"

Before the travelers could get a word out, the rest of the disciples had jumped up from the table as well and surrounded the pair, offering hugs, hearty slaps on the back, and kisses on the cheek. They told Cleopas and James that Thomas was still absent from them. Some had seen him about the city a few times, but he was still in hiding…and sulking. For now, though, even several who had been outside of what was left of the Eleven were also there, including some of the women.

"No matter what anyone else might tell you, it's true," Matthew belted out. "The Lord *has* risen indeed! He has appeared to Simon—and Mary Magdalene has seen Him, too! She was overflowing with excitement as she described her encounter to us! She should be here later this evening— then you can ask her about it yourselves!"

"Yes!" James responded. "That's why we're here. Yeshua appeared to us as well—just a few hours ago!"

"Just wait until we tell you what He told us," Cleopas chimed in. "You'll never believe all we have to share with you—and everything we've learned from Him. It's all true! Yeshua brought the Scriptures to life for us as we walked along the road to Emmaus."

"Tell us!" Peter pleaded. "*Please!* Tell us everything!"

So, Cleopas told the group what happened as they had been on the way to Emmaus—and at the inn, and during their brief meal—and how they had recognized Yeshua when He broke the bread and finally pulled back the hooded part of His garment. They told of how they had glimpsed the scars on His wrists, as well as how Yeshua had disappeared from their presence in the twinkling of an eye.

While they were still talking about these marvels and celebrating among themselves—some praying, some openly worshiping, others weeping and praising God—the One they were talking about suddenly stood among them.

Yeshua simply materialized; it was as though He had been there all along.

8

THE REVENANT

"Come! Sit with Me," He entreated, patting the floor beside Him.

Those in that room of communal hiding were momentarily unable to move. They were speechless, flabbergasted. *This can't be! There He is! Yeshua is right here…in the locked room, with us!*

Where has He come from? How did He get here? Is this some sort of hallucination? Is it a ghost? How in the world?

"Peace be with you." The familiar voice was uniquely His. *No—this isn't a vision! He is literally right before us!*

To say the men and women gathered there were stunned is an understatement. A few were on the verge of fainting from the shock. Others had their senses awakened more vividly, hair standing up on the back of their necks.

It was in this moment that Yeshua said to them, "Why are you afraid, and why do doubts arise in your minds? *Behold My hands. Behold My feet.* It is I! Touch Me and see! A ghost does not have flesh and bones, as you can clearly see that I have."

As Yeshua was saying this, He was rolling up His sleeves and unlashing His robe to show those in the room His hands, His feet, His side. But they no longer needed the proof. Once they recovered their bearings and returned to normal breathing, they knew. This *was* Him!

Their momentary fright turned to indescribable joy. Now there was an unleashing of unrestrained emotion. Raucous laughter. Open weeping. Praise and adulations. All of it brought the room to a glorious new life.

Then, suddenly, in the midst of the rising jubilation, Yeshua matter-of-factly asked, "Do you have anything to eat? I'm famished! What smells so good?" Many of the gathering chuckled at His request, while Andrew darted to the table, snatched up a bowl, and offered Him a piece of broiled fish.

"He wants to eat!" Peter cried out. "*He really is back!*"

After an explosion of laughter at Peter's jab, Yeshua nodded at Andrew in thanks, took the fish, and let out His own uniquely infectious laugh… one they had heard so many times before. He stood there and ate the food in their presence, savoring each huge bite that He took, playfully smacking as He ate. "Well!" He said, "Will you not join me? Or, will you simply stand there and watch Me eat this whole bowl of fish?"

His friends and followers couldn't stand it any longer. They rushed to Him at once, wrapping Him in embraces. Some started weeping again. Others broke into laughter. He was really here! Alive! And with *them*! And eating…*fish*!

As soon as the joyful commotion had settled a bit, Yeshua began to speak. "This is what I told you while I was still with you," He said. "Everything must be fulfilled that is written about me in the Law of Moses, the Prophets, and the Psalms." He looked around, surveying the floor for a place to sit so that He might speak.

"Come! Sit with Me," He entreated, patting the floor beside Him. "Get cushions for everyone! We have a lot to talk about!"

When all were finally seated around Him, Yeshua said, "I have many things to show you—mysteries hidden in the Word, and even within creation itself. The revelations are deep treasures, hidden since the beginning of time, but now unveiled for you—especially for you. You will share some of them with the world in the coming days, and you'll learn more over the years. Others after you, many years into the future, will continue to uncover the deepest truths of those treasures as the days of My return draw nearer. The manifold wisdom of Heaven will now be revealed to the coming church, and then, through that church, it will be dispersed to the ends of the earth!"[15]

Like wide-eyed children on their first day in a synagogue Tanakh[16] class, Yeshua's audience sat at His feet and listened, clinging to every word He spoke. It was really Yeshua! They longed for this moment to never end.

Yeshua began teaching with these words: "So now you will see, now you'll understand, like never before. This is what is written: 'The Messiah will suffer and rise from the dead on the third day…'"

Then He shared with them, one after the other, what used to be mysterious passages from the Tanakh that were now being brought to life from the mouth of the Living Word Himself. He cited all the Scriptures wherein repentance for the forgiveness of sins would be preached to all the nations, beginning at Jerusalem and eventually spreading to the global population of the last days. He assured them that this gospel of the Kingdom would survive until the very end, and it would be broadcast throughout the growing world, among all the nations and peoples—even those living in the last days.

Cleopas meditated on these wondrous revelations as he looked across the room while Yeshua was teaching. James was listening, too, thinking to himself, *What a difference a day can make! I thought our lives were over. Now I realize, we've actually just begun to live, really live!* Just then, he let out a sigh of overwhelming contentment as he savored the moments at Yeshua's feet.

Several hours passed, but they seemed to be only moments. Then, as Yeshua wrapped up His teaching, He declared, "You are now witnesses of these things."

He looked into the eyes of each of those sitting around Him. "Not many days from now," He said, "I am going to send you the gift My Father has promised, the Holy Spirit of God. He will continue to lead you into all truth.

"But for now, you must stay in the city until you have been clothed with power from on high. Also, there are still a few from our closest circle who must hear Me and see Me before these things happen."

He looked at Cleopas and James and laughed. "No more running off, okay?" The two men looked at each other, their faces flooded with expressions of delight.

"Soon, you'll see our dear brother Thomas," Yeshua said, and concluded with an instruction: "Tell him I want to see him. Bring him here to Me, if he'll come. Be gentle with him."

Then, in the same way it had happened with Cleopas and James hours earlier at the inn in Emmaus, *Yeshua was gone.* It was as though He had easily passed from one realm to another.

For a long while, none of those present dared to move. What a holy moment this had been. The Resurrected Yeshua had been among them. *He was alive!* This was exactly what they had been yearning for. And now they were living in the midst of their answered prayers. They knew this was no dream, vision, hallucination, or ghost. They had *all* heard Him, eaten with Him, touched Him, and learned from Him…for hours.

Cleopas caught James' attention, then made a fist and held it to his heart. James' face radiated a newfound zest for life. But there was more to come for these two friends, and for the others as well. Yeshua would appear to them again several times in the coming days and weeks. Many others would see Him, too. Hundreds of others would experience His physical presence among them.

But for now, these in the Upper Room would simply bathe in the holy moment of *today.*

Part II

THE LINKS

The mystery that has been kept hidden for ages and generations, but is now disclosed to the saints.

~Colossians 1:26

9

VITAL CONNECTIONS

*No, we speak of God's secret wisdom, a wisdom that has been hidden
and that God destined for our glory before time began.*
~1 CORINTHIANS 2:7

What if I told you that a mysterious prophecy in the Old Testament book of Daniel directly connects with another prophecy in the New Testament book of Matthew—one spoken by Jesus Himself—and very few people have ever made the crucial link between the two? Additionally, what if it was clearly demonstrated that these two passages, whose connections were hidden for thousands of years, were ultimately meant for you?

How It Works

Here's an example of how connecting revelations work in real life. When the angel Gabriel visited Mary and Joseph, telling them what their own eternally famous place in history would be, they had to have been overwhelmed by all they heard. But their incredulousness would be put on a dose of adrenaline once the truth finally hit home.

Can you imagine what they must have thought when it dawned on them that the words in the book of Genesis were about *them*, specifically, and had been about them since the beginning of time? God had announced to Satan, "And I will put enmity between you and the woman, and between your seed and her seed. He will crush your head, and you will strike his heel" (Berean Study Bible; see Genesis 3:15). Mary and Joseph now understood! Their personal lives were actually veiled within the Word of God, spoken out of the mouth of humanity's Creator in the Garden of Eden thousands of years ago. *Mary* would ultimately be that one woman out of all others who would finally bring forth the One who would crush Satan's kingdom![17]

Or, how about when they made the link between their own lives and Isaiah's enigmatic prophecy that speaks of Mary's state of virginity at the outset of the bearing of the Christ child: "Therefore the Lord himself will give you a sign: The virgin will conceive and give birth to a son, and will call him Immanuel"[18] (see Isaiah 7:14).

I also wonder when the same prophet's words foretelling the birth of what now was to be *her Son, the Creator of the Universe,* hit Mary and Joseph as also being about them. Think of it! They were going to give birth to the One who would be known for eternity as "Almighty God and Everlasting Father"! (See Isaiah 9:6–7.)

Surely both Mary and Joseph had heard, read, and studied all these Scriptures in synagogue classes since they were children. Yet, until Gabriel's visit, they never dreamed those prophecies had been about *them.* Nor could they have even considered, before this moment, the specific manner in which those prophecies would now be fulfilled. Pretty amazing, wouldn't you agree?

Hidden Knowledge?

Don't forget this tidbit: More than seventy times within the pages of the New Testament, the authors of the Scriptures proclaim—either with these exact words or something like them—"This was to fulfill what the prophet said...."

I imagine those writers—especially Peter, John, and Matthew—received most of their understanding of those revelations from Jesus Himself. The disclosures would have been given during His lengthy teaching sessions, especially *after* His resurrection. Those men were, after all, a collection of fishermen and tax collectors. They certainly were not theologians with formal training in the rabbinical interpretations of the Scriptures. Who was it, then, that made them privy to the myriad intricate and previously hidden connections of the most perplexing passages in the Bible? Jesus Himself, of course! The Bible tells us it was Him, but we seldom even consider that morsel of revelation.

> Jesus said to them, "This is what I told you while I was still with you: **Everything must be fulfilled that is written about me** in the Law of Moses, the Prophets and the Psalms." **Then he opened their minds so they could understand the Scriptures.** (Luke 24:44–45, emphasis added)

Some time back, I was seeking the best scholastic information I could find to begin the tedious research for this book. In so doing, I landed on a trusted site that I had quoted in some of my previous works. Imagine my shock when I read the writer's bold assertion: "God condemns *any method* of discerning hidden knowledge."

I knew in my soul this certainly was *not* a biblically correct statement. I wondered if I had misread or simply misunderstood what I had read, so I kept reading. As it turned out, I hadn't missed a thing. The writer meant exactly what he stated, evidenced by the fact that the only proof text upon which he illustrated that conclusion was a single verse from the book of Deuteronomy:

> There shall not be found among you anyone who burns his son or his daughter as an offering, anyone who practices divination or tells fortunes or interprets omens, or a sorcerer. (Deuteronomy 18:10)

The writer of the piece appeared to be saying that searching for disclosures of God's hidden mysteries was tantamount to some form of witchcraft![19]

No Denying It

I use the illustration of that article's summary only to demonstrate a greater truth. Even though we have the Word of God by which we can make contextual comparisons, Yahweh also tells us—*within the pages of that very same Word*—that He truly does keep some things veiled. Sometimes He obfuscates the ultimate fulfillment of His Word only until it's the proper time to reveal the mystery to His children. Even the early church became aware of that, and Peter wrote about it with great emotion.

> Concerning this salvation, the prophets, who spoke of the grace that was to come to you, searched intently and with the greatest care, trying to find out the time and circumstances to which the Spirit of Christ in them was pointing when he predicted the sufferings of the Messiah and the glories that would follow. It was revealed to them that they were not serving themselves but you, when they spoke of the things that have now been told you by those who have preached the gospel to you by the Holy Spirit sent from heaven. Even angels long to look into these things. (1 Peter 1:10–12)

> Above all, you must understand that no prophecy of Scripture came about by the prophet's own interpretation of things. For prophecy never had its origin in the human will, but prophets, though human, spoke from God as they were carried along by the Holy Spirit. (2 Peter 1:20–21)

In other words, there were occasions when the ancient prophets themselves didn't understand the details of the great obscurities about which they were instructed to write. They knew they were writing and speaking to people in times other than their own. Even the angels of Heaven didn't understand many of the details of the prophecies. So, how are God's people, through the ages, supposed to discover the revelation of those mysteries—secrets, temporarily veiled revelations, coded words, and so forth?

The answer is that we must search out the obscurities by using sound protocols of biblical investigation, and we must seek with great diligence to discern the times in which we're living. The Holy Spirit then guides us, sometimes incrementally, into the truth that applies to our own specific time.

Then, only when the time is right, the fullest and ultimate fulfillment of those divine mysteries will be right in front of those who have the spiritual *eyes to see*.

10

PROBING THE MYSTERIES

And he said to them, "To you has been given the secret of the kingdom of God, but for those outside everything is in parables."
~MARK 4:11, ESV

Think about the prophecies of the expected coming One who would, only in God's own timing, be made manifest in the flesh of Jesus Christ.[20] The Old Testament was filled with detailed announcements concerning that appearance. Yet, the religious elite, for the most part, missed the event when it finally occurred. The Apostle Paul described the wonder like this:

> Though I am less than the least of all the saints, this grace was given me: to preach to the Gentiles **the unsearchable riches of Christ,** and **to illuminate for everyone** the stewardship of **this mystery,** which **for ages past was kept hidden in God,** who created all things. **His purpose was** that **now, through the church, the manifold wisdom of God should be made known** to the rulers and authorities in the heavenly realms. (Ephesians 3:8–10, emphasis added)

The bottom line: God *encourages* us to seek His hidden knowledge; these are His treasures of purposely placed mysteries. He even says He delights in us when we do so—but only if our seeking is done within the confines of the precepts of His Word.

To illustrate, here are a few validations from both the Old and New Testaments.

- **The secret things belong to the Lord** our God, but the **things that are revealed belong to us** and to our children forever, **that we may do all the words** of this law. (Deuteronomy 29:29, ESV; emphasis added)
- It is **the glory of God to conceal things**, but the glory of kings is to search things out. (Proverbs 25:2, ESV; emphasis added)
- From now on **I will tell you of new things, of hidden things unknown to you.** They are created now, and not long ago; you have **not heard of them before today.** So you cannot say, "Yes, I knew of them." (Isaiah 48:6–7, emphasis added)
- See, the former things have taken place, and **new things I declare; before they spring into being** I announce them **to you.** (Isaiah 42:9, emphasis added)
- I will give you **the treasures of darkness**, riches **stored in secret** places, **so that you may know that I am the Lord**, the God of Israel, who summons you by name. (Isaiah 45:3, emphasis added)
- He gives wisdom to the wise and knowledge to the discerning. **He reveals deep and hidden things.** (Daniel 2:21–22, emphasis added)
- But we impart **a secret and hidden wisdom** of God, which **God decreed before the ages** for **our glory.** (1 Corinthians 2:7, ESV; emphasis added)
- And he said to them, "To you has been given **the secrets of the kingdom of God,** but for those outside everything is in parables." (Mark 4:11, ESV; emphasis added)

- Now to him who is able to strengthen you according to my gospel and the preaching of Jesus Christ, according to the revelation of **the mystery that was kept secret for long ages.** (Romans 16:25, ESV; emphasis added)
- So then, men ought to regard us as servants of Christ and as those **entrusted with the secret things** of God. Now it is required that **those who have been given a trust must prove faithful.** (1 Corinthians 4:1–2, emphasis added)
- **The mystery that has been kept hidden for ages and generations,** but is **now disclosed** to the saints. To them **God has chosen to make known** among the Gentiles the glorious **riches of this mystery,** which is Christ in you, the hope of glory. (Colossians 1:26–27, emphasis added)
- No, **we speak of God's secret wisdom,** a **wisdom that has been hidden** and that God **destined for our glory before time began.** None of the rulers of this age understood it, for if they had, they would not have crucified the Lord of glory. (1 Corinthians 2:7–9, emphasis added)
- **These things God has revealed to us** through the Spirit. For the Spirit searches everything, **even the depths of God.** (1 Corinthians 2:10, ESV; emphasis added)
- How **the mystery was made known to me by revelation,** as I have written briefly. (Ephesians 3:3, ESV; emphasis added)

The Lord reveals that kind of information to His children only when He determines the moment has arrived for its disclosure to burst forth into fruition. Only He knows the day and the hour.

Now, before we dive into our own mystery-solving quest, let me offer a taste of what's in store in the chapters ahead.

II

THERE IT IS!

God's up to something in these last days.

Uri Mendel had taken a seat beside me on the couch in the living room of my home on the Florida Gulf Coast in the very early 2000s.

We were enjoying a cup of coffee, having just finished our evening meal. Uri—an Israeli-born tour guide whose first language is Hebrew—had traveled from Israel to visit my wife and me based upon a friendship we had formed a few years earlier on a tour of the Holy Land.

I was holding a book when we sat down together. As we got comfortable, I opened the book to a page I had marked to show him. I couldn't wait to find out what he might say about it.

I took a sip of coffee and pointed to a block of Hebrew text, then asked Uri what he saw when he looked at those letters. I wanted to know his interpretation. He scanned it and exclaimed, "Wow! What in the world is *this?*"

He plunked his coffee cup down on the table beside him, becoming very serious about what he was looking at. "Where did you get this?" he asked. "What am I seeing here? This is not possible!"

I have to be honest—his initial response shocked me. I didn't expect that reaction from the normally calm man I had come to know, but he was clearly stunned by what he was reading. I knew this conversation was soon going to become very interesting.

Uri reached for the book so he could turn to its cover for a closer look. He wanted to see its title and who wrote it. I had already mentioned both of those facts to him when we sat down, but apparently he had dismissed the information as unimportant, having claimed no knowledge of the author or the book. Now, after what he'd seen, the information suddenly became important to him.

I laughed and firmed my grasp on the book, playfully keeping him from seeing the cover. "Don't look at the cover yet," I teased. "I'll show you everything in a few minutes. But right now, just tell me what you see."

He chortled, then half-heartedly relented. "This block of letters—" he pointed at it with his index finger, "I can read the text! I'm familiar with it. It comes from the book of Daniel." He paused and kept staring, at the passage, mesmerized.

"Carl," he said, as he finished reading aloud the block of words, putting them together into sentences, "it's the passage in Daniel that says 'seal up the scroll, until the time of the end.'"

"Yes," I replied. "That's Daniel chapter 12, particularly verse 4."

Just then, I was going to ask Uri to tell me more about the portion of the text that was highlighted, but he beat me to it. His countenance was flushed as he readied himself to spill out what he was thinking. For a few seconds, he seemed like a child about to explode in uncontrollable delight over what he had discovered.

"I've got to tell you," he said, "this is impossible! This just can't be here...but there it is!" He pointed to a word in the text as he spoke.

"Why do you say that?" I asked.

In a few more seconds, I would find out why...and I would be floored by what he told me.

Before Our Eyes

Yes...*there it is.* That's the *aha* moment that often shocks us as God reveals one of His previously hidden treasures.

And that's the whole point, isn't it? What do we do when we see something that brings illuminating, life-changing glory to the name of Yawheh and His Holy Word, and it's right before our eyes? And what if there's no way to deny its presence…and we didn't expect to see such a thing in the first place—especially when there are no tricks, illusions, twisting, or stretching of the facts involved? What do we do with *that*?

If these considerations sound intriguing, just wait! We've only just begun.

The account of Uri, and what he saw that day, along with many other stunning disclosures, will be fully revealed in the pages that follow. But first, let's dive into the depths of our journey by making the promised connections between that mysterious prophecy in the Old Testament with its direct ties to a striking prophetic pronouncement of Jesus in the New Testament.

Part III

THE KEY

You know how to interpret the appearance of the sky, but you cannot interpret the signs of the times.

~MATTHEW 16:3

12

UNTIL THE TIME OF THE END

As those seals are broken and unlocked, the entire book of the disclosure of the time of the end begins to unfold before our eyes.

We'll start our journey by looking at the two linking passages mentioned earlier. Together, they hold a seemingly cryptic biblical key, and it's been hiding in plain sight for almost two thousand years. The linkage begins at the end of the book of Daniel.

The prophet Daniel's renowned treatise on end-time events is the definitive apocalyptic book of the Old Testament, in much the same way the book of Revelation is for the New Testament.[21] Because of this, practically every serious scholar agrees that Revelation is impossible to properly interpret without a diligent comparison to the book of Daniel.[22]

For example, the first words of Daniel's closing chapter sound almost like they've come straight out of the New Testament, especially from certain parts of the book of Revelation itself.[23]

Have a look at those first four verses of Daniel 12:

And at that time shall Michael stand up, the great prince which standeth for the children of thy people: **and there shall be a time of trouble, such as never was since there was a nation even to that same time: and at that time your people shall be delivered,** every one that shall be **found written in the book.**

And many of them that sleep in the dust of the earth shall
awake, some to everlasting life, and **some to shame and everlasting contempt.** And **they that be wise shall shine** as the brightness
of the firmament; and **they that turn many to righteousness** as
the stars for ever and ever.

But thou, O Daniel, shut up the words, and seal the book
[scroll], **even to the time of the end:** many shall run to and fro,
and knowledge shall be increased. (Daniel 12:1–4, KJV; emphasis
added)

A Sealed Scroll

In that last verse, Daniel is told to seal up the scroll of the prophetic disclosures he had received.[24] Then, he's informed that many of the things
he was shown would ultimately be exposed—but only at the time of *the
end.*[25]

Dr. Gary Everett's Study Notes on the Holy Scriptures (Daniel 12):[26]

Daniel's vision comes to a close with a few brief remarks **about
the last times and the coming of the Lord and the final Day of
Judgment.** Thus, the first few verses of Daniel 12 tell us that this is
a time of trouble, which we now call the Tribulation Period. **This
lengthy vision that Daniel is given takes biblical prophecy up
to the Second Coming of the Messiah** when the "Times of the
Gentiles" will come to an end.[27] (Emphasis added)

Now compare Daniel 12:4 to what John the Revelator sees at the
throne of God in the fourth through sixth chapters of Revelation.[28] There,
we find John in the physical presence of Heaven's court witnessing the
risen and glorified Jesus Christ holding, of all things, a scroll that is sealed.
As those seals are broken and unlocked, the *book of the disclosure of the time
of the end* begins to unfold in our presence.[29]

Then I saw in the right hand of him who sat on the throne a scroll with writing on both sides and sealed with seven seals. (Revelation 5:1)

I watched as the Lamb opened the first of the seven seals. Then I heard one of the four living creatures say in a voice like thunder, "Come!" (Revelation 6:1)

The comparative imagery between Daniel and Revelation is striking. It appears that Daniel was told the "sealing" of the things he was allowed to experience in his prophetic visions were to stay sealed, but only *until the time of the end*.[30] That unsealing would be left to another age and another people. It would only come at the direction of Yahweh Himself.[31]

Only One Place

In Revelation 5, we are informed that Jesus alone is worthy of breaking the seals and opening the scroll, thus beginning the unveiling.[32] But, here's the crucial point: Prior to that passage in Revelation, no other place in the Bible speaks of a sealed scroll—especially one that would be unsealed in the last days—*except* Daniel 12:4. If all we had was the Bible itself, with no outside sources whatsoever, we would have to make the connection between the passage in Daniel 12 and Revelation 5 as referring to the same scroll and event.

G. K. Beale—*Commentary on the Greek Text:*[33]

The only other place in the Bible, before Revelation 5, wherein a scroll is sealed, is in Daniel chapter 12.... **There's only one place in the future where a scroll is unsealed.** It's found in **Revelation 5 and 6.**

The metaphor of seals can be found outside Daniel elsewhere in the OT and Jewish apocalyptic, **but the seals in Rev. 5:1 come from Dan. 12:4, 9.**[34] (Emphasis added)

Following is the Revelation 5 account of Jesus unsealing the scroll:

He [Jesus] went and **took the scroll from the right hand of Him who sat on the throne.** And when He had taken it, the four living creatures and the twenty-four elders fell down before the Lamb. Each one had a harp and they were holding golden bowls full of incense, which are the prayers of God's people. And they sang a new song, saying:

"You are worthy to **take the scroll and to open its seals,** because you were slain, and with your blood you purchased for God persons from every tribe and language and people and nation. You have made them to be a kingdom and priests to serve our God, and they will reign on the earth." (Revelation 5:7–10, emphasis added)

Our generation is now in the midst of numerous disclosures that were written in the scroll of Daniel, then unsealed in the pages of Revelation. Those unsealed disclosures continue to come to life, even more so in our generation of humanity's existence. You'll see that in a much clearer light in the next couple of chapters.

Think of it: We are the only generation that has ever looked at some of the most mysterious visions found within the pages of Revelation and are now able to say: "Yes! I can see that happening—perhaps in our own lifetime, or in the very near future!" In fact, *all* of the technologies required to bring these things to fruition—either implied or directly revealed—are right before us.

We are the first generation to be able to say these things with a straight face, and to have a large number of students of the Word of God agree with us when we say them.

There's a reason this is so.

13

LIVING IN SCIENCE FICTION

There can no longer be any doubt:
The unsealing is happening now.

No generation before ours could have imagined the entire planet observing real-time global events unfold before their eyes, as foretold two thousand years ago. Yet today, that phenomenon happens around the clock, day in and day out. We watch these things develop as they happen.

The images of our daily happenings are displayed on screens we carry in our hands, or are mounted on our walls, resting in our laps, and sitting on our desktops. We watch them almost everywhere, even from thirty-six thousand feet in the sky as we rocket forth, traveling at speeds of close to six hundred miles per hour—almost the speed of sound. These screens are displayed in airports, train and bus stations, cruise ship corridors, office buildings, doctors' offices, automobiles, mass transit vehicles, and public outdoor plazas in major cities around the globe. We almost cannot escape the myriad "living" images that continually pour out among us.

Neither could any other generation before us imagine the reality of a planet-wide human identification system. Nor could they have conceived of the techno gadgetry required to make it happen. That's not to mention a worldwide allegiance to a singular man who, according to Revelation

13–14, will eventually preside over a global government. This doesn't even take into account our unprecedented technological ability to "call fire down from the heavens,"[35] or the capability of everyone on the planet to instantaneously communicate personally with anyone else anywhere.[36]

And think of this: Since the entire global population will eventually be forced to receive a mark, as the book of Revelation asserts, how would that "beast system" know which people are obeying or disobeying? It wouldn't, unless there were some way of monitoring every human on the earth in real time, *all the time!* The tech systems required for that monumental task would have seemed unachievable for almost two thousand years after John wrote those words. We are now the only generation to possess the technology to do that very thing, and we are actually laying out the plans to implement the technology. That tech is advancing farther into Orwellian scenarios of application every single day.[37]

Let's look at a couple of examples of how quickly all this is happening. Early in the writing of this book, I was typing the last words of the preceding paragraph. About an hour after that, an Internet newsfeed popped up on my computer. This is one of the first headlines I read: "Clearview Plans Facial Recognition Database That Knows Every Person on Earth."[38]

Here are some of the opening words of that article:

Clearview AI…aims to build a facial recognition database that includes you. Yes, you. But not only you. Clearview wants its database **to include every human being on Earth**, and it thinks it can get there by **siphoning up 100 billion photos from the internet**…. The Company told investors that **it already has 10 billion images**, and it is currently **adding 1.5 billion more every month.**[39] (Emphasis added)

Then there's this scenario, also seeming to jump right out of the pages of the book of Revelation, published online by the World Economic Forum in February 2022:

Our days are filled with myriad discrete data collection moments. Even when we have genuine intent to affirmatively consent to each moment of data collection, it is practically impossible to do so: **No individual has the time to provide affirmative consent on a near constant basis.** This reality arguably **undermines our individual agency.**

What if technology allowed you to **outsource your decision-making** even further—**to a digitally automated agent**, potentially **using artificial intelligence (AI)**, which could **actively make those decisions for you?**[40] (Emphasis added)

Now Is the Time

Each of the previously listed techno-marvels, whether used for good or evil, would have appeared to be impossible from the time John was given the book of Revelation until today, with most occurring only in the last few years. Now, they are no longer insurmountable challenges. We're either presently using these technologies or envisioning and devising their soon appearance. There can no longer be any doubt: *The unsealing is happening now.* And, to a growing number of scholars, it seems increasingly likely that Daniel was giving us *hints* of future advancements in various types of wondrous technologies that would mark the days of the ultimate *unsealing*.

What was the hint Daniel revealed? For starters, we must understand that the divine clue was given in a code. The code is right there in the surface text of the Bible, in plain language, but only the generation of humanity that begins to see it unfold will be able to comprehend its fullest scope. Look again at verse 4 of Daniel's final chapter:

Many shall run to and fro, and knowledge shall be increased. (Daniel 12:5, KJV)

What do these shadowy words mean?

The Great Debate

That single prophetic utterance of Daniel 12:4 has been the subject of heated scholarly debate almost from the time it was written.[41] One can certainly imagine why. It is because these words, as I've already stated, are *coded*. They were Holy Spirit-inspired glimpses of a future world. Daniel's iterations would, no doubt, take on different meanings for successive generations until they were perfectly fulfilled as God intended.

As you will soon discover, the words in Daniel 12 are also directly linked to a revelatory end-time announcement made by Jesus Himself. *There's* the real key for unlocking its meaning. When Yeshua straightforwardly explains the prophecy, it's settled. At that point, there's simply no more argument about the proper interpretation.

So, as we continue, let's explore several vital connections that will help give us a larger understanding of those last incredible declarations the prophet Daniel laid out.

ONLY IN OUR DAY

Does the Bible say anything at all about a never-before-seen
technological eruption that will occur within the last days?

his is a good place to recap an important truth I've been preaching
and teaching for several decades.

I often state it like this: "We are now living in the most prophetic
times humanity has ever witnessed since the First Coming of Jesus Christ."
Sadly, when I say these words, most of the folks look at me like I have a
third eye planted in the middle of my forehead. But even that reaction is
what the Word of God said would happen: *The coming of the Son of Man*
will be just like it was in the days of Noah and just like the days of Lot (para-
phrased; see Luke 17:26–30). I am convinced we are there now, at least
on the leading edges.

Unparalleled

I also believe a truly observant student of the Word of God would recognize the following unparalleled signs of our times as either directly or
indirectly jumping right off the pages of the Bible's ancient predictions.

Some of the most important examples are as follows: First, there was
the stunningly prophetic return of the nation of Israel—a 2,700-year-old

prophecy occurring in 1948.[42] Following that was the world-changing return of Jerusalem as the legally recognized "chief city" of Israel in 2018. Next, there's the ever-unfolding alignment of the Ezekiel 38–39 nations that are foretold to organize an unholy coalition to eliminate the prophetically revenant nation of Israel and retake the restored Jerusalem!

There's also the exponential explosion of technology that began its sharp upsurge in the early 1950s,[43] only a few years after Israel's miraculous return. That upwelling included nuclear technology, computers, the Internet, global information/communication, planetary exploration of our own solar system, deep-space investigation, satellite warfare, and drone warfare, as well as satellite communications and weapons guidance, deep-fake video and audio, holographic imaging, virtual reality (VR), artificial intelligence (AI), and always-advancing high-speed transportation technologies.

But there's more—so much more! There's also biometric identification, DNA/mRNA, mRNA vaccines, advanced medical diagnostics, and robotic surgery. Further, there's Crispr-Cas9 genetic editing, globally pervasive spying and intel gathering, and the most current explorations of quantum physics that attempt to pierce the veil of "multiple dimensions of reality" we now know *are* genuinely there. And the list goes on.[44]

Global Mobilization

Think about it: Until the early 1900s, just a little over one hundred years ago, all of humanity, for the preceding six to ten thousand years of recorded history, had only *walked* wherever they went—or they rode upon beasts, or traveled in wagons and carriages pulled by those beasts. It wasn't until 1825 that the world's first steam-engine train grunted down its rudimentary railway. But even then, most of the world was still walking or riding animal-pulled carts of some sort. They would continue to do so for decades.

It wouldn't be until sixty years after the appearance of the steam-driven locomotive that the first basic automobile was invented, in 1886. That early, open-air, two-seat vehicle looked a lot like a glorified lawnmower.

It was almost another forty years after that, well into the 1920s, before the more "modern" Model T and Model A cars became increasingly pervasive, at just about the same time that propeller-driven airplane travel began to take hold. The "running to and fro" of Daniel's budding prophecy was beginning to open its bloom just a little over one hundred years ago. But if the world *then* had only known what was just up the road.

Today we travel in highly personalized "metal boxes" on massive and looping interstate highway systems. We do this while adjusting the comfort level of our vehicle's temperature-control systems as we sit on our heavily cushioned passenger seats…which are often equipped with back massagers.

We navigate our massive high-speed steel ships to circumnavigate the entire world with few limitations. And, almost three football fields' length below the oceans' surfaces, our nuclear-powered submarines slip along at speeds that can have us almost anywhere on the planet within days, delivering, if necessary, mega tons of nuclear weapons.

Every day, multitudes fly through the air in gleaming aluminum tubes at speeds of many hundreds of miles per hour…while passengers take naps, talk to friends, and drink cocktails as they soar. About 115,000 of those "metal birds" are coursing and crisscrossing their way across the globe twenty-four hours a day, seven days a week…transporting a mass of people each year that adds up to more than half the planet's total population.[45]

Additionally, there are currently more than 6,500 satellites orbiting our earth, and many more scheduled to be launched. Some are communications satellites, some are mapping and spy devices, and others are used as weapons of war. We've also launched a couple of deep-space probes that have now gone beyond our own solar system and, recently, beyond our galaxy, yet still communicate with us back on earth.[46]

Exabytes

Within that stunning sphere of recent massive technological advancement, we have also determined that over 90 percent of the world's entire storehouse of recorded knowledge has been generated in only the last several years of humanity's existence.[47] The amount of stored global data was estimated to be 44,000 exabytes[48] at the dawn of 2020. By 2025, the amount of global data generated is expected to reach 463 exabytes…each and every single *day*. As a point of reference, all the words ever spoken by all the humans who have ever lived could fit into only 5 exabytes of stored data.[49]

All of the preceding genres of technology show no signs of slowing down. And that's not counting the tech on the near horizon that we don't yet even know about. In fact, the speed of this massive upgrading phenomenon is so rapid that much of the info you've just read will probably be outdated in only a few short years after the writing of this book.[50]

Foundational Question

In light of what we've considered thus far, another question has to be asked: Does the Bible say *anything at all* about a never-before seen technological eruption that will occur within the last days?

After all, if the answer to that question is no, then think of the ramifications of this next question: If there truly is absolutely *nothing* in the Bible about this mind-boggling explosion of tech and knowledge, then how could we ever again trust the Word of God to be relevant to our own days? The short answer is *we couldn't*!

But, I assure you, the Bible hasn't missed a thing. We are the ones who've missed it.

15

NAYSAYERS

The message is right there, albeit in relatively coded language.

Shockingly, several of today's online resources, as well as a number of classical scholars, flatly claim that the Bible *nowhere* addresses the issue of a futuristic burgeoning of technology.[51]

This is a formidable claim, considering the types of tech advancements required to bring about the last-days condition of the Antichrist world alone, as catalogued in Revelation 13–14. Yet, the contextually mistaken notion that the Word of God does not prophesy vast advancements of techno applications in the last days still persists.

As an example, consider a contemporary commentary from a generally respected and often-quoted biblical research website. It asks the following question in its headline, "Does the Bible say that an increase in technology is a sign of the end times?"[52]

The article then attempts to explain away the works of many renowned people who understood certain scriptural prophecies—especially the prophecy of Daniel 12:4—to answer a resounding "Yes" to the headline's question. Then, that piece goes on to categorically declare: "The short answer is 'No.'"

As it turns out, the general message of the piece is that the Bible says *absolutely nothing substantial* about last-days technological advancements. The article concludes with the following:

> Many passages of Scripture refer to what will happen at the end of the age, **but no other passage** [The "other passage" is referring to Daniel 12:4][53] **seems to deal with increasing knowledge or technology as a sign for us.**
>
> **A greater sign** is the **advancement of the gospel** which Jesus spoke of in **Matthew 24:14** and which He commanded us to proclaim in Matthew 28:19–20. God's goal for mankind isn't to advance as far as we can or to know all we can discover, but rather that all should come to repentance (2 Peter 3:9, emphasis added).[54]

How to Miss the Revelation

Remarkably, the article also refers to the words of Jesus in Matthew 24:14. The author's implied admonition in using that particular verse is: "We shouldn't concern ourselves with uncovering mysteries of God's Word. We should primarily be about the business of preaching the gospel."

While there is a measure of admirable truth in that contention, the writer of the piece has actually missed the very *code* Jesus intended for us to discern, and it is embedded within the verse to which the writer referred![55]

Here is Jesus' prophetic declaration found in Matthew 24:14:

> And this gospel of the kingdom will be preached in the whole world as a testimony to all nations, and then the end will come.

There it is!

In that statement, Jesus announced that technology would explode just before His return and that certain technological developments would be used to take the gospel to the world. He also proclaimed that all this would be a definitive sign of the last days.

I can guess your thoughts right now: *Wait a minute, Carl. That passage doesn't say anything like that! Where in the world did you get that notion?*

Look very closely again at Jesus' words. The message is right there, albeit transmitted in a relatively coded language. Don't worry if you don't see it yet. Many others don't either—at first reading anyway. But it's there.

And…it was meant to be there.

It was meant for us. It was meant for you.

16

CONTEXT, CONTEXT, CONTEXT

And this gospel of the kingdom will be preached in the whole world
as a testimony to all nations, and then the end will come.
~MATTHEW 24:14

First, let's break down Jesus' Matthew 24:14 prophetic declaration in its proper context. Then we can use what we learn as we next dissect Daniel's prophecy.

We know without any doubt that Jesus' assertion in this verse is a foretelling of the end times. His straightforward words scream the truth of that. His announcement was not a prophecy merely about His current days on earth, nor was He speaking only of the near future of His disciples. He was speaking specifically of the very last days, because His numinous forecast is tied to His words: "and then the end will come."[56]

Jesus also tells us that one of the most defining signs of the end-time generations would be the global dissemination of the gospel message—and He says it twice![57]

However, some will still insist that Jesus doesn't literally mean the *entire earth*; He only means the Roman Empire. That was the whole world of His day.

The problem with that assertion, however, is that it ignores the greater context Jesus Himself laid before His disciples. After all, the initial question the disciples had asked Him, as recorded in Matthew 24:3, was: "What will be the sign *of your coming* and of *the end of the age?*"[58]

We can safely say the "end of the age"[59] has not yet come. Yeshua has not returned. His Kingdom certainly has not been set up on the earth in a literal sense. But, for the first time in history since He spoke those words, the crux of His prophecy is being fulfilled, right before our eyes. And, since Jesus was indeed speaking of "the end," He had to have been ultimately speaking of at least our day, and perhaps beyond.

Gospel Technology

Think of it! Twenty-four hours a day, every day of the year, and only for the last several decades, the gospel of Jesus Christ has been sent into every nation and tribe on the planet, among practically all the many billions of its citizens. The message of God's Word is being broadcast to the nations through all manner of burgeoning instantaneous information and communications technologies.

Essentially, every Christian from almost anywhere on the planet can now reach the entire world with the gospel of Jesus Christ through personal digital communication devices. We don't even have to be a traditional preacher or evangelist to do so. We don't have to get on an airplane, or a ship. We don't have to be officially commissioned as a missionary by a particular ecclesiastical denomination. We don't have to hold seminary degrees. All we have to do is punch a few buttons on a device we hold in our hand and start talking or typing to share the good news of Jesus Christ to whomever—whenever and wherever we wish, and in practically any language of the world! No other generation before us has ever been able to do this. There can be no doubt: Jesus' prophecy was about our days and beyond. His words could be referring to nothing less.[60]

The Starting Point

Also consider that, when Jesus said the "gospel of the Kingdom" had not yet been completed,[61] He hadn't gone to the cross. He hadn't yet risen from the grave. He had not ascended into Heaven. He had not yet given the Holy Spirit to His born-again people. The Church had not been born. The first gospel message had not yet been preached.[62]

Moreover, the entire world had not even been discovered and mapped when Jesus gave that prophecy. That wouldn't happen in the way we now recognize the globe until the mid-1800s.[63] Furthermore, the seemingly supernatural technology it would take to saturate the entire population with the gospel had not been invented when Jesus spoke those words and would not be developed until our generation. And that tech is *still* developing at mind-boggling speeds. The fact that the gospel of Jesus Christ should have gone forward more than a few decades after His crucifixion must have seemed impossible to those who conspired to bring about His death! Yet, not only did it happen, but the life-changing message is still being preached throughout the globe, with no apparent end in sight, and almost two thousand years after the prophecy was made. There is no human explanation for such a fact.[64]

As it turned out, everything Jesus prophesied all those years ago *would* happen—but only in the very last days, according to His own words in their context. Context makes all the difference in the world, wouldn't you agree?

The Real Journey Begins

Now let's jump back into Daniel 12:4. By applying the same contextual approach we just took with Matthew 24:14, we can discover what Daniel was trying to say within the similarly coded language of his words. It's one of the Bible's most important keys to understanding the days in which we now live.

17

MULTI-MILLENNIAL LEAP

But you, Daniel, shut up the words and seal the book, until the time of the end. Many shall run to and fro, and knowledge shall increase.
~Daniel 12:4, ESV

nraveling the mystery of Daniel's last-days prophecy can only be accomplished if we faithfully employ two very important protocols of biblical interpretation. We've already used these principles as we dissected the words of Jesus in Matthew 24:14. Now, we'll give these interpretive tools a working definition.

1. **The context of time frame:** First, determine the correct *time frame* at which the prophecy is ultimately *aimed.* This includes ascertaining if there is a *compound nature*[65] to the prophecy, especially within its time-frame declaration.

2. **The context of word meanings:** Determine the *proper word usages* of the biblical languages employed in that passage and consider whether they are *relevant to the time frame upon which the prophecy is ultimately focused.*

In reference to the first principle—just like with Jesus' prophecy in Matthew 24—Daniel 12:4 answers the question for us. Daniel was told the prophecy he was shown was *actually* meant for the "time of the end."[66]

Answering the Critics

A sizable number of classical commentators on Daniel 12 through the ages have desperately tried to make those words—"the time of the end"— refer *only* to the end of Daniel's days, and not the actual *end of days* before the return of the Lord Jesus Christ. A quick comparison of several biblical commentaries reflects that dichotomy.[67]

Admittedly, there are passages in the book of Daniel that refer only to the prophet's specific era[68] as well as the days immediately afterward, especially during the times of the Greek domination of Judea by Antiochus Epiphanes.[69] However, from chapters 7–12, we're also consistently confronted with snippets and/or entire treatises on prophecy that could have no meaning—in proper context—other than that of the age of the Antichrist, or the days approaching it. As a result of that seemingly multi-branched interpretation, I and many other biblical expositors have come to view Daniel's words within the scope of their compounded sense. That is, the words in Daniel 12 specifically address the literal "time of the end."

Albert Barnes, American theologian and author of *Barnes' Notes on the Bible,* states the matter succinctly. (Please see endnote for additional examples from other respected scholars.)[70]

> This is **such language** as would be used on the supposition that the reference **was to far-distant times,** and to **the scenes of the resurrection and the final judgment,** when Daniel would be present.... **I do not see that it is possible to explain the language on any other supposition than this....**
>
> **No other interpretation,** therefore, **can be affixed to this....** With this great and glorious doctrine the book appropriately closes... "at **the end of days"—when time shall be no more, and when the consummation of all things shall have arrived.**[71] (Emphasis added)

Daniel 12 Connects to Matthew 24

Look at what Daniel asserts regarding the same thing Jesus would later speak of in Matthew 24:14:

> **Those who are wise will shine** like the brightness of the heavens, **and those who lead many to righteousness**, like the stars forever and ever. (Daniel 12:3, emphasis added)

There's only one way God's people *of the last days* will "shine" and "lead many to righteousness," and that's through the preaching of salvation found through the blood of Jesus/Yeshua alone. Jesus told us this would be accomplished through broadcasting the "gospel of the kingdom" to "all nations."[72]

Jamieson-Fausset-Brown Bible Commentary (Daniel 12):

> Turn…to righteousness—literally, "justify," that is, **convert many to justification through Christ** (James 5:20).[73] (Emphasis added)

A number of respected scholars acknowledge that this is exactly what Daniel was speaking about.[74] He saw into the future. He saw into our days, the last days, and he saw the global preaching of the gospel of salvation in a way that must have looked like science fiction.

Jesus Settles It

But that's not all. Scholars have also long been aware that Jesus' prophetic message of the last days, found in Matthew 24, draws heavily from the book of Daniel.[75] In so doing, Jesus Himself removes all doubt as to the specific timing of Daniel's prophecy. That's a crucial point to remember as we move forward. Compare the following two passages. First, the opening words of Daniel 12:

**There will be a time of distress such as has not happened from
the beginning of nations until then.** But at that time your people—everyone whose name is found written in the book—**will be
delivered.**[76] (Daniel 12:1, emphasis added)

Next, these are Jesus' words, from Matthew 24:

**For then there will be great distress, unequaled from the begin-
ning of the world until now**—and never to be equaled again....
[This verse from Matthew 24:21 is practically a direct quote of
Daniel 12:1.]
     Then will appear the sign of the Son of Man in heaven. And
then all the peoples of the earth will mourn when they see the Son
of Man coming on the clouds of heaven, with power and great
glory. **And he will send his angels with a loud trumpet call, and
they will gather his elect from the four winds, from one end of
the heavens to the other.** (Matthew 30–31, emphasis added)

While Daniel didn't tell his readers exactly how that "deliverance"
would take place in the last days, Jesus filled in many of those details.
That divine process would occur at the sounding of a heavenly trumpet,
as well as at the command of Jesus Himself. The *delivery* process would be
put into effect through a host of angelic agents.[77] Jesus was "decoding" a
portion of Daniel's prophecy, and at the same time, He was quoting some
of it almost word for word! Yet much of today's Church has missed this
huge, divine clue.

What Daniel Beheld

But, you might ask, did Daniel actually see the types of things that are
now a part of our everyday lives? Most assuredly he did! He probably saw
much more than what we even know at this point. This is the purpose of
the *coded* language in Daniel 12. Its message was designed to give instruc-

tion and inspiration throughout future generations, but it would only develop into its final fulfillment in the generations of the very last days.

Next, let's examine Daniel's words recorded in chapter 12:4 to determine their truest meanings.

18

TO AND FRO

Daniel saw our days. He saw the exponential advancements in travel, communication, and information-exchange technologies.

D r. James Burton Coffman was a contemporary of our own age, having passed away in June of 2006 at the age of 101. He was a prolific teacher, preacher, and biblical scholar who wrote an extensive and renowned set of commentaries on the entire Bible. His work is valued by biblical students the world over.

In his hundred-plus years of life, Dr. Coffman experienced the transition from the modes of travel that had been used for the previous six thousand years to the travel and technology innovations of our current days. What an amazing chunk of history to have lived through! In his voluminous work, *Coffman's Commentaries on the Bible*, he wrote the following concerning Daniel 12:

> "Men shall run to and fro, and knowledge shall be increased." Some interpreters **have tried to apply** this to persons letting their eyes run to and fro searching for the truth; **but we cannot find anything like that in the passage.**
>
> **If men will just look at the travel to and from upon the planet earth by men of all nations throughout this whole century, they**

could not fail to be impressed with the truth that this going "**to and fro" on the earth has been multiplied fantastically above everything that was even dreamed of a hundred years ago.** Is not this prophesied here as being a development "at the time of the end"?

Likewise, has not knowledge been "increased"? In the field of medicine, more knowledge has been learned in the past century than in all previous centuries put together. Furthermore, this same phenomenon may be noted in any one of a hundred different fields of knowledge. Take transportation, chemistry, biology, agriculture, space travel, etc., is it not a fact that "knowledge has been increased"? Does this mean, therefore, that we are indeed approaching the time of the end? Our own conviction is that the answer is undoubtedly affirmative.

The prophecies of knowledge being increased and men going "to and fro" **could never have been fully understood** by any person living prior to the 20th century!

In this connection, **one should read 1 Peter 1:10-12,** where this phenomenon of the prophets not understanding their own prophecies is specifically stated.[78] (Emphasis added)

Here's the passage Dr. Coffman was referring to in his closing paragraph:

Concerning this salvation, the prophets who foretold the grace to come to you searched and investigated carefully, **trying to determine the time and setting to which the Spirit of Christ in them was pointing** when He predicted the sufferings of Christ and the glories to follow.

It was revealed to them that they were not serving themselves, but you, when they foretold the things now announced by those who preached the gospel to you by the Holy Spirit sent from heaven. **Even angels long to look into these things.** (1 Peter 1:10–12, Berean Study Bible; emphasis added)

A Leap in Knowledge

Only three years before Dr. Coffman passed away, the Human Genome Project[79] was completed, and the "code of life" for all humanity had been fully sequenced and mapped. That monumental leap in knowledge once again turned a corner of "changing everything" regarding the way we will continue to live now, as well as in the future. These increases in knowledge are exactly what the Word said would occur. Dr. Coffman was bold enough to confront the status quo and declare the truth of what he saw. That truth is in *the code* given by the prophet Daniel.

Multiplication Processes

Many shall run to and fro, and knowledge shall **increase**. (Daniel 12:4, emphasis added)

Daniel uses the word "many" to indicate the extent of the last-days travel around the world and the nations. In the Old Testament text, that word is the Hebrew *rab.*

Strong's Exhaustive Concordance defines *rab* as: "**Abundant** (in quantity, size, age, number, rank, quality), **exceedingly populous, to multiply**.... The word is often translated in other biblical passages as 'multitudes,' the implication being *practically uncountable.*"[80] (Emphasis added)

The poignant way *rab* is used in the first book of the Bible gives us a clue as to its fullest gravity of meaning:

The LORD saw **how great** [*rab*; globally ubiquitous] the wickedness of the human race **had become on the earth** [through an exponential growth process, over time], and that **every inclination of the thoughts of the human heart** was only **evil all the time.** (Genesis 6:5, emphasis added)

Encompassing the Planet

The words "to and fro" in the English (actually, a fairly archaic form) come from the Hebrew word *shuwt*, which means to "travel about, over long distances—encompassing the entire globe."[81]

Here are several examples of its use:

- After they had **gone through the entire land** [*shuwt*], they came back to Jerusalem at the end of nine months and twenty days. (2 Samuel 24:8, emphasis added)
- For the eyes of the LORD **range throughout the earth** [*shuwt*] to strengthen those whose hearts are fully committed to him. (2 Chronicles 16:9, emphasis added)
- And the LORD said to Satan, 'Where have you come from?' Satan answered the LORD, "**From roaming throughout the earth, going back and forth on it** [*shuwt*]. (Job 2:2, emphasis added)

Thus far, we understand that Daniel was shown modes of transportation like nothing he could have imagined. He was also allowed to "see" the vast numbers of people participating in this travel, numbers that would exceed any the world had experienced in any age before. One would think Daniel's vision would have completely boggled his mind—perhaps even terrified him. In fact, that's exactly what he said happened:

As [the angel] came near the place where I was standing, **I was terrified and fell prostrate.** "Son of man," he said to me, "**understand that the vision concerns the time of the end.**" (Daniel 8:17, emphasis added)

Apparently, the only thing that alleviated Daniel's immediate fright was understanding that the things he saw were visions of the last days of humanity's existence, before the return of Yeshua.

Daniel saw *our* days. He saw the exponential advancements in travel, communication, and information-exchange technologies, as well as the global chaos that eventually comes as a result. What he saw...*petrified* him.

But, how about the phrase in Daniel 12:4 that says "knowledge will increase"?

This is where yet another "aha!" usually occurs.

19

KNOWLEDGE WILL INCREASE

Armed with these deeper understandings of the word usages within the language Daniel employed, let's do a little experiment.

What do Daniel's words, "knowledge will increase," actually mean? Once more, a study of the original words sheds enormous—practically indisputable—light.

The Hebrew term Daniel used for "increase" is *rabah,* which is frequently found in the Bible to speak of an explosive increase.[82] As an example, have a look at the first usages of the word in the book of Genesis, starting in the first chapter. In these verses, where we see the English "multiply," the Hebrew word is *rabah.*

- And God blessed them, saying, "Be fruitful **and multiply and fill** the waters in the seas, and let birds **multiply on the earth.**" (Genesis 1:22, ESV; emphasis added)
- And God blessed them. And God said to them, "**Be fruitful and multiply and fill the earth** and subdue it, and have dominion over the fish of the sea and over the birds of the heavens and over every living thing that moves on the earth." (Genesis 1:28, ESV; emphasis added)
- When **man began to multiply on the face of the land** and daughters were born to them. (Genesis 6:1, ESV; emphasis added)

- Bring out every kind of living creature that is with you—the birds, the animals, and all the creatures that move along the ground—**so they can multiply on the earth and be fruitful and increase in number** on it. (Genesis 8:17, emphasis added)

The words "multiply and fill" are how we would describe consistently increasing growth, until the numbers reach a practically incalculable amount. Our modern English expression of this idea would be "exponential growth." This is exactly how Daniel said knowledge would increase in the last days. How could anyone deny that we, and *only we*, are now there?

To illustrate what Daniel was speaking about, consider the following from *Bell's Commentary on the Bible:*

From the time Christ died to the year 1700, knowledge on earth doubled. It took 1700 years for all of the previously accumulated knowledge to double on earth. In the year 1900 it doubled again, only 200 years later. In the year 1950 it doubled again, only 50 years later. In the year 1970 it doubled again, only 20 years later. Today information doubles every 2 years. Prognosticators are pointing to a day very soon when knowledge on earth will double every single day.[83]

Bell's Commentary was published in 2017. As this book is being written, in 2022, accumulated knowledge is said to be already doubling every thirteen months. However, because of additional giant leaps in tech development just on the horizon, accumulated knowledge is very soon expected to reach a doubling rate of *every twelve hours!*[84] I'm convinced Daniel saw it. Are *you* convinced yet?

Knowledge and Technology

The word "knowledge" is also rich with hidden meaning. Consider how it is used elsewhere in Scripture:

- In the middle of the garden were the tree of life and **the tree of the knowledge** of good and evil. (Genesis 2:9, emphasis added)
- Huram was filled with wisdom, with understanding **and with knowledge** to **do all kinds of bronze work.** He came to King Solomon and did all the work assigned to him. (1 Kings 7:14, emphasis added)

Interestingly, the ancient Hebrew text does not have a word that translates to "technology." This is because that word, as we know it, had not yet come into use. But, the word "technology" derives from the word "knowledge." We cannot look up the etymology or definition of the word "technology" without finding the word "knowledge" in practically every explanation.[85]

Word Swap

Now let's do a little experiment.

We will substitute the word "technology" for "knowledge" in the verses we've just examined. We'll do the same with the words and phrases "many," "to and fro," "increase," and "time of the end." We'll exchange these with the fuller concepts we've just uncovered.

Each of the replacement terms is a legitimate use of the original Hebrew, as evidenced from the Hebrew concordance entries and the Scripture we've already examined. In doing this, see if you might also spot what a number of students of the Word during our own times are now discerning.

- In the middle of the garden were the tree of life and **the tree of the** [**technologies**] of good and evil. (Genesis 2:9, emphasis added)
- Hiram was **filled with** wisdom, with understanding **and with** [**the technological know-how**] to **do all kinds of bronze work.** He came to King Solomon and did all the work assigned to him. (1 Kings 7:14, emphasis added)

Now for the biggest shocker. Let's do the same with Daniel 12:4:

- But you, Daniel, shut up the words and seal the book, until the [**the days just before the return of Yeshua**]. [**Vast masses of people**] shall [**travel throughout the earth**], and [**knowledge and technology**] shall [**exponentially multiply**]. (Daniel 12:4, ESV; emphasis added)

That legitimate exercise of modern word exchange makes the concept pretty clear, doesn't it? Jesus, of course, knew the truth of Daniel's words. That's why He quoted from Daniel 12 in His Matthew 24 discourse on the Mount of Olives and interpreted Daniel to be speaking about the time of the end...*our days*. If you don't remember anything else about Daniel 12, please remember that vital truth. If someone asks you what you believe about that passage, you can simply say, "I believe what Jesus said *He believed* about it!"

Thankfully, not all of the classical scholars missed what Daniel meant. Several understood it completely. In fact, one nailed it, at least as far as the limits of his knowledge of future discoveries could have stretched. That man was Sir Francis Bacon.

Sir Francis Bacon

Bacon, who lived from the mid 1500s through the early 1600s, was a renowned English philosopher and statesman who served as attorney general and lord chancellor of England. His works are widely acknowledged as the nascent development of today's modern scientific method. His treatises remained influential throughout the entire systematic knowledge revolution. His writings and advancements in various fields of scientific discovery and methodology are central points of scholarly debates to this day.[86]

Bacon indisputably saw the meaning and importance of the prophecy of Daniel 12:4, "Many shall run to and fro, and knowledge shall increase," (Daniel 12:4, ESV). The *Cambridge Bible for Schools and Colleges* acknowledges Bacon's thoughts on that passage:

> [Many shall run to and fro, and knowledge shall be increased] A famous passage, prefixed by [Francis] Bacon in its Latin to the first edition of his *Novum Organum*, and interpreted by him (1. 93) as signifying that the complete exploration of the world, which seemed to him to be then on the point of accomplishment, would coincide with great discoveries in science [including, of course, the resulting technologies].[87]

Following are Bacon's own prophetic words. This is only one example of his prescient explanations of Daniel 12:4. We find various, but equal, restatements of this postulation throughout his other important works as well:

> And this **Proficiency in Navigation, and discoveries**, may plant also an expectation of the **further proficiency, and augmentation of all Sciences**, because it may seem **they are ordained by God to…meet in one Age.** For so the Prophet Daniel **speaking of the latter times foretelleth: as if** the openness and **through passage of the world, and the increase of knowledge were appointed to be in the same ages,** as we see it is already performed in great part.[88] (Emphasis added)

Now we know that Sir Francis Bacon—and others like him—was correct all along, in spite of myriad cynics who have thought otherwise. It is now evident that Bacon accurately predicted the heart of what we're now living in, and he foretold it four centuries before his words became reality. He made those predictions based upon Daniel's seemingly coded prophecy. Mr. Bacon has been vindicated, entirely. We are his witnesses.

Modern scholars now have little excuse as to the proper interpretation and understanding of Daniel's prophecy, which was intended, in the ultimate sense of fulfillment, for a certain generation.

That generation is the generation of the end time: *our generation.*

20

HIDDEN THINGS

From now on I will tell you of new things,
of hidden things unknown to you.
~Isaiah 48:6

Only twice in this book will I illustrate a scriptural truth with the relatively recent science of Equidistant Letter Sequencing (ELS), sometimes called "skip codes."[89] Actually, the theory that these kinds of codes might truly exist within the pages of Scripture goes back over 1,500 years.[90]

As we examine these two spectacular and significant instances, we'll follow an academically sound, biblically balanced approach to our analysis. I'll be the first to admit the ELS computer-search program has sometimes been misapplied. Then again, the surface text of the Word of God itself has been similarly mishandled, even by God's own people. But we surely don't stop studying the Bible because of those who don't "use it properly." Instead, we insist on a set of protocols to ensure its proper interpretation.[91]

Operating within the parameters of the strictest procedures, it is my opinion that we simply can't depart from our current discussion about Daniel 12:4 without exploring one of these stunning ELS instances. I think you'll agree with me once you see it. It's one of those things that will likely compel you to say, "Wait a minute! How can this be?"

An Illustration

If you're not familiar with ELS, the best way to explain it is to present a brief hypothetical model. We'll use a passage from Isaiah 52. I will reproduce it here in English, but for the sake of our illustration, let's pretend our reproduction is written in Hebrew—the language the ELS program was originally designed to research.

You'll notice the passage we'll use is about preaching the good news (gospel) to all the nations, specifically to God's people, Israel. It also speaks of the importance of glorifying the name of God. A part of Isaiah's prophecy is also quoted by the Apostle Paul in Romans 10:15.

Since both preaching the Word to all the nations and bringing glory to the name of God are also foundational ministry passions of mine, how amazing would it be if we happened to find my name in this passage using ELS? Impossible, you say? Yes. I would certainly suppose it would be *impossible*—humanly speaking.

> And all day long my name is constantly blasphemed. Therefore **my people will know my name**; therefore in that day they will know that it is I who foretold it. Yes, it is I.
>
> **How beautiful on the mountains are the feet of those who bring good news,** who proclaim peace, **who bring good tidings, who proclaim salvation** [Yeshua/Jesus], who say to Zion, "Your God reigns!" Listen! **Your watchmen lift up their voices; together** they shout for joy. **When the Lord returns to Zion, they will see it with their own eyes.** (Isaiah 52:6–8, emphasis added)

Following the proper ELS program conventions, we would start our hypothetical exploration by first taking out all the punctuation, capitalization, and spacing between each letter. This is one of the first protocols of the actual ELS program. Thus, the verses would appear as one block of text—a run-on sentence that would look like this:

andalldaylongmynameisconstantlyblasphemedtherefore
mypeoplewillknowmynamethereforeinthatdaytheywillknow
thatitisiwhoforetoldityesitisihowbeautifulonthemountains
arethefeetofthosewhobringgoodnewswhoproclaimpeace
whobringgoodtidingswhoproclaimsalvationwhosaytozion
yourgodreignslistenyourwatchmenliftuptheirvoicestoge
thertheyshoutforjoywhenthelordreturnstoziontheywillseeit
withtheirowneyes

With the text arranged in this manner, the ELS program can simply search through each segment of text in a strictly defined skip code without being skewed by spaces, capital letters, punctuation, and other anomalies. The program would then look only for the letters it was encoded to find. Next, we would direct the program to look for two words: "carl" and "gallups."

The Search

Let's say we instructed the program to use a *skip parameter* to be anywhere between *every two to thirty letters* only. This is because, for a revelation to hold genuine significance, the search could not be just a willy-nilly hunt for a bunch of specified letters separated by any number of ridiculously far-spaced or indiscriminate intervals. Of course, with those kinds of searches, the letters for my name could be found in every book on the planet.

The properly encoded ELS protocol would then start the examination by looking for the first "c" in the passage. Then it would search for the first "a" located after that "c." Let's say the program found the letter "a" exactly twenty letters over from the first "c."

Now the program has a *specific parameter* with which it *must* proceed. The program would then check to see if—using the same skip number of twenty letters from the "a"—an "r" might be found. Of course, that would be highly improbable.[92]

However, let's say the "r" was indeed twenty letters over. Then, twenty more letters over, the "l" was there as well. At this point, you would probably be scratching your head, wondering how this could be. Yet, right before your eyes would be an ELS twenty-letter skip code for "carl" within the very text we chose to search.

But wait! What if, twenty more letters over from the "l," the letter "g" was also discovered? Then another twenty letters over, another "a" was found, and so on, until finally the words "carl" and "gallups" were found in that text. And, each letter of both words was spaced horizontally[93] through the text exactly twenty letters from each other! What might you think *then*?

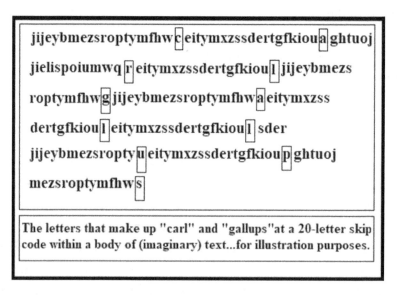

jijeybmezsroptymfhw c eitymxzssdertgfkiou a ghtuoj

jielispoiumwq r eitymxzssdertgfkiou l jijeybmezs

roptymfhw g jijeybmezsroptymfhw a eitymxzss

dertgfkiou l eitymxzssdertgfkiou l sder

jijeybmezsropty u eitymxzssdertgfkiou p ghtuoj

mezsroptymfhw s

The letters that make up "carl" and "gallups" at a 20-letter skip code within a body of (imaginary) text...for illustration purposes.

Our hypothetical discovery would reveal that something on the verge of the supernatural might have been disclosed. At least it would certainly appear to be.

Do you see the implications of such an occurrence being discovered by using scientifically sound search parameters? The discovery might turn out to "mean" nothing, in the end of it all. But it's there, regardless—and almost impossibly so. For that reason alone, the phenomenon demands

serious consideration before we simply dismiss it. Welcome to the phenomenon of skip-code research, or *ELS technology*. That tech has only
been available to our own generation.

The illustration we've just examined is, of course, merely hypothetical.
My name, as far as I am aware, does not exist in that or any other passage.

Nevertheless, scores of legitimate biblical ELS codes have been discovered within the last several decades by researchers and mathematicians.
Those discoveries have been proven through accredited peer review to be
next to statistically impossible to even exist.[94] Yet, the revelations are certainly there, regardless of who "likes" it and who doesn't.[95]

In the next chapter, you'll read the full story I spoke of earlier regarding the Israeli tour guide, Uri Mendel, who visited my home while he
was in the United States. It is a true account of the impact a genuine ELS
revelation makes upon someone who is unprepared to "see" it.

Uri saw something incredible in Daniel 12:4 that stunned—even
unnerved—him.

21

REVEALING THE UNSEARCHABLE

Call to me and I will answer you and tell you great
and unsearchable things you do not know.
~JEREMIAH 33:3

By 1997, I had been the pastor of Hickory Hammock Church in Milton, Florida, for ten years. In honor of that anniversary, our gracious church family treated my wife and me to a tour of Israel.

On that trip, we became good friends with our Israeli guide, Uri Mendel.[96] Mr. Mendel had been an officer in the Israeli Defense Forces (IDF) in years past and, after his service, had worked as a licensed Israeli/US tour guide. The company for which he worked took Americans all over Israel; it also took Israelis all over the United States.

As mentioned earlier, Uri was born in Israel and speaks Hebrew as his native language. He also speaks fluent English and takes great pride in his work as an international tour guide. He and I hit it off on the first day of our tour, and our friendship continued to blossom for years.

In the early 2000s, Uri called my wife and me from New York City to say he was in the United States finishing up a tour for a large group of travelers. He said the tour group was returning to Israel the next day, but that he, instead, wanted to fly to Florida and see us for a couple of days, if at all possible. We quickly made the arrangements, and he was on his way.

First Exposure to ELS

In the meantime, back in 1997, a *New York Times* bestseller was rocking the world in a manner unlike few books I had ever read. The book was titled *The Bible Code*, written by Michael Drosnin. Prior to writing the book, his first, Drosnin had been a journalist for the *Washington Post* (1966–1968) and the *Wall Street Journal* (1969–1970).

The release of Drosnin's book shook the global core of religion, biblical scholarship, secular worldviews, and even statistical sciences. It was reportedly based upon weeks of personal meetings over a five-year period with Dr. Eliyahu Rips, the discoverer of the ELS codes in the Bible. In the first chapter of the book, Drosnin says:

> The code was discovered by Dr. Eliyahu Rips, one of the world's leading experts in group theory, a field of mathematics that underlies quantum physics. It has been confirmed by famous mathematicians at Harvard, Yale, and Hebrew University. It has been replicated by a senior code-breaker at the U.S. Department of Defense. It has passed three levels of secular peer review at a leading U.S. math journal....
>
> I have known about this [code phenomenon] for five years. I have spent many weeks with the Israeli mathematician, Dr. Rips. I learned Hebrew, and checked the code on my own computer every day. I talked to the man at the Defense Department, who independently confirmed that the Bible code does exist. And I went to Harvard and Yale and Hebrew University to meet with three of the world's most famous mathematicians. They all confirmed that there is a code in the Bible.[97]

Drosnin followed that first book with two more, *The Bible Code II* (2002), another runaway bestseller, and *The Bible Code III* (2010). At his death in 2020, the *Boston Globe* reported on his passing with these words:

> "The Bible Code" **had its roots in science. In the early 1990s, Israeli mathematician Eliyahu Rips and his colleagues performed an experiment** in which they laid out the 304,805 letters of the Torah like a giant crossword puzzle and then performed a **"skip-code" computer search. They discovered uncanny [word and name] combinations.**[98] (Emphasis added)

When I read Drosnin's first book around 1999, I was cautious yet stunned by its findings. All of the revelations were clearly illustrated so readers could see the startling discoveries for themselves. But one of Drosnin's findings particularly interested me, and I knew just who to ask about it.

In My Living Room

When Uri Mendel made that visit to my home, I decided to do my own verification with a man who spoke Hebrew as his native tongue. I invited him to sit with me on the couch in my living room and then I asked Uri if he had heard of Drosnin and *The Bible Code*. He said he had not heard of the man, nor was he familiar with the book.

I then told Uri I wanted him to verify something in the book. I explained that certain "tables" in it were written in Hebrew; I needed him to translate and verify the proper use of the Hebrew language in those tables. He said he'd be glad to and seemed quite willing to help with my otherwise mysterious appeal.

I gave Uri no hint as to what the book was about, or what I wanted him to look at. I didn't even mention that he would be looking at Scripture. I just wanted his raw reaction to what I would show him.

I opened Drosnin's book to page 99, pointed to a specific ELS illustration, then asked Uri, "What do you see here?"

Upon taking a quick glance at the chunk of biblical text—consisting of nothing but Hebrew letters, laid out in a block-text style, with no punctuation or letter spacing—he exclaimed, "Wow!

"What is this?" Uri insisted. "Where did you get this? What am I looking at here?"

22

NO MERE COINCIDENCE

We are that generation of "running to and fro"
over the face of the earth.

Uri reached for the book, still firmly held in my hands, so he could turn to its cover for a closer look. He was staggered by what I had just shown him. He wanted to see the book's title and author's name again.

I laughed as I eased the book away, keeping him from seeing the cover. "Don't look at the cover yet," I teased. "Just tell me what you see. I'll explain everything after you show me what's there, in Hebrew."

He relented with a chuckle, and said, "This block of letters," he pointed with his index finger, "I don't know why they're written this way, without spaces and punctuation…but I do understand the text. I'm very familiar with it. It comes from the book of Daniel." He paused and kept staring at it, mesmerized.

"I know these words!" he said. "It's the passage that says 'seal up the scroll, until the time of the end.'"

"Yes," I replied, "that's Daniel, chapter 12." I was going to ask him to speak to the four letters in the *circled text* highlighted by Drosnin, but Uri beat me to it.

He pointed to the letters again, and continued, "These Hebrew letters that are highlighted in the squares are from the regular text, like we have in our Bibles. There are no spaces between them, but my mind can see the sentence. They say, 'Shut up the words and seal the scroll, until the end.'"

"Right," I said. "But what about these letters?" I pointed to the ones running vertically, starting from the first letter of the sentence he had just quoted. Those four letters ran at a skip code of only thirty spaces, which placed all of them one on top of the other. The letters were highlighted within circles.[99]

"That's why I'm shocked!" Uri said. "It says 'computer'!" It seems to mean this 'unsealing' Daniel was talking about would be done with computers!"

"So," I asked, "the word 'computer' is definitely there, in Hebrew?"

"Oh yes!" he replied. "But that's not the only thing."

He sat there silent for a moment longer, then said, "What you might not know is that the word for 'computer' is a relatively new word in Hebrew. It only came about with the invention of the computer. This word was not in the ancient Hebrew of Daniel's day, not even close. It's virtually impossible that what I am looking at is there—but there it is!"

I thanked him for his confirmation. We talked about the book for several more hours, as he continued to thumb through its pages, looking at each code chart and reading as much as he could.

The Code

Following is a reproduction of the chart of Daniel 12 that Uri was examining. You can see the encircled letters that make up the Hebrew word for "computer." That word is spelled in Hebrew like this: מַחְשֵׁב.

In the chart, the word runs vertically, from bottom to top, and intersects with Daniel's prophecy that states, "and knowledge will increase." What do you think are the chances of finding the word "computer" in that location, and connecting with that sentence—a word that didn't even exist for more than 1,500 years after Daniel wrote the prophecy? It's a statistical impossibility. Yet...*there it is.*

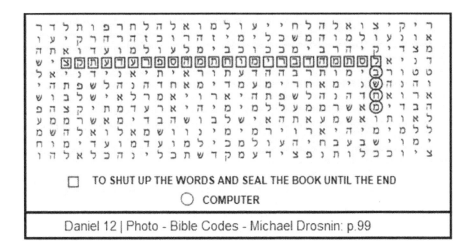

TO SHUT UP THE WORDS AND SEAL THE BOOK UNTIL THE END

COMPUTER

Daniel 12 | Photo - Bible Codes - Michael Drosnin: p.99

Unfortunate Turn

Sadly, it was Drosnin himself—according to various mainstream news reports—who finally cast doubt upon how to "use" the discoveries. In the opinion of a number of detractors, Drosnin seemed to have developed an almost obsessive fascination with trying to use the codes to "predict the future." Some of his prophetic speculations, in my estimation, bordered on the bizarre. He even made the following claim in his book:

> I talked to the man at the Defense Department, who independently confirmed that the Bible code does exist. And I went to Harvard and Yale and Hebrew University to meet with three of the world's most famous mathematicians. **They all confirmed** that there is **a code** in the Bible **that predicts the future.**[100] (Emphasis added)

However, the main source of Drosnin's research, Dr. Eliyahu Rips, resoundingly rebuffed Drosnin's handling of the ELS information. What follows are pertinent excerpts from Dr. Rip's 1997 rebuttal statement, published shortly after *The Bible Code* had been released on the global market:

I have seen Michael Drosnin's book "The Bible Code." **There is
indeed serious scientific research being conducted with regard to
the Bible Codes.**

[But I had to address] whether we can, **from a scientific point**
of view, **attempt to use the Codes to predict future events.** After
much thought, **my categorical answer is no.** All attempts to
extract messages from Torah codes, or **to make predictions based
on them,** are **futile and are of no value.**

This is not only my own opinion, but **the opinion of every
scientist who has been involved in serious Codes research. The
only conclusion that can be drawn** from the **scientific research
regarding the Torah codes is that they exist** and that **they are not
a mere coincidence.**[101] (Emphasis added)

Statistical Impossibility

Here's the crux of the matter regarding the ELS codes and Daniel 12.
The word "computer" is indeed in that passage, starting with the exact
sentence wherein Daniel predicts an "unsealing" of prophecy in the last
days. It's about as statistically impossible for that word to be in that exact
spot as it would be for "carl gallups" to be found in Isaiah 52. Similarly, the
Daniel computer skip code is also a short one, it's a picture of perfect symmetry, and again, it's connected to the very verse to which it would apply.

What do you think? Is it a coincidence that, in Daniel 12:4, a last-days
"unsealing" is mentioned in connection with the verse that also predicts a
technological explosion in the last days, and then that explosion actually
does occur? We're currently living in it!

Think of this: Out of that technology explosion of our day, predicted
by Daniel, came the invention of the computer. Computer technology is
the precise tool that would enable us to invent the ELS code search system that then empowered us to see the word "computer" in Daniel 12:4.
Further, the word "computer" intersects with the prophecy that appears to
hint, in the surface text, of its eventual appearance.

I don't believe this to be a coincidence. Nor could Daniel have some-how encoded it on purpose. It had to be divinely implanted in the text. If it is a coincidence, then it certainly is one of the biggest flukes of happen-stance I've ever laid my eyes upon. It would also seem to imply that God is not really in "control" of every "jot and tittle" of His Word after all. Yet, we know He most certainly *is* in control. So…how did the word "computer" get there—right there, in that exact verse and spot?

I am certain we are the generation Daniel spoke of that is "running to and fro" over the face of the earth. We are also the generation of ever-increasing knowledge, and we are now globally using the technology that emanated from that knowledge!

The puzzle pieces are still falling into place; the bigger picture is still emerging.

PART IV

THE POWER

In the beginning was the Word, and the Word was with God, and the Word was God. He was with God in the beginning.

Through him all things were made; without him nothing was made that has been made. In him was life, and that life was the Light of all mankind. The light shines in the darkness, and the darkness has not overcome it....

The Word became flesh and made his dwelling among us. We have seen his glory, the glory of the one and only Son, who came from the Father, full of grace and truth.

~JOHN 1:1–5, 14

23

THE TIE THAT BINDS

If quantum mechanics hasn't profoundly shocked you,
you haven't understood it yet.
~Niels Bohr

With our understanding of what Daniel and Jesus said about the explosion of technology and knowledge in the last days, let's now talk about current scientific knowledge and its stunning links to the Word of God.

An Extraordinary Realm

Less than a hundred years ago, humanity gained a fundamental understanding of one of life's deepest scientific mysteries. The early explorers of that enigma were increasingly shocked by what they were finding as they continued to dig ever deeper into the abyss of its obscurities. The shock factor of it all continues to this very day.[102]

Starting in the mid 1920s, we were just beginning to theorize—within a fair degree of scientific certainty—about the existence of "unseen" particles at the atomic level. These particles were thought to be the tiniest building blocks that make up the foundational *stuff* of everything that exists. In other words, that's when we began to grasp that every single thing we could physically experience was actually made up of miniscule particles we could *not see*. And those particles were made up of even tinier particles…seemingly to the point of infinity. I am, of course, speaking of the world of atomic science and quantum physics.[103]

John Archibald Wheeler, director of the Center for Theoretical Physics at the University of Texas, is one of the world's leading theoretical physicists. In 1939, he and Niels Bohr published a paper, "The Mechanism of Nuclear Fission." That document laid the underpinning studies for atomic and hydrogen bombs.

Around 1979, Wheeler was reported to have become increasingly concerned about the curious world of quantum mechanics and its many paradoxes that suggested that, on the atomic level, "reality seems more like magic than like nature" on the physically experienced level.[104]

What we are witnessing today within the realm of that knowledge, compared to just a few decades ago, is an indescribable advancement… and it's still barreling forward at lightning speed. Once again, here is a certain class of knowledge like the world has never before possessed, an explosion of scientific information impacting practically *everything* in the world of advancing technology. This is just as Daniel and Jesus told us would happen as the last days draw closer.

The Stuff of Matter

Simply put—for the purpose of this chapter—here is how we can understand quantum physics at a basic working level. Atoms and their quantum particles are the smallest foundational materials of physical reality presently known to humanity. We know that certain atoms have the ability to bond together. When they make those bonds, they form molecules. Specific molecules are able to connect with other certain molecules in order to create *matter*, which is defined as any substance that occupies space and has mass.

An example of this would be when two atoms of hydrogen join with one atom of oxygen. That combination produces a molecule of water—H_2O. That molecule has mass and takes up space. Therefore, it is qualified as "matter." The atomic bonding that produces all the molecules of matter known to humanity create every physical *thing* in our universe.[105]

But where did the ability for atoms to bond with other atoms originate? And *why* did it originate? How does an atom *know* what it is and what it's supposed to do in the first place? For example: What are the orbits in which their elements travel, and how do they make certain their movements are uniformly compliant enough so that the universe itself doesn't fall apart? What instructs a particular atom that it's supposed to *do* anything at all? And, once the atom *starts* doing what it needs to do, how does it know it must *keep* doing it?

Besides the fundamental components of the atom—which consist of the nucleus (made up of neutrons and protons), along with its orbiting electrons—we now have discovered there are still *smaller elements* that create the framework of the atomic structure. Those smaller particles are comprised of ever-smaller particles, or waves, or packets of particles. They are also made up of important energy sources, especially electromagnetic energy forces called photons.[106]

It seems the deeper we look, the more we find within the fascinating world of atomic quanta particles.[107] Moreover, every one of these microscopically infinitesimal and elemental components is operating in ways that drastically differentiate one atomic structure from another. To this day, physicists are still trying to unravel the deepest secrets of how it all works.

Here's another stupefying truth about atoms. The ways in which the tiny elemental components of an atom interact are currently understood to operate outside every boundary of the known physical laws of the universe! It is as if they have their own laws of dynamic activity that is decidedly otherworldly—and not directly related to anything we know in our own physical world. This fact, as previously mentioned, was what Dr. John Archibald Wheeler was most concerned about when he asserted that "reality seems more like magic than like nature."

The Problems

Lawrence Maxwell Krauss is a theoretical physicist and cosmologist who taught at Arizona State University, Yale University, and Case Western Reserve University. He explained the problems of quantum physics like this:

> **No one intuitively understands quantum mechanics** because all of **our experience involves a world of classical phenomena** where, for example, a baseball thrown from pitcher to catcher seems to take just one path, the one described by Newton's laws of motion. **Yet at a microscopic level, the universe behaves quite differently.**[108] (Emphasis added)

Yet, these subatomic particles—apparently acting completely outside the realms of uniformly reliable prediction—make up everything within the realms of "reliable calculation" known to humanity, and I mean *everything*, including all the laws of the universe that we understand, measure, and predict.[109]

To this day, there are only a limited number of "known" operating protocols of the quantum particles. Yet, it is through the info we do possess, at the quantum level, that we are able to consistently create several of our more astounding technologies, such as lasers, MRIs, and the soon-coming quantum-computing and weapons-engineering tech.[110] A whole new universe of knowledge and technology has been unlocked—only in our generation. And, apparently, there's much more quantum tech headed our way.[111]

The Bond

Have you ever wondered what holds an atom together? Why is it that the elemental parts of an atom don't just fly apart, shoot off into oblivion, then disintegrate? No shell, skin, or container of any type surrounds the particles. They're just *there*, operating in perfect cooperation. What is the adhesive substance or energy that somehow connects the quantum particles to each other?

The scientific answer to that can get a little complex. However, a basic and sound answer is that the atomic structure is predominately held together by *electromagnetic forces* (photons)—otherwise known as *light*.[112]

Information posted on Oregon State Science Department's website states it like this:

> **The law of electrostatics** says that like charges repel. So, if a nucleus contains two or more positively charged protons, they should repel each other. But in that case, **why doesn't the nucleus [of the atomic structure] fly apart? The answer to this question involves…electromagnetic force.**[113] (Emphasis added)

And an article published on a University of Chicago website confirms the foundational definition of electromagnetic force:

> **Electromagnetic force** is responsible for generating **visible light,** as well as radiation in **other wavebands** not detectable by the human eye.[114] (Emphasis added)

Since *light* is the glue of all reality, then everything we perceive as matter could be described as frozen or solidified light! This is exactly how Albert Einstein described it. Have a look at the following excerpts from a Universe Today: Space and Astronomy News website article titled, "How Are Energy and Matter the Same?"

> As Einstein showed us, light and matter are aspects of the same thing. **Matter is just frozen light**. And light is matter[115] on the move.
>
> A neutron, for example, can decay into a proton, electron, and anti-neutrino. The mass of these three particles is less than the

mass of a neutron, so they each get some energy as well. **Energy and matter are really the same thing. Completely interchangeable.**[116]

So in a way, energy, matter, space and time are all aspects of the same thing.[117] (Emphasis added)

At this point, you might be wondering: *What does all of this have to do with the theme of this book?* I'm looking forward to showing you the answer.

24

SEEING THE WIND

Science is finally catching up to what the Word of God has been telling us all along.

Let's start this chapter by having a look at the very beginning—the opening words of the Bible:

> **In the beginning** God created the heavens and the earth. Now the earth was formless and empty, darkness was over the surface of the deep, and the Spirit of God was hovering over the waters. **And God said, "Let there be light,"** and there was light. God saw that **the light was good**, and he separated the light from the darkness. (Genesis 1:1–4, emphasis added)

Imagine! The first "elemental reality" that God created was *light.*

We know it is *light* that holds everything together at the subatomic level. But, we've only known this since our techno world began to explode with the discoveries of quantum physics—right in line with Daniel's prophecy.

Here's what the Word of God is really telling us: *Light had to be created first.* Without it, the entire framework of the atomic structure could not even exist. Without atoms and their dependable stability, there could be no molecules. Without molecules, there would be no molecular bonding. Without molecular bonding, matter itself could not exist. And, since all of that is true, then nothing in our universe could exist, either; neither could *you or I*. First, there had to be light.

Unseen

All we've learned thus far means that everything *seen* by us as reality was originally made from what was *not seen*. It wasn't seen, because it didn't even exist!

Where have we heard that before?

By faith we understand that the **universe was formed at God's command,** so that **what is seen was not made out of what was visible.** (Hebrews 11:3, emphasis added).

Ellicott's Commentary for English Readers explains Hebrews 11:3 in layman's terms:

As the **visible universe did not take its being out of what was apparent,** so **what** from time to time **is seen does not arise of itself out of what is manifest to man's natural perceptions.** Not only is the **eternity of matter denied,** but from the beginning a **warning has been given** against a materialistic philosophy.[118] (Emphasis added)

How could God's Word have revealed these deep matters of quantum physics, in both the Old and New Testaments, many thousands of years before humanity discovered the scientific reality of it?

Again, you might be thinking: Now that we can finally observe with our own eyes these smallest elemental particles of the atomic structure, what's the big deal? Now we can see them!

The truth is we still can't "see" them. Yes, you read that correctly. Rajat Kumar Pradhan, PhD, is a professor in the physics department at Utkal University in Utkal, India. He explains:

> **We can never see the subatomic particles directly**, but can only **infer from observation of such indirect effects**, like tracks.
>
> **If there are many of them and they are emitting some radiation**, and also if we shine some radiation on them and receive back the response, **this will also constitute a kind of seeing.**
>
> Finally, we of course **see everything with the "mind's eye", not the physical eye**, whether direct or indirect!
>
> **The mountain that we see with our eyes is but an interpretation of the data** that forms the neural correlate in the brain.[119] (Emphasis added)

When explaining this concept, I usually equate "seeing" quantum particles as being similar to "seeing" the wind. Humanity has yet to truly "see" the element of wind with our physical eyes. However, we certainly know it's there. We feel it, we can measure it, we can harness its power, and we can see and experience its effects—especially in the aftermath of its occasionally devastating presence. This is how we "see" the wind and, similarly, it's the way we "see" quantum particles.

It seems science is finally catching up to what the Word of God has been telling us all along, and not the other way around. And, just like Daniel and Jesus have said, the deepest truths of His Word would be reserved only for those with "eyes to see."

25

LIGHT

Now we see it. Now we understand it in its fullest sense.

B y this point, you might have already guessed where I'm headed next. The upcoming revelation is indeed profound, yet, it has been right there in God's Word since the very beginning.

Dozens of times, from Genesis to Revelation, the divine concept of *light* is emphasized. Usually those passages speak of light as it is equated with God Himself and, of course, with Yeshua, who is the physical image of the otherwise invisible God. Light is also the description given to those who are born again in Yeshua.[120]

- **He wraps himself in light** as with **a garment**; he stretches out the heavens like a tent. (Psalm 104:2, emphasis added)
- I saw that from what appeared to be his waist up he looked like glowing metal, as if full of fire, and that from there down he looked like fire; **and brilliant light surrounded him.** This **was the appearance of** the likeness of **the glory of the Lord.** (Ezekiel 1:27–28, emphasis added)
- This is the message we have heard from him and declare to you: **God is light**; in him there is no darkness at all. (1 John 1:5, emphasis added)

- **God, the blessed and only Ruler,** the King of kings and Lord of lords, who alone is immortal **and who lives in unapproachable light,** whom no one has seen or can see. (1 Timothy 6:15–16, emphasis added)
- **When Jesus spoke again** to the people, he said, "**I am the light of the world.** Whoever follows me will never walk in darkness, but will have the **light of life.**" (John 8:12, emphasis added)
- In [Jesus] was life, and that life was the light of men. (John 1:4)
- [Jesus said to them,] "**You are the light of the world....** In the same way, **let your light shine before others**, that they may see your good deeds and glorify your Father in heaven." (Matthew 5:14–16, emphasis added)

Now that we've established the most *elemental force* of life and matter to be *light,* and that light is what holds atomic structures together, we're ready to connect the dots that make up the backbone of the next *coded* revelation about Yeshua. Observe the declaration of Colossians 1:

The Son is the image of the invisible God, the firstborn over all creation.

For **in him all things were created:** things in heaven and on earth, **visible and invisible,** whether thrones or powers or rulers or authorities; all things have been created through him and for him.

He is before all things, and **in him all things hold together.** (Colossians 1:15–17, emphasis added)

There it is—buried in the Word of God for more than two thousand years, a declaration of quantum physics, attributed to Jesus Christ as the Creator and Sustainer of it all!

He is the *energy source of light* that holds everything together. He is *the light* that existed from the beginning and before the beginning. And this truth has only been knowable in the sense of quantum physics for less than a hundred years!

The next three commentary entries were written in the late 1800s, decades before the most nascent quantum physics understanding was coming into view. These scholars certainly got the theological implications of Colossians 1:17 correct, as well as the crux of the science itself. Words and phrases they used, such as "the primeval law of their being," "sustaining power," "organic stability," "continuance," and "maintained in their present state" seem pretty advanced for scholars living long before we understood about photons and electromagnetic energy forces within subatomic and submicroscopic structures, wouldn't you say?

Ellicott's Commentary for English Readers:

That is, **hold together in unity**, obeying **the primeval law of their being.** In this clause is **attributed to our Lord**, not only the creative act, but also **the constant sustaining power**, "in which all lives and moves and has its being."[121] (Emphasis added)

Meyer's New Testament Commentary:

[In Him all things hold together] expresses **that there is in Christ not merely the creative cause,** but also the **cause which brings about organic stability and continuance** in unity (preserving and governing) for **the whole of existing things.**[122] (Emphasis added)

Jamieson-Fausset-Brown Bible Commentary:

[All things are] Not only are **called into being from nothing,** but are **maintained in their present state.** The Son of God is **the Conserver, as well as the Creator** of all things.[123] (Emphasis added)

The Light of Life

Here is another well-known passage—the first few verses of the Gospel of John.

In the beginning was the Word, and the Word was with God, and the Word was God. He was with God in the beginning. **Through him all things were made**; without him nothing was made that has been made. **In him was life, and that life was the light of all mankind.** (John 1:1–4, emphasis added)

John begins his book with a declaration that hearkens all the way back to Genesis 1:1–3. It speaks of Creation itself and reiterates that Jesus was/ is Creator of all things. John also states Jesus is the "light" that holds creation together. Without that *light*, we are told, there would be no *life* at all. Once again, our most recent technological explosion has confirmed the truth of God's ancient declarations.

Consider the words of the following excerpt from a *U.S. News and World Report* article posted on April 2016. The article is titled, "During Conception, Human Eggs Emit Sparks: This Is the First Time the Phenomenon Has Been Observed by Scientists."

> **When a sperm meets an egg, sparks fly—literally.** According to a study published in Scientific Reports, an **explosion of zinc fireworks occurs when a human egg is activated by a sperm enzyme**…. A press release explains the science behind the phenomenon: "As the zinc is released from the egg, it binds to small molecule probes, which emit light in fluorescence microscopy experiments. Thus, the rapid zinc release can be **followed as a flash of light that appears as a spark**."
>
> This is the **first time scientists have observed these sparks** in a human egg.
>
> "We discovered the zinc spark just five years ago…and to see the zinc **radiate out in a burst** from each human egg **was breathtaking**," said one of the study's senior authors, Teresa Woodruff, Thomas J. Watkins Memorial Professor in Obstetrics and Gynecology at Northwestern University Feinberg School of Medicine (Rachel Dicker, www.usnews.com, 4/26/16). (Emphasis added)

Think of that! Yeshua really is the literal *Light of Life*, just like His Word asserts. And we are the first generation to know that the energy force of *light* genuinely holds everything in the known universe together; even at the moment of conception, there is an observable *burst of light*.

This truth has been embedded in God's Word all along, visible in the surface text that much of humanity has been reading and memorizing for thousands of years. But, the genuine depth of the meaning of those words, in just the right time—our time—have finally been brought forth for all the world to see. We are the first generation of humanity to have the technology to expose that glorious truth!

I stated at the beginning of this book that I'm building a case. This investigation is truly going somewhere. However, at this moment, we're still connecting the dots as the evidence consistently unfolds before us. Therefore, note that we'll see the evidence of Jesus being the Light of Creation again, and in a place we might least expect it.

26

UNSEEN REALMS

But we impart a secret and hidden wisdom of God,
which God decreed before the ages for our glory.
~1 Corinthians 2:7, esv

The Word of God undeniably speaks of multiple dimensions of physical realities. This important truth often escapes the attention of the modern church.

Beginning in the Bible's very first pages, Yahweh is presented as existing outside of the universe. Even the universe itself is set forth as only one of God's glorious "containers of creation" in the midst of His overall creative exploits.

Conceiving the Inconceivable

To be sure, no human allegory is perfect when attempting to illustrate God's glory, but the following will suffice here. Consider a desktop, or even a laptop computer, or whatever digital-quantum device that might be in vogue when you are reading this book—even perhaps years after its initial publication.

The inventor and programmer of that technology exists outside of it. The article of that tech is not the inventor's residence, or even his place of day-to-day presence. The intelligence that enables its systems to operate was first coded into its internal components. That coding creates *artificial intelligence* (AI). We call it that precisely because an intelligence much greater than what is actually operating the system was placed there, by design, for specific functions.

But the creator of that digitally intelligent "universe" is always outside of it. The creator might interact with it or even adjust its code from time to time, but its internal structure is not the abode of its inventor. Nor can the resultant technology even conceive of its creator's existence. The creator existed long before it did, and it will exist long after the tech device has stopped working.

Outside of the device's existence, there are many other worlds of existences and unseen realms of reality. But the internal intelligence of the mechanism can't comprehend those realms. It has no idea anything else exists at all. Yet those physical realities are genuinely there. Now, compare that illustration to what God's Word tells us about our own existence.

God Doesn't Lie

In the book of Job, chapter 38, we are assured that God already had another creation that existed long before ours. It was outside of our universe. It was, and still is, inhabited by living, thinking, choosing, and intelligent beings—the *bene elohim*, the sons of God—what most would call the angelic realm. This realm existed long before our earthly reality was ever spoken into existence.[124]

By the conclusion of Genesis 3, we're shown that God sealed off one of His created dimensions—the originally created Paradise, also known as the Garden of Eden. That was the earthly dimension created solely for the communal fellowship Yahweh would enjoy with all of His creation, both human and angelic. Since the Fall of Man in Eden, God has kept it sealed from all the other dimensions of reality and it will remain so until He restores all things to their former glory. This, of course, is the crux of the gospel message and the reason for Yeshua's redemptive work on earth.

When we reach the closing pages of the book of Revelation, we are shown that this same Paradise will finally be restored and revealed as our eternal home.

As we read through the pages of the Bible, by faith we understand that these other dimensions of reality exist, because the Word of God and our Redeemer assure us they are real.

Also, consider Paul's *catching-up* experience to the third Heaven, as recorded in 2 Corinthians 12:2–4. And don't forget the account of the Apostle John entering through a portal—described as a "door" that was opened—that led him to the throne of God, where he was given the entire book of Revelation (Revelation 4:1ff). Even Philip, the bold evangelist of the nascent church, was supernaturally transported[125] from one place to another during the early days of his ministry endeavors (Acts 8:39).

Each of these biblical people was apparently conducted through portals, dimensions, and time warps—if we were to use our modern language to explain these narratives. Further, these kinds of experiences are not foreign, even to the Old Testament Scriptures. They are all right there and have been for thousands upon thousands of years.

The Bible also speaks of the *unseen realms* as they are connected to spiritual warfare.[126] Additionally, we read of Jesus describing Himself as "the door," "the way," and "the gate." We read about the sky being "rolled up like a scroll" in the last days, as well as the coming *Lake of Fire*, the new Heaven and the new earth, and so forth.

The Word of God also discloses the "realms" of Heaven, Hell, the great chasm between them both, and Paradise, as well as "doors" that lead to Heaven's throne room, the demonic abode, the angelic abode, and the keys to life and death—mysterious portals only Jesus Himself can open.

From Genesis to Revelation, we are guaranteed that these realms are as real as the physical world and universe in which we currently exist. We are also assured that Jesus Christ is the Creator and Lord of every single one of them.

Jesus spoke of the authenticity of the dimension in which life continues at another level, a divine and completely redeemed level, one completely separate from our own.

- Jesus answered him, "Truly I tell you, today you will be with me in paradise." (Luke 23:43)
- Simon Peter asked him, "Lord, where are you going?" Jesus replied, "Where I am going, you cannot follow now, but you will follow later." (John 13:36)
- No one has ever gone into heaven except the one who came from heaven—the Son of Man. (John 3:13)
- Jesus answered, "I am the way and the truth and the life. No one comes to the Father except through me." (John 14:6)
- I am the Living One; I was dead, and now look, I am alive for ever and ever! And I hold the keys of death and Hades. (Revelation 1:18)
- The rich man also died and was buried. In Hades, where he was in torment, he looked up and saw Abraham far away, with Lazarus by his side. So he called to him, "Father Abraham, have pity on me and send Lazarus to dip the tip of his finger in water and cool my tongue, because I am in agony in this fire." (Luke 16:22–24)

Once we wrap our minds around these truths, we are well on our way to acquiring a treasure trove of additional insight into the living Word of God. That insight more thoroughly equips us to understand what God is really up to. It speaks of what life is all about—what the concept of "eternity" means, and what our divinely appointed purpose is in the midst of it all.

27

FOLLOW THE SCIENCE

These things God has revealed to us through the Spirit.
For the Spirit searches everything, even the depths of God.
~1 Corinthians 2:10, esv

Certain scientific revelations have existed within the pages of God's Word for many thousands of years, long before they were discovered by modern science. Let's go back, for just a moment, to the subatomic level of scientific conundrums.

A Phys.org scientific article explains some of the most recent scientific understanding coming from the quantum world of knowledge.

The **existence of parallel universes** may seem like something cooked up by science fiction writers, with little relevance to modern theoretical physics. **But the idea** that **we live in a "multiverse" made up of an infinite number** of **parallel universes has long been considered a scientific possibility.**...

It is important to keep in mind that **the multiverse view is not actually a theory, it is rather a consequence of our current understanding of theoretical physics.** This distinction **is crucial.**

We have not waved our hands and said: "Let there be a multiverse." Instead the idea that the universe is perhaps one of infinitely many is derived from current theories like quantum mechanics and string theory.[127] (Emphasis added)

A recent *Discover Magazine* article, titled, "Three Totally Mind-bending Implications of a Multidimensional Universe," asserts that the cosmos more than likely exists in far more than the three dimensions we are familiar with in the context of our own physical existence on earth. They claim that what we now believe exists, with a very high degree of certainty, is actually *many dimensions* of physical reality—and that existence is reliably predicted by current physics models.[128]

Dr. Michio Kaku, a world-famous theoretical physicist, agrees.[129] He is the cofounder of *string field theory*, which asserts that multiple universes and multiple dimensions do indeed exist. Dr. Kaku claims the models can now be tested to "1 part in 100 billion in accuracy, making it the most successful physical theory of all time."[130]

But there's more. The following was written by Adam Milton-Barker, a network engineer and Intel software innovator in the fields of artificial intelligence (AI), internet of things (IoT), and virtual reality (VR). This is some of the information he presents concerning the internationally acclaimed CERN Hadron Collider located in Switzerland.[131]

The Large Hadron Collider or LHC is the world's most powerful particle accelerator, [located] 300 ft. below the ground at the CERN Control Centre in Geneva, Switzerland.[132] The machine is the result of thousands of scientists and engineers planning and building over the last few decades. **To explain simply what the machine does, it sends sub-atomic particles at the speed of light** hurtling around the loop in opposite directions and then **smashes them into each other.**

CERN wants to use the LHC to find out the **fundamentals of our universe** and **how it was created.** [They are also] **expecting to find other dimensions** and [then] **open portals to these dimensions.**[133] (Emphasis added)

Another leading global online tech publication—with more than nine million unique browsers worldwide each month—reported this ominous quote from Sergio Bertolucci, CERN's director of research and scientific computing:

A top [scientific researcher] at the Large Hadron Collider (LHC) says that the titanic machine **may possibly create or discover** previously unimagined scientific phenomena, or "unknown unknowns"—for instance "**an extra dimension.**"

"**Out of this door might come something, or we might send something through it,**" said Sergio Bertolucci.[134] (Emphasis added)

NBC News even reported on this topic with the sensational headline, "Scientists Are Searching for a Mirror Universe. It Could Be Sitting Right in Front of You."

At Oak Ridge National Laboratory in eastern Tennessee, physicist Leah Broussard is **trying to open a portal to a parallel universe.**… if she unequivocally detects even a single mirror particle, it would prove that **the visible universe is only half of what is out there**—and that the known laws of physics are only half of a much broader set of rules. "If you discover something new like that, the game totally changes," Broussard says…. **Broussard's goal is to find out if that portal really exists and, if so, to open it in a methodical way.**[135] (Emphasis added)

Shortly thereafter, the mainstream global media breathlessly announced that on July 5, 2022, the CERN Large Hadron Collider would begin an entirely new and intensified series of experiments that could go on for at least four years.[136] These never-before-attempted super-experiments would supposedly include the most involved research yet, seeking to uncover the deepest secrets of dark matter and of gravity itself.

The research states many physicists are convinced that both of these topics, and others like them, could be ultimately explained by the existence of several extra dimensions of physical realities.[137]

In a July 2022 NPR article announcing CERN's restart, Dr. Sarah Demers, a physics professor at Yale University, said, "There has to be more out there because we can't explain so many of the things that are around us." Demers, who is also at CERN working on the third run, added, "There's something really big missing, and by really big, we're talking about 96 percent of the universe really big."[138]

Once again, "modern" science appears to be playing a quickly advancing game of catch-up regarding the deep truths of God's revealed Word. Physicists are only recently urging us to understand that there may very well be "many more" visible and physical dimensions just beyond our current level of discovery. However, regardless of what scientists are able to "prove," the fact of unseen realms of reality is exactly what the Bible has been telling us about all along. For the scientists who insist on ignoring this, there truly is something "big" missing—something "really big."

Consider what the Apostle Paul said:

For we are not fighting against flesh-and-blood enemies, but against evil rulers and authorities **of the unseen world**, against **mighty powers in this dark world**, and against evil spirits **in the heavenly places**. (Ephesians 6:12, NLV; emphasis added)

The unsealing of the last-days knowledge spoken of by Daniel and Jesus appears to be roaring forward, right in our own lifetime.

What We Don't Know

I suppose the bottom line is that we simply don't know what we don't know!

We're like the fish living at the deepest levels of our oceans' floors. They live and die in that realm thinking their "world" is all that exists.

They have no way of knowing that, directly over their heads live many billions of earth's life forms known as human beings. Nor are they aware of the thirty million other species that exist among those multiplied billions of humans.

They can't begin to fathom the world we live in, the worlds beyond our worlds, or the fact that they are really living in the bottom of an oceanic system that almost entirely envelopes a planet, a giant ball of matter hanging in space…on nothing. Neither can they comprehend that all this is also revolving around a gargantuan nuclear reactor called the "sun" in a solar system located in a spiral galaxy—that's only one of many trillions of other galaxies in a universe that extends beyond the reaches of imagination. They simply *don't know what they don't know.*

Why should we think we are the exception?

The next revelation will further illustrate my point.

28

ETERNAL ENTANGLEMENT

*The distinction between past, present, and future
is only an illusion, however persistent.*
~ALBERT EINSTEIN[139]

One of the strangest characteristics of quantum physics is "entanglement." That term is most simply explained in this manner: A particle from a specific atom in one place and another particle taken from that same atom—located even light years away—will instantly respond to the same stimuli, as if the two are connected by a mysterious channel of communication.

Scientists have now observed this phenomenon in action. Albert Einstein colorfully dismissed quantum entanglement as "spooky action at a distance." Over the past few decades, however, physicists have demonstrated the reality of that "spooky action" over increasingly greater distances—even from Earth to a satellite in space![140]

Following are the opening two paragraphs from a Phys.org article titled "Record Quantum Entanglement of Multiple Dimensions":

An international team [of quantum physicists] **has managed to create an entanglement**[141] **of 103 dimensions** with only two photons. **The record had been established at 11 dimensions.**

The states in which elementary particles, such as photons, can be found have **properties which are beyond common sense.** Superpositions are produced, such as **the possibility of being in two places at once,** which defies intuition. In addition, **when two particles are entangled, a connection is generated: measuring the state of one affects the state of the other particle instantly, no matter how far away from each other they are.**[142] (Emphasis added)

Dr. Micho Kaku explains quantum entanglement like this:

If I have two electrons close together, they can vibrate in unison.... **Now, separate those two electrons so that they're hundreds or even thousands of light years apart,** and **they will keep this instant communication bridge open.** "If I jiggle one electron, the other electron 'senses' this vibration instantly, faster than the speed of light."[143] (Emphasis added)

Biblical Application of the Science

Not only is quantum entanglement now scientifically proven, but it is used in several of our most current technologies.[144] Furthermore, understanding quantum entanglement might also help explain a few things about certain biblical narratives.

Consider what we've discussed in the last several pages: *instantaneous communication at the speed of light, from one dimension into another.* That sounds awfully close to the supernatural concept of prayer, doesn't it? Surely prayer is an interdimensional form of communication—wouldn't you agree?[145]

Moreover, quantum entanglement even shines a bit of light on the concept of *God the Father* being present within the dimension of His own cosmic glory, while at the same instant He is existing in human flesh on earth—even on a cross—as *God the Son.* Let's look at God's own words regarding this interdimensional truth.

The Pierced One

The book of Zechariah was written more than 2,400 years ago, a full four hundred years before Yeshua went to Golgotha's cross. Yet God plainly asserted that He would one day, be in two places at one time! He doesn't *explain* it—there are no scientific arguments or long dissertations. We are simply called upon to believe by faith what He declares in His Word. [146]

> **The Lord, who stretches out the heavens, who lays the foundation of the earth**, and who forms the human spirit within a person, **declares**....
>
> "**And I will pour out** on the house of David and the inhabitants of Jerusalem **a spirit of grace** and supplication.
>
> "[On that day] **They will look on me, the one they have pierced**, and **they will mourn for him as one mourns for an only child** [all happening at the same time], and **grieve bitterly for him as one grieves for a firstborn son**." [147] (Zechariah 12:1, 10, emphasis added)

Observe how contemporary scholars understand the multidimensional nature of God's declaration in that passage. [148]

Coffman Commentaries on the Bible (1905–2006): [149]

> **Me whom they pierced**, and they **shall mourn for "him**...." This passage **sends the critics into a frenzy**.... But, "'**They shall look unto me** whom they have pierced' **is the authentic reading**." Baldwin spoke of **some who were embarrassed** by the "apparent contradiction that God had been put to death." **Unregenerate man has difficulty** with the proposition that **God indeed died in the person of his Son on the Cross**. (Emphasis added)

Expository Notes of Dr. Thomas Constable: [151]

The **unusual combination** "they will look to me **whom they have pierced**" and "they will mourn for Him" **suggests two different individuals,** but the **deity of the Messiah solves this problem. Yahweh Himself would suffer for the people in the person of Messiah.**[152] (Emphasis added)

Even the Apostle John understood this truth and recorded it in his Gospel.

These things happened **so that the scripture would be fulfilled:** "Not one of his bones will be broken," and, as another scripture says, "**They will look on the one they have pierced.**" (John 19:36–37, emphasis added)

Wait a minute! Does Yahweh actually declare that He is both God *and* man—at the same time—in the person of Jesus Christ? *Really?* Yes, that's exactly what the Bible states, from the beginning of the Old Testament through the end of the New Testament. Zechariah 12 offers one of the most striking examples.[153] These are just a few wonderful things to ponder as they relate to the scientific discoveries of our times.[154]

Armed with what we've learned thus far, let's continue to delve deeper into the Word of God. There we'll discover that not only is Yeshua the physical manifestation of YHWH in the flesh, but His name is scattered throughout the Old Testament—and in places that open up nothing short of breathtaking revelations.

PART V

THE SALVATION

Who has gone up to heaven and come down? Whose hands have gathered up the wind? Who has wrapped up the waters in a cloak? Who has established all the ends of the earth? **What is his name, and what is the name of his son?** Surely you know! Every word of God is flawless; he is a shield to those who take refuge in him.

~Proverbs 30:4–5, emphasis added

29

HIDING IN PLAIN SIGHT

Substituting "Jesus" for Yeshua, *look what we discover!*

Of course, the English word "Jesus" does not appear in the Old Testament.

To be sure, there *are* foreshadowing "images" of Him within those pages. And, there are stunning prophecies and undeniable *types* of Him, but we don't see the actual name "Jesus." However, in the Hebrew language, it's a different matter, because the name *is* there. And it's there almost a hundred different times, *if* you know what you're seeing in the plain text.

Since the name "Jesus"—*Yeshua* in Hebrew—literally means "salvation" in English, it is interesting to look at the context in which "salvation" is most often used.[155]

To make this part of our excursion visual, we will place the word "Jesus" in each of the following Old Testament passages wherein the English word "salvation" is found, knowing the Hebrew word in that verse is actually *Yeshua*. We won't look at every one of the almost one hundred instances, but the following samples will prove to be dramatic enough. By employing this word substitution, we see major doctrinal themes take on a fresh new depth of understanding.

God with Us

The first example we'll examine is in the book of Exodus, in reference to the Israelites' successful escape into the wilderness from Egypt.

> The LORD (Yahweh) is my strength and my defense; **he has become my [Jesus]**. He is **my God**, and **I will praise him**, my father's God, and **I will exalt him**. (Exodus 15:2, emphasis added)

The Song of Moses not only spoke truth to God's people of that day, but it also carried prophetic meaning, because God literally *did* become Jesus/Yeshua! Jesus *is* with us as our strength and defense. Jesus *is* God in the flesh. And we *do* praise Him and exalt Him, precisely because He *is* our Creator and our Deliverer. Here is a very visible compound understanding of the verse, right there in the text…*if* we know what we're looking at!

- **In the beginning was the Word, and the Word was with God, and the Word was God.** He was with God in the beginning. **Through him all things were made**; without him nothing was made that has been made…. The **Word became flesh** and made his **dwelling among us**. We have seen his glory, the glory of the one and only Son, **who came from the Father**, full of grace and truth. (John 1:1–3, 14, emphasis added)
- **The Son is the image of the invisible God**, the firstborn over all creation. **For in him all things were created:** things in heaven and on earth, visible and invisible, whether thrones or powers or rulers or authorities; all things have been created through him and for him. (Colossians 1:15–16, emphasis added)
- In these last days **he has spoken to us by his Son**, whom he appointed heir of all things, and **through whom also he made the universe. The Son is** the radiance of God's glory and **the exact**

representation of his being, sustaining all things by his powerful word. (Hebrews 1:2–3, emphasis added)

The Rock

In the New Testament, Paul harkens all the way back to those forty years of wilderness wanderings of Exodus and how God supernaturally provided water for the Israelites from a huge rock. In 1 Corinthians, the apostle reminds us the rock that provided their *life-saving water* was a picture of Jesus Himself—the Rock from which flowed the *Living Water*.

And all drank **the same spiritual drink.** For they drank from the **spiritual Rock** that followed them, and **the Rock was Christ.** (1 Corinthians 10:4, ESV; emphasis added)

A striking image of the Rock is found in Deuteronomy 32:15, part of a prophetic lament concerning Israel's present and future rebellion, during the time of Moses and long after they would enter the Promised Land.[156] Once again, substituting "Jesus" for *Yeshua*, like we did in Exodus 14, look what we discover:

Jacob [Israel] dined until satisfied; [Israel] grew fat and kicked. He grew fat, coarse, and gross, so that he **abandoned the God who made him** and **spurned the Rock that was his [Jesus]**. (Deuteronomy 32:15, ISV; emphasis added)

We find the same declaration in 2 Samuel:

My God, **my Rock,** in him I will take refuge, my shield, and the horn [**strength**] of **my [Jesus]**, my high tower, and my refuge, **my savior;** from violent people **he saves me.** (2 Samuel 22:3, NEW HEART ENGLISH BIBLE)

The Gospel

Here's yet another example of this amazing form of a Yeshua code, also lining up with several New Testament declarations.

> Sing to the LORD, all the earth! **Tell of His [Jesus] from day to day. Declare His glory among the nations,** His marvelous deeds **among all peoples.** (1 Chronicles 16:23–24, ESV; emphasis added)

In 1 Chronicles we are told to proclaim the good news (gospel) of *Jesus* to all the earth—to all the nations and all peoples. Furthermore, we're instructed to do it with an abundance of praise and song every day. This is precisely what the New Testament attests as well:

- And **this gospel** of the kingdom will be **preached in the whole world** as a testimony **to all nations,** and then the end will come. (Matthew 24:14, emphasis added)
- **Therefore go** and **make disciples of all nations,** baptizing them in the name of the Father and of the Son and of the Holy Spirit. (Matthew 28:19, emphasis added)
- And **the gospel** must first be **preached to all nations.** (Mark 13:10, emphasis added)
- Then I saw another angel **flying in midair,** and **he had the eternal gospel to proclaim** to those who live on the earth—to every nation, tribe, language and people. He said in a loud voice, "**Fear God and give him glory,** because the hour of his judgment has come. **Worship him who made the heavens, the earth,** the sea and the springs of water." (Revelation 14:6–7, emphasis added)

The Light of Life

Consider the following from Psalm 27, remembering what we've already learned about Jesus being the *light,* and that in Him "all things hold together." This passage proclaims every one of those New Testament truths in Jesus!

> The LORD [*Yahweh*] is **my light** and **my** [**Jesus**]—whom shall I fear? The **Lord is the stronghold of my life**—of whom shall I be afraid? (Psalm 27:1, emphasis added)

Yahweh became, and at the same time has always been, Yeshua/Jesus. He is our Creator, and He is the ultimate *stronghold*—the *light*—holding together our very being and life, and every element that makes up the universe.

It's as if, when Jesus said He would show His disciples all the places in the Scriptures that were about Him, He actually knew what He was talking about!

30

HE HAS BECOME MY JESUS

*From beginning to end, Yeshua/Jesus is right
there in the Old Testament, and quite dramatically so.*

More than six dozen times, from Exodus to Zechariah, the name
of *Yeshua*/Jesus appears in the middle of God's Old Testament
promises.

The books of Psalms and Isaiah are the two most-quoted Old Testament
works found within the pages of the New Testament. Those two Old Testament books also contain the bulk of the "salvation"-*Yeshua* word connections.

We've already seen how amazing some of those associations really are.
Let's look at several more samples from the Psalms and Isaiah, as well as
from the books of Zechariah, Job, and Jonah. Again, I will substitute the
word "Jesus" for *Yeshua*/ "salvation" in each instance. Notice how many of
these word swaps also give a richer meaning to New Testament doctrinal
revelations about Jesus Christ.

The Psalms

- But I trust in your unfailing love; **my heart rejoices in your**
  [Jesus]. I will **sing the Lord's praise**, for he has been good to me.
  (Psalm 13:5–6, emphasis added)

- But may all who seek you rejoice and be glad in you; may **those who long for your** [Jesus] always say, **"The** LORD **is great!"** (Psalm 40:16, emphasis added)
- Those who sacrifice thank offerings honor me, and to the blameless **I will show my** [Jesus]. (Psalm 50:23, emphasis added)
- My soul finds rest in God alone; **my** [Jesus] **comes from him. He alone is my Rock** and **my** [Jesus]; he is **my fortress,** I will never be shaken. (Psalm 62:1–2)
- May God be gracious to us and bless us and make his face shine on us—**so that your ways may be known on earth, your** [Jesus] **among all nations.** (Psalm 67:1–2, emphasis added)
- But may all who seek you rejoice and be glad in you; **may those who long for your** [Jesus] **always say,** "The LORD is great!" (Psalm 70:4, emphasis added)
- Sing to the LORD a new song, for **he has done marvelous things**; his right hand and his holy arm **have worked** [Jesus] for him. The LORD has **made his** [Jesus] **known** and revealed his righteousness **to the nations.** He has remembered his love and his faithfulness to Israel; **all the ends of the earth have seen the** [Jesus] **of our God.** (Psalm 98:1–3, emphasis added)

Isaiah

"Surely **God is my** [Jesus]; I will trust and not be afraid. The LORD, the LORD himself, is my strength and my defense; **he has become my** [Jesus.]" With joy **you will draw water from the wells of Jesus.** (Isaiah 12:2–3, emphasis added)

Does this bring to mind images of Jesus with the woman at the well in John 4?

Jesus answered her, "If you knew the gift of God and who it is that asks you for a drink, you would have asked him and **he would have given you living water.**"

"Sir," the woman said, "**you have nothing to draw with and the well is deep.** Where can you get this living water? Are you greater than our father Jacob, who gave us the well and drank from it himself, as did also his sons and his livestock?" Jesus answered, "**Everyone who drinks this water will be thirsty again, but whoever drinks the water I give them will never thirst. Indeed, the water I give them will become in them a spring of water welling up to eternal life.**" (John 4:10–14, emphasis added)

There are still more examples:

- In that day they will say, "**Surely this is our God**; we trusted in him, and **he saved** us. **This is the** Lord, we trusted in him; **let us rejoice and be glad in his** [Jesus]." (Isaiah 25:9, emphasis added)
- Turn to me **and be given** [Jesus], all you **ends of the earth**; for **I am God**, and there is no other. By myself I have sworn, my mouth has uttered in all integrity a word that will not be revoked: **Before me every knee will bow; by me every tongue will swear.** (Isaiah 45:22–23, emphasis added)[157]
- I will also **make you a light for the Gentiles** that **my** [Jesus] **may reach to the ends of the earth.** (Isaiah 49:6, emphasis added)
- This is what the Lord says: "**In the time of my favor** I will answer you, and **in the day of** [Jesus] I will help you." (Isaiah 49:8, emphasis added)
- Then all mankind will know that **I, the Lord, am your** [Jesus], your **Redeemer**, and the **Mighty One of Jacob.** (Isaiah 49:26, emphasis added)
- But **my righteousness** will last forever, **my** [Jesus] through **all generations.** (Isaiah 51:8, emphasis added)

- The Lord will lay bare his holy arm **in the sight of all the nations, and all the ends of the earth will see the Jesus of our God.** (Isaiah 52:10, emphasis added)

Here's one of my favorites from Isaiah. It mirrors the great truths of Romans 10.[158]

- **How beautiful on the mountains are the feet of those who bring good news** [the gospel], who proclaim peace, **who bring good tidings, who proclaim** [Jesus], who say to Zion, "Your God reigns!" (Isaiah 52:7, emphasis added)

And…they just keep going deeper and deeper. The next two passages, for example, simply shout out the words of the book of Revelation![159]

- I delight greatly in the LORD; my soul rejoices in my God. **For he has clothed me with garments of** [Jesus] and arrayed me **in a robe of his righteousness,** as **a bridegroom adorns** his head like a priest, and **as a bride adorns** herself with her jewels. (Isaiah 61:10, emphasis added)
- The LORD **has made proclamation to the ends of the earth:** "Say to Daughter Zion, '**See, your** [Jesus] **comes! See, His reward is with him,** and his recompense accompanies him.'" **They will be called the Holy People, the Redeemed of the LORD.** (Isaiah 62:11–12, emphasis added)

Zechariah

This is also a favorite:

Rejoice greatly, daughter of Zion. Shout, daughter of Jerusalem. **Look, your king comes to you.** He is righteous, **and having** [Jesus]; lowly, and **riding on a donkey,** even on a colt, the foal of a donkey. (Zechariah 9:9, NEW HEART ENGLISH BIBLE; emphasis added)[160]

Jonah

We certainly can't forget the Yeshua code that's found in the words of the prophet Jonah:

- But I, **with a song** of thanksgiving, **will sacrifice to you.** What I have vowed I will make good. **[Jesus] comes from the Lord.** (Jonah 2:9, emphasis added)

Job

Then there's incredible testimony from the book of Job.

The Hebrew word "salvation"/*Yeshua* is not in the text of Job. But the person of Jesus certainly is! Here, He is called "Redeemer," which is a synonym for "Savior," or even for "Jesus" Himself.[161] In fact, that word is found seventeen times from Job through Jeremiah. In every instance, the declaration is made that it is God who is our Redeemer/"Jesus."

Notice Job declares this "Redeemer" will eventually exist in the earthly dimension of reality—in the flesh. Yet, at the same time, He is also God. Job additionally speaks of his own eternal, yet "fleshly," life because of the power of this One who is the Redeemer. By now, we simply can't miss the code.

- For I know that **my Redeemer [Jesus] lives,** and at the last **he will stand upon the earth.** And after my skin has been thus destroyed, yet **in my flesh I shall see God.** (Job 19:25–26, ESV; emphasis added)

From beginning to end, Yeshua/Jesus is right there in the Old Testament, and quite dramatically so. In each of the many times the name is found, it can be tied directly to New Testament promises and declarations found only in *Yeshua Ha' Mashiach.*

The Amidah Prayer for the Messianic King

Before we close this chapter, I must share one of the most striking examples of the Orthodox Jewish people literally imploring the LORD of Heaven to send them Yeshua! Of course, they don't even realize this is what they are asking. Sadly, their eyes are still blinded to that eternal truth.

The Hebrew Amidah Prayer[162] is the central prayer of Jewish liturgy and is, therefore, the core of every Jewish worship service. This prayer, among others, is found in the *siddur,* the traditional Jewish prayer book. In Hebrew, the prayer is called *Tefilat HaAmiday*—"The Standing Prayer." The original prayer constituted eighteen blessings. Today, nineteen blessings are used. The Amidah has been recited among the Jews since the first century—from the days of Yeshua until today.[163]

Blessing number fifteen of the Amidah Prayer is titled as a prayer "For the Messianic King." Where the word "salvation" is spoken in Hebrew (*Yeshua*), I will again substitute the English form: "Jesus":

Speedily cause **the offspring of your servant David** to flourish, and let him be **exalted by your saving power,** for **we wait all day long for your** [Jesus]. Blessed are you, O Lord, **who causes** [Jesus] **to flourish.** (Emphasis added)

As the whole world is being immersed in the disclosure of every kind of Yeshua code we can imagine, please fervently pray for the Jewish people…that their eyes might be opened to the name and person of the true Messiah and Savior, *Yeshua,* the One for whom they have so desperately longed.[164]

PART VI

THE LANGUAGE

I will give you the treasures of darkness, riches stored in secret places, so that you may know that I am the Lord, the God of Israel, who summons you by name.

~Isaiah 45:3

THE MYSTERIOUS HEBREW LANGUAGE

The secret things belong to the Lord our God,
but the things that are revealed belong to us and to
our children forever, that we may do all the words of this law.
~DEUTERONOMY 29:29, ESV

The most ancient precursor to what we know as the Modern Hebrew alphabet is the Proto-Sinaitic alphabet. That script consisted of letters drawn as stick figures, or *pictograms*. Those letters were rudimentary portrayals of animals, tools, human body parts, and other generally recognizable objects of everyday life.[165] (See appendix 1.)

Each picture was meant to represent the predominant sound of a specific letter. For example, if this applied to today's English alphabet, a depiction of a fish might indicate the "f" sound. A figure of a man could represent the sound "m," an outline of a hand would indicate the "h" sound, and so forth.

Most language experts agree that the Proto-Sinaitic script was the predecessor of what would eventually evolve into a number of modern alphabets of the world, including the one used in the original manuscripts of the Bible[166]—the *Paleo Hebrew*.[167] (See appendix 4.)

Hebrew Ideograms

Every letter representation in the Proto-Sinaitic alphabet also had a meaning or idea associated with it. Those meanings are referred to as "ideograms," or "ideographs." For example, the sound made by the letter *ayin* was represented by a pictogram of an eye. However, the *ayin* also held the ideographic meaning of the eye itself, as in "the eye of God," or "to see," or even the idea of "salvation."[168]

Additionally, the Hebrew ideographic letter meaning might portray a spiritually cryptic message, especially when combined with other letters that made up a name. Even today, many Hebrew people around the world try to decipher the meanings associated with significant names or even their own names by combining the Proto-Sinaitic meanings of each Hebrew letter into a single supposed message.[169] (See appendix 2.)

Hebrew Language Evolution

Today, the most primitive Proto-Sinaitic fragment samples we possess are dated somewhere between the mid-nineteenth and the mid-sixteenth centuries BC. These kinds of fragments are still being found in archeological digs in the Middle East.[170] (See appendix 1.)

As the early Hebrew alphabet evolved into the Modern Hebrew alphabet, many of its ideographic meanings were also transferred to modern times. It is true that those ancient pictograms are seldom depicted in the Modern Hebrew alphabet schematics, nor are they usually referenced in strictly academic circles. Despite this, a large number of Hebrew-speaking individuals, as well as an assortment of Hebrew scholars, continue to be ardent researchers of the ancient letter meanings.[171]

To be academically honest, a few critics still maintain that those ancient ideograms are not used in today's Hebrew life and are not connected to the Modern Hebrew alphabet in any way. However, those protestations are simply incorrect on several levels. Let's look at a few examples.

Ideogram Carryover

Israel's *Haaretz*[172] is a premier Orthodox-leaning Israeli news publication. Its English edition is also published and sold together with the *International New York Times*. In 2013, *Haaretz* categorically verified the existence of the modern recognition of the Hebrew ideograms in an article titled, "In the Beginning: The Origins of the Hebrew Alphabet":

> **The names of the Hebrew letters have meaning** [ideas] in the Hebrew language. That **doesn't actually matter when writing or reading**, but it is **nice to know**.[173] (Emphasis added)

Additionally, Hebrew Today, an Israeli organization that describes itself as a professional Hebrew-language learning institute, is also in line with *Haaretz*'s assessment concerning the alphabet ideograms. Hebrew Today is used by a number of teachers in Israel's public and private schools. Its language services are employed within several educational and news publication services as well.[174]

As an example of the modern ideographic carryover, here is what Hebrew Today says concerning the meaning of the first letter of the Modern Hebrew alphabet—*aleph*:

> Aleph is one of the **most important** and noteworthy letters in the Hebrew alphabet for a **number of reasons, some spiritual and some practical.**... It therefore **symbolizes** oneness and **unity.**... It is often associated with the **oneness of monotheism** [God]. It also has **connotations of greatness.**... Despite the fact that the Aleph is the first letter in the alphabet, **there is actually an element of humility to the letter** [as well].[175] (Emphasis added)

Hebrew Today also states:

Each letter in the Hebrew alphabet **has both a literal and mystical meaning.** This means that **each name has a mystical significance, based on the letters** which form the name.[176] (Emphasis added)

Another example is provided by Dr. George W. Benthien, who earned his PhD in mathematics from Carnegie Mellon University, specializing in continuum mechanics.[177] His assertion was issued in a 2013 publication titled, "The Hebrew Language and Way of Thinking."

In 1905 Flinders Petrie, a renowned Egyptologist, discovered an inscription written using previously unknown pictograph symbols. Due to the limited number of pictographs employed, it was determined that the language was alphabetic.

Another renowned Egyptologist Dr. Alan Gardiner studied this inscription in detail. **He was able to determine that the pictograph symbols were related to the Hebrew alphabet since the names of the Hebrew characters had ancient meanings related to the pictographs,** i.e., For example, the first letter of the Hebrew alphabet is named **aleph meaning "ox;"** the tenth letter is named **yod meaning "hand,"** and the sixteenth letter is named **ayin meaning "eye."**[178] (Emphasis added; also see appendix 2.)

The Mezuzah

The Shin

The widely acknowledged ideographic element of Hebrew history is also demonstrated by the fact that affixed on the doorposts of almost every Jewish household and business around the world is the Hebrew mezuzah.[179] On practically every one of those mezuzahs is emblazoned the singular Hebrew letter *shin/sin.*[180]

The *shin* is placed on the mezuzah precisely because its symbolic spiritual meaning represents the name of God—and that letter has held that ideographic standing since the most ancient usage of the Hebrew language Most specifically, it stands for *El Shaddai*—God Almighty.[181] The *shin*, used in this way, is an ancient Hebrew alphabet ideogram still in global use today. It delivers a "message" that attests to the blessings of God Almighty upon the home or business to which it is attached.

Mathematical Letters

Another interesting feature of the Hebrew alphabet, one shared with several other ancient languages, is that each of its twenty-two letters is also assigned a *numerical value.* (See appendix 3.)

This numbering system was inherited from the Aramaic and Phoenician script from about 800 BC, and was the earliest precursor to an actual system of numbers expressed as unique characters or symbols, as they are seen today. At first, individual numbers were expressed by letters of the alphabet. In the original Hebrew Scriptures, there were no actual numbers as we know them today. Instead, *numbers of things* were spelled out in words.[182]

We even find what many scholars believe to be a direct reference to this well-known fact in the book of Revelation. It is the familiar passage that refers to the "number of the beast":

> This calls for wisdom. Let the person who has insight calculate the number of the beast, for it is the number of a man. That number is 666.[183] (Revelation 13:18)

With all of this important historical background in mind, I want to share with you a dramatic true story. It directly connects to what we've been speaking of and, more importantly, to what we'll continue to investigate as we move forward in our journey.

The saga comes straight out of Israel. It concerns the ministry of the late Rabbi Kaduri, the most venerated rabbi in Israel's history.

32

THE CRYPTIC CASE
OF THE MISSING CROSSES

He reveals deep and hidden things;
he knows what lies in darkness, and light dwells with him.
~Daniel 2:22

Following is yet another revelatory Yeshua code first leveled upon the world in 2007. For those who know about it, it's nothing short of earth-shattering, especially considering its source. Yet, the "religious" Orthodox powers prevalent in Israel and around the world have desperately tried to cover up the revelation.

The Rabbi, the Secret Note,
and the Identity of Messiah

In January 2006, Rabbi Yitzhak Kaduri, the most recognized rabbi in Israel's modern history, fell gravely ill. Within weeks, he passed away in a Jerusalem hospital at the age of 108.[184]

More than 250,000 people attended the rabbi's funeral. In fact, Jerusalem was effectively closed down for nearly two days because of the crowds pouring into the city to attend the service.

The deeply Orthodox rabbi was also a close confidant and supporter of Prime Minister Benjamin Netanyahu. In other words, this was no ordinary rabbi. Kaduri was *the rabbi of rabbis*, and almost every Jewish person to this day knows it. Today, many businesses, billboards, and institutions of education still prominently display his photo throughout Israel and around the world.

The Note

The vast majority of the massive funeral crowd didn't have a clue that, only a few months earlier, Kaduri had scribbled a mysterious note on a nondescript scrap of paper. He announced to his 2005 Yom Kippur service attendees in his downtown Jerusalem synagogue that he had received a personal "visitation" and knew who the Messiah truly was; he told them he had put the revelation in a note. The content of the note was promised to reveal the *actual name* of the soon-coming Messiah. But the disclosure of the note's contents, Kaduri informed, was to take place one year after his death.[185] At that time, the note was to be placed on his highly visited website for all the world to see.

However, in January 2007, when the note was posted on Kaduri's website—precisely one year after his death—its actual words revealed no specific name of the Messiah, at least not on its surface. In fact, the message appeared to be rather benign. A number of Kaduri's global contingent of followers expressed their frustration.

The Messiah

However, those who were disappointed would soon be in for a huge surprise. Within weeks of the original posting, a group of Kaduri's closest disciples pointed out the note's true message. Not only had their beloved Rabbi Kaduri done exactly what he had promised, but the name of the Messiah had actually been right before the world all along. To his followers' delight, it turned out that Rabbi Kaduri had ingeniously encoded his note. The encryption key used to unravel the coded portion appeared in the very first sentence—hidden, but in plain sight.[186]

When the name Kaduri promised to deliver was finally revealed, the disclosure stunned many who saw it. There were others, however, who were not at all surprised. These were a select handful of Kaduri's private students. The rabbi had often spoken with them, behind the closed doors of his classes, about the revelation. But now, Kaduri had literally pulled it off—from beyond the grave. He finally told the world what his students already knew. The news of the decrypted riddle blazed around the world, as it dramatically disclosed what billions had been proclaiming for over two thousand years: *Yehoshua/Yeshua* is the name of the real Messiah.

Global Scandal

On April 30, 2007, the widely read print magazine *Israel Today* published a feature about Kaduri's note. The piece claimed it had been decoded, and that its message might well prove to be spiritually momentous. The publication also posted an article, in conjunction with the magazine story, on its Internet website at israeltoday.co.il. Both the print and the online piece bore the sensationalized title, "Rabbi Reveals Name of the Messiah."

The article's author, Aviel Schneider, was quoted as saying, "The worldwide reaction to news of Kaduri's note has been 'crazy.' I have never received so many emails and calls from around the globe."[187]

But soon, a peculiar fact was discovered. Only the original Internet article, not the magazine article, included a section entitled "The Rabbi's Followers React," which presented a striking and important piece of information:

> Israel Today was given access to many of the rabbi's manuscripts, written in his own hand for the exclusive use of his students. **Most striking were the cross-like symbols painted by Kaduri all over the pages.**

In the Jewish tradition, one does not use crosses. In fact, even the use of a plus sign is discouraged because it might be mistaken for a cross. **But there they were, scribbled in the rabbi's own hand.** When we asked what those symbols meant, Rabbi David Kaduri [Rabbi Yitzhak Kaduri's son] said **they were "signs of the angel."**

Pressed further about the meaning of the "signs of the angel," he said he had no idea. Rabbi David Kaduri went on to explain that only his father had had a spiritual relationship with God and had met the Messiah in his dreams. Orthodox Jews around the Nahalat Yitzhak Yeshiva told Israel Today a few weeks later that the story about the secret note of Rabbi Kaduri should never have come out, and that it had damaged the name of the revered old sage.[188] (Emphasis added)

Why would Kaduri plaster his manuscripts with a symbol that looked like the cross? Using such a blatantly Christian image would indeed be considered highly offensive to any Orthodox Jew. Yet there they were—crosses splashed all over the pages of the rabbi's notes.[189]

Vanished?

Surprisingly, the original *Israel Today* article eventually disappeared from the Internet. The conspiracy theories began to churn. Some who were closely following the Kaduri saga suspected *Israel Today* might have been pressured to take down its Internet accounting of the event.

In response to the uproar, I contacted officials at *Israel Today* in early 2013, when I first verified the missing Internet story. They assured me the original April 30, 2007, article would soon be reposted, and that the entire website had only recently been removed and was merely undergoing an "upgrade process." I was also assured *Israel Today* was categorically standing by the original article.[190]

Adjusted Reappearance

Sometime later, the Rabbi Kaduri article was indeed reinstated on the website. However, the newly posted article was under a somewhat less sensational title: "The Rabbi, the Note, and the Messiah."

Additionally, the editor's note at the top of the reposted page claimed: "*This is a reprint* of a cover story that first appeared in the April 2007 issue of *Israel Today Magazine*." While that statement might be technically accurate concerning the magazine article, it did not account for the fact that the reprinted Internet article had been significantly adjusted as compared to the original. Oddly, the reinstated Internet version did not include the section with the heading initially titled "The Rabbi's Followers React." The comments about the "many" Kaduri manuscripts, the "signs of the angel," the "cross symbols," and the observation about damaging "the revered old sage's name" had mysteriously vanished.

Because of this obvious anomaly, I again contacted a key figure within the *Israel Today* organization and requested information regarding these omissions. The next day, I received a lengthy response stating, "The website version of any article also appearing in our print magazine is not definitive. The original version in the magazine is the definitive version."[191]

Then, only a few days after receiving that response, the same representative *emailed* me a photocopy of the entire original article. Noticeably absent from it was the subject matter concerning the cross symbols and the statement about the potential of "damaging" Rabbi Kaduri's name. When I asked for an explanation of these lingering incongruities, I received no reply. Communication from the publication abruptly ceased. I was beginning to feel I might have hit upon something.

It was Israeli-born Messianic Jew Zev Porat who offered up the key for the most probable answer to this mystery. As you will soon see, Rabbi Porat's reasoning is sound, and once again demonstrates the dramatic depth of the overall Orthodox elite's attempted cover-up of the truth of Kaduri's Messiah revelation.

33

A RABBI SPEAKS

This is what the LORD *says—Israel's King and Redeemer,
the* LORD *Almighty: I am the first and I am the last;
apart from me there is no God.*
~ISAIAH 44:6

Messianic Rabbi Zev Porat is a long-time friend of mine and a valued ministry partner. He and his wife live in Tel Aviv, Israel. Zev was born into a deeply Orthodox family and was raised in Israel.

I have written two books about the detailed and historically accurate account of Rabbi Kaduri. The latest, updated one—*The Rabbi, the Secret Message, and the Identity of Messiah*—was coauthored with Rabbi Zev Porat. Zev has familial connections to Rabbi Kaduri himself, as well as deep Orthodox connections to this entire story.[192]

It's important to note that Hebrew is Zev's native language. His great-grandfather, grandfather, and father were influential rabbis in Israel. Some even served on the *batei din*, Israel's rabbinical court.[193] Even former Prime Minister Arial Sharon spent the night in the home of Zev's grandparents. On his mother's side of the family, Zev has close relatives who've worked in the Israeli government under the Netanyahu administration. Rabbi Porat's family was personally connected to Rabbi Kaduri and his ministry,[194] and Zev also completed the official rabbinical training required to

serve on Israel's nascent Sanhedrin Council. He received certification of
the completion of those studies, but long ago renounced that certification
when he was born again in *Yeshua Ha Mashiach*— "Jesus the Messiah."
I relate Zev's extensive background and credentials to assure you that his
testimony throughout this book is trustworthy and astute.

Zev's Insight

Rabbi Porat offered the following valuable insight:

> This is an amazing thing, about the disappearance of the cross
> symbols from *Israel Today's* piece. Several of Kaduri's *yeshiva* [rab-
> binical training school—much like a seminary] students have
> been telling me about something that matches this very thing. In
> fact, they are still talking about it today. And in light of the miss-
> ing information from the second printing of the Internet article,
> what the students are telling me now makes perfect sense.

He continued:

> The students tell me that Rabbi Kaduri had been teaching them
> about the Hebrew letters—the Aleph (א) and Tav (ת). As you prob-
> ably know, these are the first and last letters of the Hebrew alpha-
> bet. According to the New Testament language of Greek, Yeshua
> called Himself the Alpha and the Omega. But in the Hebrew, it is
> the Aleph and the Tav. The Tav is especially interesting because in
> the most ancient pictographic representations, the Tav was desig-
> nated by a symbol that looks exactly like the sign of the cross! Its
> meaning is the mark, or the sign.
>   On the other hand, the Aleph, the first letter of the Hebrew
> alphabet, was represented by the ancient pictographic form of an
> ox head. That particular symbol meant the leader, or the One

who is most powerful. In the most ancient times the Aleph represented God himself—and was pronounced *El*.[195]

The rabbi stated further:

Based upon the information in that *Israel Today* article, and what Kaduri's students are telling me, I believe those cross symbols were *Tav depictions* that Rabbi Kaduri was drawing on his documents. I think he was preparing the world for his eventual Messiah note—declaring that Yeshua is the Aleph and the Tav—and that the sign of the cross, *the Tav*, is further proof that Yeshua is the Messiah—the King of kings, the most powerful One, who became our ultimate sacrifice for sin, bringing us peace with God. Yeshua is *the mark* of God's plan of salvation![196]

Zev elaborated:

The fact that *Israel Today* published the information about the cross symbols is further verification that what Kaduri's students have been telling me is true. Since they ultimately backed off that part of the original article, to me, it might be an indication that they received persecution for printing this amazing part of the story. It appears that the reprinted Internet story may have been changed for this very reason. We probably will never know the absolute truth of the matter. However, the pressure to shut down this story, or at least these particularly revealing elements of it, is real.[197]

Two Little Letters

Let's wade in a little deeper and find out what the uproar about the *aleph* and *tav* is really all about. After all, they're just two little letters in the ancient Hebrew alphabet, correct? So what in the world could be the problem?

34

THE ALEPH AND THE TAV

Why should our people not know these eternal truths?
~MESSIANIC RABBI ZEV PORAT

Yeshua declares in the book of Revelation that He is the *Alpha* and the *Omega*. This title is taken straight from the Greek language, the original language of the New Testament documents.

> I am the Alpha and the Omega, the First and the Last, the Beginning and the End. (Revelation 22:13)

But in the Semitic/Aramaic/Hebrew language, Yeshua would have actually said, "I am the *Aleph* and the *Tav*." This is because the Hebrew letters *aleph* and *tav* are the first and the last letters of the Hebrew alphabet, directly corresponding with the first and last Greek letters, *alpha* and *omega*.

The collective *aleph and tav* carries the same message used by Yahweh in the Old Testament when He calls Himself the "first and the last" in three different passages. In each of those passages, all of which are found in the book of Isaiah, Yahweh also calls Himself "the Redeemer" in conjunction with being the "First and the Last."

- "Who has performed this and carried it out, calling forth the generations from the beginning? I, the LORD—**the first and the last—I am He.**... For I myself will help you," declares the Lord, **your Redeemer**, the Holy One of Israel. (Isaiah 41:4, 14, BEREAN STUDY BIBLE; emphasis added)

- This is what the Lord says—Israel's **King and Redeemer**, the Lord Almighty: I am **the first and I am the last**; apart from me there is no God. (Isaiah 44:6, emphasis added)

- I am he; **I am the first and I am the last. My own hand laid the foundations of the earth**, and my right hand spread out the heavens; when I summon them, they all stand up together.... This is what the Lord says—**your Redeemer**, the Holy One of Israel: "I am the Lord your God." (Isaiah 48:12–13, 17, emphasis added)

As disclosed several chapters earlier, one of the direct synonyms for "redeemer," as used in the English language, is "Jesus."[198] We also discovered that God identifies Himself as our Redeemer/Yeshua seventeen times in the Old Testament. And, of course, there is simply no question concerning the New Testament affirmation that Yeshua/Jesus is exalted as the ultimate manifestation of our Redeemer.[199]

The *Aleph*

Proto-Sinaitic | Paleo-Hebrew | Modern

The ancient Proto-Sinaitic *aleph*, the first letter of the Hebrew alphabet, was originally represented by the pictographic form of an ox head. That symbol meant "the leader" or "the one who is most powerful." This is further confirmed by the *Harvard Theological Review* in an article titled "Yahweh and the God of the Patriarchs," which asserts that, since the most ancient times, the Hebrew letter *aleph* represented God Himself[200] and was pronounced "*El.*"[201]

The *Tav*

Proto-Sinaitic | Paleo-Hebrew | Modern

What about the *tav*? This letter conveys the most startling revelation of all concerning the "first and the last." In our day of almost instantaneous global communication and information systems, the entire planet is now being made privy to this amazing Yeshua code.

In the most ancient pictographic representations, the *tav* was represented by a symbol that looks just like the crucifixion cross of Yeshua. It retained a similar appearance, even in the Paleo-Hebrew, which is the original script of the Hebrew Scriptures, and remained in use until nearly the second century BC.[202] And, of all things, the ideographic meaning of the letter *tav* is "the mark" or "the sign." (See appendix 2.)

By declaring He is both the *Aleph* and the *Tav*, Jesus affirms He is actually "God with us," completely *one* with the Father, as well as being the Word that became flesh in order to become our Savior through the cross. Therefore, He truly is the *Aleph* and the *Tav*. He is God's "sign" to the world.[203] (See appendix 2.)

Inside Connections

For several years, Rabbi Porat has been using the teaching of the Proto-Sinaitic and Paleo-Hebrew *aleph* and *tav* symbols among the Orthodox Jewish people in Israel to lead them to Yeshua as Messiah, Lord, and Savior. Following is what he has to say about this phenomenon:

What's really amazing about this, though, is that Israel is the only nation that has ever tried to eliminate and cover up its own alphabet![204] Especially the teaching of the ideographic meanings, and the symbols for each of the letters.

Before Yeshua was crucified, the rabbis didn't understand the sign of the cross (the Tav) as being directly related to Messiah. However, after the crucifixion, they all saw it! They stopped teaching about the symbols that represented each Hebrew letter within a few decades of the crucifixion of Yeshua, because they knew it matched Yeshua's Aleph/Tav statements. This fact is verified in our own history. And, we all know that the cross is the greatest symbol by which Yeshua is known today throughout the world.

I have used this information about the ancient Hebrew alphabet in our ministry's witnessing outreach in Israel, on many occasions and in various important venues. Teaching these symbols and their meanings to today's Jewish people is such a powerful way to open their eyes to the truth of Yeshua as Messiah.[205]

Stop Teaching This!

Zev continued:

In fact, teaching the aleph/tav is so effective, that not too long ago I actually had two very prominent Israeli rabbis contact me about what I was doing. They literally pleaded with me to please not teach these ancient symbols to Jews in my outreach presentations. They claimed that it might "confuse" the people.

One of the rabbis contacted me by email, the other one called me on the phone. It's an amazing thing that for thousands of years these symbols were not confusing at all—that is, until after Jesus was crucified on a cross and fulfilled every prophecy of the coming Messiah!

After speaking with those concerned rabbis, it became very apparent to me that this one tremendous truth alone, the ancient Hebrew pictographs, was having a much larger impact in witnessing to the Jewish people about Yeshua than I had imagined. I politely told them that I would continue to use the teaching—after all, it is a historical fact of our own language, dating back thousands of years!

Why should our people not know these eternal truths? But, I can tell you—the rabbis clearly don't want this truth taught anymore, because it points directly to Yeshua Ha' Mashiach![206]

Entwined

Indeed, Rabbi Porat's revelations concerning the teaching of the *aleph* and the *tav* are amazing. These understandings will help us unveil more striking revelations in the coming chapters.

Paleo-Hebrew script

THE SILOAM INSCRIPTION

" [This] inscription records the construction of Hezekiah's tunnel in the 8th century BC and demonstrates one of the oldest examples of the ancient Paleo-Hebrew alphabet."

https://biblicalarchaeologygraves.blogspot.com/2014/12/figure-19.html
© 2014 Dr. David E. Graves

THE ETH AND THE OWTH

The Hebrew word owth *and the unpronounced Hebrew word* eth *are inextricably tied together.*

When the *aleph* and the *tav* are joined as a Hebrew word, it is called the *eth*. It is phonetically pronounced as "et" and is represented in the Modern Hebrew—reading right to left—as את.[207]

The English language has no equivalent of the meaning of the Hebrew *eth,* therefore it remains unwritten and unpronounced in English translations of the Old Testament Scriptures.[208] However, this unique two-letter Hebrew word is found well over eleven thousand times in the Old Testament Hebrew texts. It is found multiple times on practically every page of the Tanakh.[209] So…what in the world is this monumental and grammatical mystery behind the *eth*?

Mark of the Accusative Case

First, let's look at the scholarly definition of the word. *Strong's Exhaustive Concordance* defines the *eth* as:

> **Untranslatable mark** of **the accusative case.**[210] Original Word: את [*aleph* and *tav*]. As such **unrepresented in English. Apparent**

contracted from *owth* in the **demonstrative sense of entity;** properly, self (but generally used to point out more definitely **the object of a verb or preposition,** even or namely)—(as such unrepresented in English).[211] (Emphasis added)

Bible Resources:

The Hebrew word "eth" (Strong's H853) spelled Aleph-Tav **is left untranslated** because it is used to **provide emphasis** in the text **with the sense of entity; self....** There is **no equivalent English word** and for this reason, "eth" **generally is left unrepresented in English.**[212] (Emphasis added)

In other words, the *eth* is often used to direct us to another word or idea in the sentence. It can point to an entity, the object of a verb, or the object of a preposition. Oddly, in quite a few of its appearances in the Scripture, it doesn't seem to have a discernable purpose. For this reason, and in those cases, its grammatical significance draws varying opinions.[213]

Furthermore, a number of Hebrew-speaking scholars assert that there can be certain "mystical" interpretations of the *eth* as well. Those beliefs are based on several passages wherein the more spiritual meanings prove to be, according to Orthodox Rabbi Eli Brackman, "ultimately...the most satisfactory explanations" of the presence of the *aleph-tav.*[214]

The *Owth*

Since *Strong's Exhaustive Concordance* refers to *owth* as the term from which *eth* was "contracted," let's examine a magnificent revelation that *owth* holds.

In Modern Hebrew, the word *owth,* spelled אות, means "the sign." In that word we find the joining of the three Hebrew letters, reading from right to left: *aleph, vav* (or *waw,*)[215] and *tav.*

But what is the Hebrew letter *vav*, right in the middle of *owth*, between the *aleph* and the *tav*? What does that *vav* symbolize in its ideographic form in the Proto-Sinaitic Hebrew?

The *Vav*

The *vav* (ו) is the sixth letter of the Hebrew alphabet. Its ancient ideogram of that letter represented a "peg, hook, or *nail*." In fact, even in its modern depiction, that letter looks something like a nail or a peg.[216]

So it appears that the *aleph* and the *tav* are "hooked together" in the middle by a peg/nail/spike. This Hebrew word means "the sign."[217]

Here are several examples of the word *owth* in Scripture:

- And Jehovah said unto him, "**therefore whosoever slayeth Cain, vengeance shall be taken on him** sevenfold. And Jehovah appointed **a sign** [*owth*] for Cain, **lest any finding him should smite him.**" (Genesis 4:15, ASV; emphasis added)
- And God said, "**I will be with you.** And **this will** be **the sign** [*owth*] to you **that it is I** who have sent you: When you have brought the people out of Egypt, you will worship God on this mountain." (Exodus 3:12, emphasis added)
- **The LORD said to Moses, "How long will these people treat me with contempt? How long will they refuse to believe in me,** in spite of **all the signs** [*owth*] I have performed among them?" (Numbers 14:11, emphasis added)
- Again and again **they put God to the test;** they vexed the Holy One of Israel. They **did not remember his power—the day he redeemed them** from the oppressor, **the day he displayed his signs** [owth] in Egypt. (Psalm 78:41–43, emphasis added)

In the dramatic passage of Genesis 4:15, Cain is actually protected, or "saved," by having the "sign" of God placed upon him. In fact, the very word "sign" in Hebrew depicts God the Father (*aleph*) and the cross (*tav*), joined together by a nail, peg, spike, or hook (*vav*). What an astoundingly beautiful picture![218]

If you think that is a striking image, consider about the declaration of the mighty angel to Bethlehem's shepherds on the day of Yeshua's birth:

> This will be **a sign to you:** You will find a baby wrapped in cloths and lying in a manger. (Luke 2:12, emphasis added)

The word "sign" in the Greek is the direct equivalent of the Hebrew word *owth* in the Old Testament.[219] So, as it turns out, even the infant Yeshua was called an *owth* from God to the world. He is the *aleph-tav* that is joined together by a nail—God's sign to the world of His gracious act of salvation, offered through the person of Yeshua!

Now, think about this: Since the Hebrew word *owth* ("sign") and the unpronounced Hebrew word *eth* (*aleph-tav*) are inextricably tied together, then might we also surmise there's something deeper associated with the freestanding word *eth* as well?

Part VII

THE BEGINNING

I was appointed from eternity, from the beginning, before the world began.

~Proverbs 8:23

36

CREATION

The Lamb who was slain from the creation of the world.
~Revelation 13:8

Let's consider a few examples of the many thousands of uses of the *eth* in the Hebrew Scriptures. As we move forward, remember what Messianic Rabbi Zev Porat stated in a previous chapter regarding the *aleph-tav* and its connection to Rabbi Kaduri:

> Based upon the information in that *Israel Today* article, and what Kaduri's students are telling me, I believe those cross symbols were **Tav depictions** that Rabbi **Kaduri was drawing on his documents.**

Genesis 1:1

Unbeknownst to a number of Bible students, the first verse of the Bible employs the use of the word *eth*. In English, that verse is expressed in ten words:

> In the beginning God created the heavens and the earth. (Genesis 1:1)

However, in the Hebrew text, seen in the image below, we see something much more profound. In Hebrew, the verse is made up of only seven words. With that number comes the biblical connotation of completeness and perfection. This meaning is the essence of the message of Genesis 1:1.[220]

hā·'ā·reṣ	wə·'êṭ	haš·šā·ma·yim	êṭ	'ĕ·lō·hîm;	bā·rā	bə·rê·šîṯ
הָאָרֶץ	וְאֵת	הַשָּׁמַיִם	אֵת	אֱלֹהִים	בָּרָא	בְּרֵאשִׁית
the earth	(and)	the heavens	(eth)	Elohim	created	In the beginning.

Eth in the Middle

As already noted, most Hebrew grammar experts would point out that the *aleph-tav* (*eth*) functions in Genesis 1:1 merely as the accusative case pointer, indicating the object of the verb "created" is the heavens and the earth. In this instance, I would agree, except for their use of the word "merely."

Since *Aleph-Tav* is also the term employed by Yeshua as His divine title, then it can additionally indicate that this two letter, uninterpreted Hebrew word is also pointing to Yeshua as the Creator...*because Yeshua says it does!*

This is exactly what the New Testament declaration of Yeshua tells us, in the first chapter of Revelation. Consider how the Apostle Paul describes it in his letter to the church at Colossi:[221]

> **For in [Yeshua] all things were created:** things in heaven and on earth, visible and invisible, whether thrones or powers or rulers or authorities; all things have been created through him and for him. **He is before all things,** and **in him all things hold together.** (Colossians 1:16–17, emphasis added)

The message of this New Testament passage is the same one that appears to be "coded" in the first verse of the Bible. Everything about Genesis 1:1 points directly to Yeshua, the *Alpha* and the *Omega*—the *Aleph* and the *Tav*!

37

THE LAMPSTAND

From Genesis 1 to Revelation 1, the Word of God is
undeniably linked, and Yeshua stands in the middle of it all.

Finding the identification of Yeshua as the *Aleph-Tav* in the very middle of the seven-word sentence of Genesis 1:1 is indeed amazing. But to understand the gravity of that fact, let's have a look at the first chapter of the book of Revelation, where we find the same imagery:

> Then I [John] **turned to see the voice** that was speaking with me. And after turning **I saw seven golden lampstands**; and **in the middle**[222] of the lampstands I saw **one like a son of man**, clothed in a robe reaching to the feet, and wrapped around the chest with a golden sash. (Revelation 1:12–13, emphasis added)

Of course, we know the one in the middle of the lampstands of Revelation is none other than Yeshua Himself. Now we can assert that within the center of the first verse of Genesis is also a picture of the central theme of the first chapter of Revelation. From Genesis 1 to Revelation 1, the Word of God is undeniably linked, and Yeshua stands in the middle of it all.

The imagery of Revelation 1 is the menorah, the seven-channeled lampstand directed by Yahweh to be placed in the Holy Place of the

Tabernacle in the wilderness and later in the Holy Place in Solomon's Temple on Mount Moriah in Jerusalem.[223]

The imagery of Revelation 1 is found in Genesis 1:1.

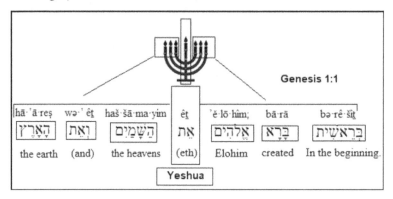

Also consider what we've already learned in a previous chapter: *Jesus is the Light* that holds all of creation together. Have a look at that passage from Colossians again:

> **For in Him all things were created:** things in heaven and on earth, visible and invisible, whether thrones or powers or rulers or authorities; **all things have been created through Him** and for Him. **He is before all things, and in Him all things hold together.** (Colossians 1:16–17, emphasis added)

The unarguable presence of the *aleph-tav* at the beginning of the Word of God, and how it links to Revelation 1, is similar to the ELS computer code we unraveled in previous chapters. It doesn't really matter what detractors might say concerning the phenomenon and exactly how it should be interpreted. The fact remains, we still have to deal with *what is there*.[224] Yet, even with this stunning image before us, there are still several more remarkable revelations in the first verse of Genesis.

38

GOLGOTHA'S HILL

Then were there two thieves crucified with him,
one on the right hand, and another on the left.
~MATTHEW 27:38

W e know from the Gospel accounts that three crucifixions were
carried out on Golgotha's hill on the day of Yeshua's execution.[225]
Jesus was in the middle. A thief was on each side of Him. Stunningly,
there are three depictions of those crosses in Genesis 1:1 as well.

Remember, the Proto-Sinaitic form of the last Hebrew letter of the
alphabet—the tav—was in the perfect shape of a cross. In the Paleo
Hebrew it was more akin to a slanted "x," of sorts, yet it was still very
similar to a depiction of the crucifixion cross. (See appendices 2 and 4)

We also saw that the *tav* carried with it the ideographic meaning of
"the sign." Indeed, the cross of Yeshua is the globally recognized *sign* of
Christianity to this day. The cross sign is found squarely in the middle of
Genesis 1:1, along with two other crosses.

Looking at the seven Hebrew words that comprise Genesis 1:1, we
find the *tav* used three times. They appear in a strikingly symmetrical
manner.

As we can also see, the *middle* cross is found in the *aleph-tav* of Genesis 1:1, the title by which Jesus identifies Himself in Revelation 1.

Imagine that. In Genesis 1:1 there exists a profound picture of Golgotha on the day of Jesus' crucifixion. The visual of those three "crosses" places Jesus on that hill exactly as the New Testament describes as *the one in the middle*, between two thieves. Think of what that opening verse to the Word of God now depicts! We can make of this resultant image whatever we wish; however, there is no disputing its presence.

In my estimation, there are just too many unexplainable biblical images here to dismiss them as coincidence. Yet, remarkably, we find still more glorious images in the midst of the Bible's first verse.

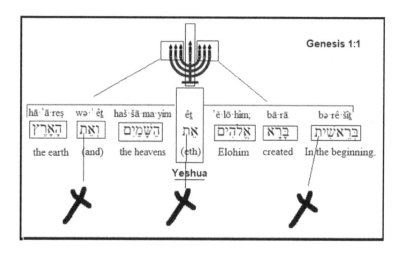

39

DIVINE SIGNATURE

*Whoever invokes a blessing in the land will
do so by the God of truth.*
~Isaiah 65:16

et me set up the next disclosure with a reminder that the Hebrew alphabet is foundationally made up of twenty-two letters. However, five of those are formed differently when they appear as the *last letter* of a word. These additional letter representations are called "sofit" ("final") forms. The five sofit letters of Hebrew are: *kaf* (ך), *mem* (ם), *nun* (ן), *fe* (ף), and *tzadi* (ץ).[226]

The entire Hebrew alphabet, then, including the five final forms, is actually made up of twenty-seven letters. They are often arranged in three

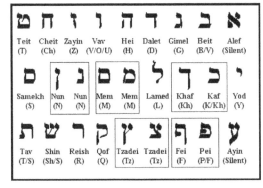

rows of nine letters each, as seen in the following illustration. The chart is read as the Hebrew language is—from the *top right* to the *bottom left*.

As you can see from the chart, the letter *mem* is exactly in the middle of the alphabet.

I Am the Truth

Let me introduce another important Hebrew word: *emeth,* which means "truth." It is represented in Hebrew as אֱמֶת: *aleph-mem-tav.* There's that *aleph-tav* again, with another letter between the two. But since the letter *mem* is also the middle letter of the Hebrew alphabet, we see something else quite startling. Running right through the alphabet, perfectly in the middle, is the Hebrew word for "truth"!

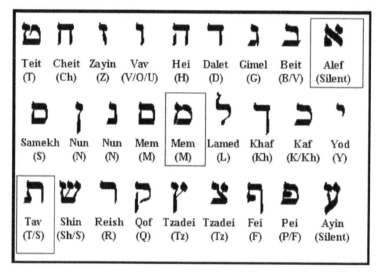

Following is how *emeth* ("truth") appears in a straight-line, symmetrical rendering of the Hebrew alphabet with its final forms included:

Finding the word for "truth" at the center of the Hebrew alphabet is no small discovery. Of course, not a single word in Hebrew can be written unless the alphabet is used. We know that Yeshua is the Word of God that encompasses and embodies all truth. This is exactly what the first words of the Gospel of John declare… connecting the deepest coded truth of Genesis 1:1 directly to the person of Jesus Christ.

In the beginning was the Word, and the Word was with God, and the Word was God. He was with God in the beginning. **Through him all things were made;** without him nothing was made that has been made.… **The Word became flesh** and made his dwelling among us. We have seen his glory, the glory of the one and only Son, who came from the Father, **full of grace and truth.** (John 1:1–2, 14, emphasis added)

At this point, you might ask, "What does the word 'truth' running right through the middle of the Hebrew alphabet have to do with the first verse in the Word of God?" That's a great question!

Now that you know what you're looking for, have another look at Genesis 1:1. Note the word "truth" begins with the first letter of the *aleph-tav*—the designation by which Jesus refers to Himself. Then, moving to the left of the *aleph*, there's the *mem*. Then, over to the left again, starting from the *mem,* is the *tav.* In another visually symmetrical arrangement, there's the word *emeth,* for "truth."

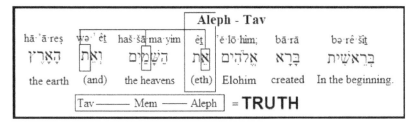

One might argue that these three letters can be found in similar combinations in almost any verse of Scripture. I assure you they cannot, especially not when we follow the protocol of finding an *aleph* that is located in the beginning of Yeshua's identification of Himself as the *Aleph-Tav.* And then that specific *aleph* is followed by a *mem,* then a *tav*—being found in a visually symmetrical layout. The vast majority of verses in the Scripture do not have this particular combination. So when it *does* occur, it's worth taking a closer look, especially in reference to the declaration in which it's found. It's yet another important observation of what is there before our eyes, but perhaps previously hidden.

Regardless of wherever else we find the *emeth*, it is hard to believe it's a coincidence that the coded word "truth" is discovered in the first verse of the Bible, and the spelling out of that word begins with the word *Aleph-Tav*—the name Jesus declared as His title in Revelation 1:13. Divine truth always begins with Yeshua.

- Jesus answered, "**I am** the way and **the truth** and the life. No one comes to the Father except through me." (John 14:6, emphasis added)
- Jesus said, "If you hold to my teaching, you are really my disciples. Then you **will know the truth**, and **the truth will set you free.**" (John 8:31, emphasis added)
- **Thy word is true from the beginning:** and every one of thy righteous judgments endureth forever. (Psalm 119:160, KJV; emphasis added)

It's almost like we're looking at some sort of Heaven-ordained "code" isn't it? Again, what are the chances? How can seven little words produce

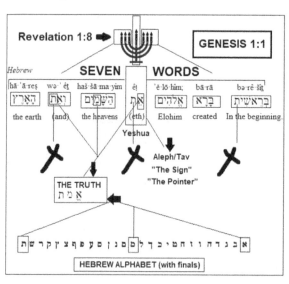

so many images from the Hebrew letters and words in that single verse? Not only that, but what would be the odds that all of those images speak directly to corresponding biblical truths throughout the Scriptures? The supernatural nature of such a discovery certainly has to be seriously considered.

In the next chapter, we'll uncover yet another picture of the disclosures we found in the first verse of Genesis. However, this time, we'll find the same coded image in the book of Psalms—and it's a passage that's quoted in the New Testament.

It's also a passage about Yeshua.

40

BEHOLD, I HAVE COME!

Psalm 40 speaks of Yeshua's redemptive work among humanity and His literal appearance on earth in order to accomplish that act of supreme salvation.

With everything we've learned thus far about Genesis 1:1 and the presence of a visible Yeshua code seemingly written all over it, still another revelation closely parallels what we've uncovered. What you will see next begins to lay out a repeating pattern throughout relevant Yeshua passages in the Old Testament.

The verse we will examine in the book of Psalms is also quoted in the New Testament book of Hebrews. That passage is Psalm 40:7, and it is wrapped up in a compound prophecy.[227]

Psalm 40 is a psalm of David and, at first glance, it might appear to be only about David and his personal journey with Yahweh. However, the storyline shifts ever so subtly and ultimately speaks prophetically of the coming of Yeshua.[228]

Then I said, "Behold, **I have come;** in the scroll of the book it is **written of me.**" (Psalm 40:7, ESV; emphasis added)

Here is the New Testament reference to that passage: Hebrews 10:7. It's a direct prophecy of the first coming of Jesus Christ:

Then I said, "Here I am—**it is written about me** in the scroll—I have come to do your will, my God." (Hebrews 10:7, emphasis added)

Before we disclose how Psalm 40 connects with Genesis 1, first look at several commentary entries—both classical and contemporary—to clearly see the connection of this Psalm with the coming of Jesus Christ into the world. (For further study, I've supplied several more commentary entries verifying Psalm 40 as a messianic prophecy at endnote 229.[229])

Barnes' Notes on the Bible:

In **Hebrews 10:7**, the apostle applies this **to the Messiah**. This is the most **simple and satisfactory interpretation** of the passage.

Lo, I come—It is difficult to see how this could be applied to David; **it is easy to see how it could be applied to the Messiah.**

In a large sense it would embrace all that had been written at the command of God at the time when this was supposed to be spoken. **That is, as spoken by the Messiah, it would include all the books of the Old Testament.**[230] (Emphasis added)

Jamieson-Fausset-Brown Bible Commentary:

Written of me—or on me, prescribed to me (2Ki 22:13). The first is the sense adopted by Paul [Hebrews 10:7]. In either case, the Pentateuch, or Law of Moses, is meant, and while **it contains much respecting Christ directly**, as Ge 3:15; 49:10; De 18:15, and, indirectly, in the Levitical ritual, **there is nowhere any allusion to David.**[231] (Emphasis added)

Guzik's Bible Commentary (a present-day commentary):

Ultimately this was fulfilled by the Son of David [Jesus]. Jesus came and was perfectly obedient, and His obedience is credited unto us…. [David] only foreshadowed the ultimate submission to God carried out by the Messiah, Jesus Christ. Hebrews 10:5–10 quotes the Septuagint (ancient Greek) translation of Psalm 40:6–8. This is a wonderful and remarkable prophecy of the work of Jesus.[232]

Another Hebrew Lesson: Bati

Again, let's appeal to Messianic Rabbi Zev Porat to find out what he has to say concerning Psalm 40:7:

The Hebrew word for "Here I come" is bati. And right in the middle of the word bati, in Psalm 40, is the Aleph-Tav! It is the same Aleph-Tav we find in Genesis 1:1, and on literally every single page of the Old Testament. Psalm 40:7 says "I come," and in the middle of bati is the symbolic Aleph-Tav name for Yeshua!

It's also important to understand that in Hebrew, the word bati, when used alone, can also be used to speak of the past or the present—depending on the context that encompasses the declaration. But in the context here, in Psalm 40, the context is future.

What Yeshua is saying here in Psalm 40, is exactly what the author of Hebrews shows us about Yeshua in chapter ten: I have come in the mystery of the Word of God—this is me!

Also notice that the word scroll is used in Psalm 40. That Hebrew word is megillah. To the Hebrew mind, especially at the Feast of Purim, they understand that the word megillah carries the nuanced meaning of "revelation" or "that which is hidden shall be revealed."[233]

I use this passage in Psalm 40:7 as an evangelistic tool here in Israel. Because the Hebrew speaking people can see it clearly when shown to them! Reading it only in the English language, you can't see it.

For example, an orthodox Hebrew scholar, or even a nonbeliever in Israel might say that the eth in the middle, or in a part of a word just means and, or the. Like the ve'et found in Genesis 1:1. [234] I say to them: But, if I take the word "and" or "the" out of scripture, you can't even have an intelligible sentence! Can you imagine reading the Bible with no and or the in a sentence anywhere?

So then I take them to Psalm 40:7 and show them the words "I come," which is made with the letters Aleph and Tav. I explain to them that without the Aleph-Tav you have no meaningful understanding of this verse. But with the Aleph and Tav, we now know who it is that is "coming"! [235]

Psalm 40:7 and Genesis 1:1

Understanding these truths, let's now compare Psalm 40:7 with Genesis 1:1. Have a look at the next two graphics.

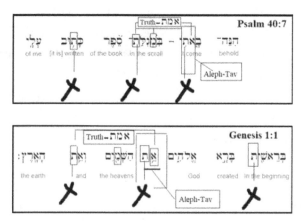

The similarities of the pattern are striking.

Both passages have three embedded crosses (*tav*), presenting pictures of Golgotha's hill. These letter-symbols would have been completely visible to the reader in the original Paleo-Hebrew text. Of course, it would be centuries later before any of the Old Testament's original readers would have an inkling of what those cross-like letters would ultimately symbolize.

Both passages also have the presence of the *aleph-tav, as well as* the word "truth," commencing with the *aleph* of the *aleph-tav*. And both passages are about Yeshua/Yahweh, the *Aleph-Tav*.

Is this a cosmic coincidence or a divinely implanted code meant for God's people to discover, especially those of the last-days generations? It appears to me the scroll is now being unsealed, opened, and revealed to the entire globe—*unto all the nations*—for a divine purpose.

41

THE FORBIDDEN CHAPTER

So, here's what we did. We took the Old Testament passage of
Isaiah 53 and printed it on a flyer in Modern Hebrew.
~Messianic Rabbi Zev Porat

One of the most remarkable Old Testament passages in the Bible that speaks of the passion, crucifixion, and resurrection of Jesus Christ is Isaiah 53. The context that sets up that chapter, however, begins within the last three verses of Isaiah 52.

> See, my servant will act wisely; He will be raised and lifted up and highly exalted. Just as there were many who were appalled at him— His appearance was so disfigured beyond that of any human being and his form marred beyond human likeness—so he will sprinkle many nations, and kings will shut their mouths because of him. For what they were not told, they will see, and what they have not heard, they will understand. (Isaiah 52:13–15)

Most modern Christians are not aware that the majority of Jewish people aren't very familiar with Isaiah 53. Many don't even know it exists. From a prominent Messianic website, Jews for Jesus, we find this insight:

Isaiah 53 does not appear in synagogue calendar readings. But its obscurity, its presence in the shadows, and the silence surrounding it shouts its importance. Its omission from the synagogue readings points to its uniqueness. One Jewish scholar, Claude Montefiore, explained: "Because of the Christological interpretation given to the chapter by Christians it is omitted from the series of prophetical lessons for the Deuteronomy Sabbaths...the omission is deliberate and striking."

Why is the omission so striking? Because when we finish the cycle of readings for the year, we haven't really finished it. We've left out a portion of our own prophets ostensibly because of what Christians think about it. Why has the Christian interpretation of Jewish Scripture placed regulations on what is or is not read in synagogues around the world?

But it isn't only because of the Christian interpretation that the Isaiah passage is omitted. After all, the services from which it is omitted aren't for Christian ears. So the problem is not what Christians think of the passage—it's what Jewish people might think.[236]

A Chinese Restaurant

How does opening a new Chinese restaurant in Israel help lead a Jewish person to Yeshua as Messiah? The question might sound ludicrous, but the answer illustrates a powerful testimony of the "living" nature of the Word of God.

Messianic Rabbi Zev Porat has often shared the account of how he and his Chinese wife, Lian, have employed a creative but surprisingly effective way to get a Jewish person thinking and talking about one of the most remarkable passages in the Old Testament concerning the Messiah. I first heard the story when Zev shared it with our listeners when he appeared on one of my live radio broadcasts. Following is his startling account:

The Israeli people generally love Chinese food. Because of that, they're very interested when a new Chinese restaurant opens in Israel, and they're usually anxious to try it out as soon as possible.

So, here's what we did. We took the Old Testament passage of Isaiah 53 and printed it on a flyer in Modern Hebrew. The little handout didn't reveal the fact that it was a passage from the prophet Isaiah's book. Instead it was written in simple paragraph form, without any verse descriptions. We never claimed this was an advertising flyer for a restaurant. But, because my wife is obviously Chinese, and we had a group from China helping us hand them out, many who took the pamphlet assumed we were advertising for a new Chinese restaurant.

When we took these leaflets to the streets of Tel Aviv an amazing thing happened. As we started handing them to the people who were walking on the sidewalk, or sitting on public benches, some of them came back to us and asked, "What is this? Are you Christians?"

Remember, there was nothing on the paper to indicate the writing was from the Bible. Neither was the name of Jesus mentioned anywhere.

I would answer, "Yes, we are—but why would you ask this?"

Their response was something like, "Because this writing declares what you Christians say about Jesus. This is the story of Jesus."

I would just look at them, smile, and say, "Really? Would it surprise you to find out this writing is actually the 53rd chapter of Isaiah? These words are not from the New Testament at all, and they are not from a Christian sermon or lesson—they are taken directly from the Jewish Tanakh. And they were written about 700 years before Jesus! Yet, you are telling me that the words sound exactly like the New Testament Yeshua? How can this be?"

At this point they are usually quite stunned. They can't believe what they are reading on our flyer is in their Scriptures. So, I open the Tanakh to Isaiah 53 and have them read it aloud.

When they are finished reading, they ask, "How is it that I've never seen this, or heard this?"

I tell them, "It is because your rabbis don't want you to know about it. They know it sounds just like Yeshua of the New Testament—and they are afraid that you might become believers. After all, without any pressure or preaching on my part, you saw it for yourself simply by reading the words—straight from the Tanakh. If the rabbis are not afraid of it, why have you never heard them read it aloud? Why have they never encouraged you to read it, or ask questions about it?"

Isaiah 53 is probably the most powerful passage in the entire Old Testament for reaching a Jewish person for Yeshua as Messiah. To be sure, there are other passages that are also mightily used of Yahweh for this purpose, but even the rabbis know that Isaiah 53 is particularly potent. This is why they try so hard to explain that this passage does not mean Yeshua—or, most often, they simply ignore the chapter completely.[237]

Relegated to Obscurity

Isaiah 53 is yet another revelation the Orthodox rabbis desperately don't want the Jewish people to see. So, through the centuries, they've crafted interpretations of that chapter in Isaiah to conceal Yeshua from the sight of those who otherwise might ask questions about it.

Overall, however, it appears they are no longer having the great success they once enjoyed. An increasing number of Jewish people are beginning to see and understand—day in and day out, seven days a week.

What once was hidden is now coming into sharp focus!

42

PROTESTATIONS

Ask those Jews who have been saved because of the passage.
Or the ones who have dared to ask their rabbis the tough
questions about this passage. They'll tell you!
~MESSIANIC RABBI ZEV PORAT

Of course, the majority of today's Orthodox Jewish leaders disavow the Messianic claims regarding Isaiah 53. To stay relevant, they pretty much have to. This is the same phenomenon Yeshua Himself faced in His years of earthly and public ministry. His "presence" threatened the very way of life for the rabbis and Jewish elite.

In pursuit of academic fairness, I will next appeal to the argument of Orthodox Rabbi Tovia Singer, who has a widespread and influential Orthodox voice in Israel and around the world among the Jewish people. In an article titled, "Who is God's Suffering Servant? The Rabbinic Interpretation of Isaiah 53," Singer gave an assessment of Isaiah 53 that is fairly typical of the general Orthodox view of the passage.

His piece begins with this paragraph:

Despite strong objections from conservative Christian apologists, the prevailing rabbinic interpretation of Isaiah 53 ascribes the "servant" to the nation of Israel who silently endured unimaginable suffering at the hands of its gentile oppressors. The speakers, in this most-debated chapter, are the stunned kings of nations who will bear witness to the messianic age and the final vindication of the Jewish people following their long and bitter exile. "Who would have believed our report?" the astonished and contrite world leaders wonder aloud in dazed bewilderment (53:1).[238]

However, a number of others whose roots are just as deeply entrenched in the Jewish faith flatly disagree with Rabbi Singer's assessment.

Holocaust Survivor

Rabbi Rachmiel Frydland was a Holocaust survivor coming from a profoundly pious Orthodox family. A former rabbinical student in Warsaw, Poland, he also became a Messianic Jewish teacher—a believer in Yeshua.[239]—who has also written about Isaiah 53.

Following are a couple of pertinent excerpts from an article Frydland wrote titled "The Rabbis' Dilemma: A Look at Isaiah 53":

> **The subject was never discussed in my pre-war-Poland Hebrew school. In the rabbinical training I had received, the fifty-third chapter of the book of Isaiah had been continually avoided** in favor of other, weightier matters to be learned. Yet, when I first read this passage, my mind was filled with questions.... Who is this chapter speaking about? The words are clear—the passage tells of an outstanding Servant of the Lord whose visage is marred and is afflicted and stricken....
>
> Rashi (Rabbi Shlomo Itzchaki, 1040–1105) and some of the later rabbis, though, interpreted the passage as referring to Israel. **They knew that the older interpretations referred it to Messiah.**
>
> However, Rashi lived at a time when a degenerate medieval distortion of Christianity was practiced. He wanted to preserve the Jewish people from accepting such a faith and, although his

intentions were sincere, other prominent Jewish rabbis and leaders realized the inconsistencies of Rashi's interpretation. They presented a threefold objection to his innovation. **First, they showed
the consensus of ancient opinion. Secondly, they pointed out
that the text is in the singular. Thirdly, they noted verse eight.**

This verse presented an insurmountable difficulty to those
who interpreted this passage as referring to Israel.[240] (Emphasis
added)

An excellent online ministry article titled "The Forbidden Chapter"
outlines of the entire history of Isaiah 53's Jewish interpretation. The sum-
mation of the article succinctly states:

It's important to understand we're not just talking about a Christian interpretation here—**the Jewish Sages of ancient times also
always interpreted Isaiah 53 to be about the Messiah.** In fact, the
well-known term "Messiah ben Yosef" is actually from this very
text.[241] (Emphasis added)

Messianic Rabbi Porat also attests, from the standpoint of his own
deeply Orthodox background, that this passage has indeed long been
avoided, hidden, and sometimes outright forbidden by the rabbis to be
read and studied among the Orthodox Jews. When it is examined, Zev
affirms, it is often adjusted so the interpretation is about Israel rather than
the Messiah.

Zev says that, frequently, the critics flat-out deny this truth, but he has
a powerful answer for those who question it: "Ask those Jews who have
been saved because of the passage. Or the ones who have dared to ask their
rabbis the tough questions about this passage. They will tell you."[242]

What does all this about Isaiah 53 have to do with the theme of our
journey? With the turn of the next page you'll find out.

43

YESHUA SHEMI

For truly I tell you, until heaven and earth disappear,
not the smallest letter, not the least stroke of a pen, will by any means
disappear from the Law until everything is accomplished.
~MATTHEW 5:18

Like the Daniel "computer" revelation discovered with ELS technology, the following is very similar in its potentially profound message. This piece of ELS evidence also follows the protocols of proper usage and application.

The Hebrew expression *Yeshua shemi,* meaning "Jesus is my name," is spelled in Hebrew as follows:

- **Yeshua:** *yod-shin-vav-ayin*
- **Is my name:** *shin-meme-yod*

Believe it or not, this exact "hidden" phrase is found in Isaiah 53 when using the proper parameters of the ELS skip code.

As with the phenomenon of the word "computer" being found in Daniel 12:4 at a skip code sequence of only thirty letters apart, the phrase *Yeshua shemi* (in reverse spelling) is similarly uncovered at the ELS skip distance of a mere *twenty* letters. That phrase, "Jesus is my name," is found in verses 7–10, beginning with verse 8. These verses just "happen" to comprise the section of Isaiah 53 universally interpreted by Christians to be a vivid portrayal and prophecy of Jesus' crucifixion.[243]

> He was oppressed and afflicted, yet he did not open his mouth; he was led like a lamb to the slaughter, and as a sheep before its shearers is silent, so he did not open his mouth.
>
> By oppression and judgment he was taken away. Yet who of his generation protested? For he was cut off from the land of the living; for the transgression of my people he was punished.
>
> He was assigned a grave with the wicked, and with the rich in his death, though he had done no violence, nor was any deceit in his mouth.
>
> Yet it was the Lord's will to crush him and cause him to suffer, and though the Lord makes his life an offering for sin, he will see his offspring and prolong his days, and the will of the Lord will prosper in his hand. (Isaiah 53:7–10)

Following is the configuration of the twenty-letter skip code that formulates the Hebrew declaration *yeshua shemi*.[244]

For a more symmetrical view of the skip, here are the same letters and words of verses 8–10, arranged so we can see the symmetry. Remember, Hebrew reads from right to left.

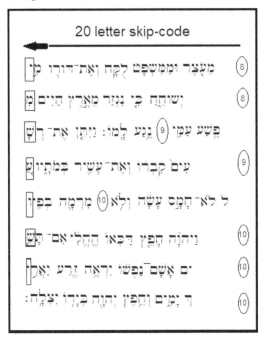

For Integrity's Sake

It is a fact that the word *yeshua* can indeed be extracted from the Hebrew Scriptures *thousands* of times using ELS. After all, many dozens of times, *yeshua* is found in the Hebrew surface text alone, and it's translated into the word "salvation" in English—as we've already examined.

Additionally, the Hebrew word *mashiach*—"messiah"—can also be extracted several thousand times. Most of the time, however, when using ELS to find these words in their "hidden" forms, the skip code has to be many hundreds of letters apart, and on a number of occasions, they are found within the spacing distance of *thousands of letters.*

Some detractors have also claimed that even the two phrases "Muhammed is my name" and "Gandhi is my name" can be found in the Hebrew Scriptures using ELS. Those claims appear to be true as well.

However, few critics seem willing to admit a huge distinction: the sparse "Muhammed" and "Gandhi" phrases are reported to be found in expansive skip codes as well. Additionally, none of those findings appear to be found in a corresponding passage wherein there would be any contextual meaning concerning whom that Scripture might be about. In other words, supposedly coded names found in that type of meaningless protocol would hold no significance whatsoever.[245]

Conversely, the *yeshua shemi* skip code we're examining in this chapter is only twenty letters long. And *yeshua shemi* is found in the surface text that speaks of an unnamed suffering servant of Yahweh, whom we now know to be Yeshua Himself.[246] Therefore, the ELS discovery provides a potential answer about the object of the passage. Considering these facts, then, the odds against this phrase being in this precise spot go up considerably—to an almost statistical impossibility.

The obvious fact of *yeshua shemi* being found in the crucifixion text of Isaiah 53, using ELS, is indisputable and therefore worthy of serious consideration. That's my primary point, and it's my reason for including it here. Once again, as the phenomenon appears before our eyes, we have to say, "There it is! I'm looking at it!"[247]

For those who do not read Hebrew, I asked Rabbi Porat to have a look at these renditions of the ELS coded phrase. As I did with Uri Mendel regarding Daniel 12:4, I asked Zev to verify whether the emphasized skip letters actually do represent the phrase *yeshua shemi*, and whether they are found in verses 8–10 of Isaiah 53.

Here is Zev's response:

Yes, the phrase is there. And these are the genuine verses of Isaiah 53. It's really quite remarkable that "Jesus is my name" is found in this exact spot.[248]

As with the ELS word "computer" being found in Daniel 12, we cannot deny that *yeshua shemi* is in Isaiah 53. I know of no one—not even the most ardent detractors of ELS technology—who denies its presence in this passage.

Remember, nestled in the vivid crucifixion imagery of the surface text of Isaiah 53, this phrase could only be "seen" with the advent of computer technology and programs designed to conduct a search of this magnitude. In this regard, it would appear that Daniel 12:4 and Isaiah 53 are inextricably tied together in a prophetic sense. No generation before ours could even attempt to search for such a thing, much less could they hope to find it. Yet, it is there, right where one might expect to find it, if it really existed. Is this visual phenomenon only a fluke, some accidental oddity?

I think not.

Consider this: Since this ELS code is truly there, then we might ask why God would do such a thing in the first place. Why would He give us "codes" and mysteries of this nature to unravel? There are two huge reasons I believe He does this.

First, it's probably because He loves doing it! We already know Yahweh operates at multidimensional levels in everything else He does. Why wouldn't He work His glory at this plane of revelation through His Word as well? I listed in an earlier chapter at least a dozen Scriptures that affirm this is exactly what God does. His graciousness extends to us at many levels. Truly, the surface text of the Scriptures is always enough, yet, apparently, He still gives us more!

- See, the former things have taken place, and new things I declare; before they spring into being I announce them to you. (Isaiah 42:9)
- It is the glory of God to conceal a matter; to search out a matter is the glory of kings. (Proverbs 25:2)

Second, it could well be that we are nearing the last of the *very last days*. If that's the case, these kinds of revelations would be especially important to the Jewish mindset regarding *seeing some hard evidence* that the person whom they have previously denied as Messiah might in fact be the One they have longed for all along![249]

God's heart is for the Jewish people *first*.[250] His Word speaks of the ingathering during the last days that will involve the Jewish people coming to Yeshua as Messiah and Lord in great numbers.[251] So, a coded message of this magnitude could be just what it takes to bring a number of Jewish souls to Jesus Christ. And don't forget: It was distinctly Jewish scholars, mathematicians, and computer experts who discovered the ELS codes and invented the technology to employ them, in the first place.

However, as striking as the Isaiah 53 ELS code is, there are still several more hidden gems in that text. Believe it or not, those treasures go all the way back to the mysteriously repeating Genesis 1:1 cycle we've already discovered.

44

THE SURFACE TEXT

He was chosen before the creation of the world,
but was revealed in these last times for your sake.
~1 Peter 1:20

By taking a deeper look at the surface text of Isaiah 53, we'll discover several more amazing revelations about that chapter. Let's inspect the text as it is written in the Modern Hebrew, but with the understanding that it was originally written in Paleo-Hebrew letters.

Isaiah 53 is divided into twelve verses.[252] Verse 6 initiates the narrative of verses 7–10. It was in those last four verses where we discovered the ELS code, "Jesus is my name." However, in verse 6, within the surface text only, we discover yet another layer of potential identification verification.

Here is that verse in English:

We all, like sheep, have gone astray, each of us has turned to our own way; and the LORD **has laid on him** the iniquity of us all. (Isaiah 53:6, emphasis added)

Here it is in Modern Hebrew, reading right to left. Look what we find in that verse, the one that actually commences the crucifixion scene of Isaiah 53.

Based upon what we've already learned about the *aleph-tav* "pointer,"
this discovery is quite remarkable. The marker of the *aleph-tav* is indeed
grammatically pointing to the "Him" of the sentence and connecting it
with the "what" of the sentence. On the *Aleph-Tav* was laid the iniquity of
us all. We were the ones who deserved "the cross" because of our sin. But
Yahweh laid that punishment upon the *Aleph-Tav* instead!

Golgotha's Hill

When we get to the next two verses—7 and 8—we find another coded
message, one reminiscent of what we found in Genesis 1:1:

> He was oppressed and afflicted, yet he did not open his mouth;
> he was led like a lamb to the slaughter, and as a sheep before its
> shearers is silent, so he did not open his mouth. By oppression and
> judgment he was taken away. Yet who of his generation protested?
> For he was cut off from the land of the living; for the transgression
> of my people he was punished. (Isaiah 53:7–8)

As in Genesis 1:1, we also find in Isaiah 53:7–8 three "crosses" and the
aleph-tav. The revelation of these truths looks like this:

- Following is what these revelations of Isaiah 53:6–10 look like when shown together. Once you see it, it's awfully difficult to un-see.

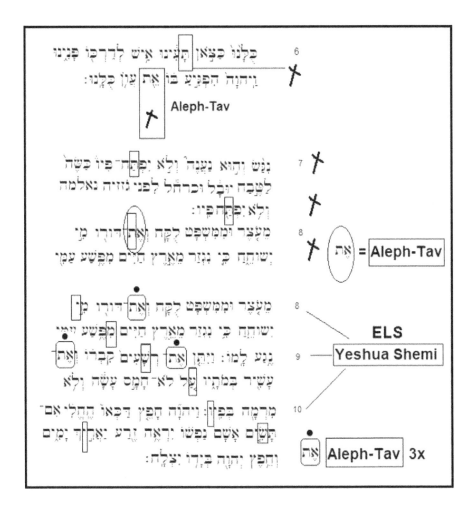

PART VIII

THE NAME

Therefore God exalted him to the highest place and gave him the name that is above every name, that at the name of Jesus every knee should bow, in heaven and on earth and under the earth.

~PHILIPPIANS 2:9–10

45

SAY MY NAME

Of course YHWH wants us to speak His name!
Why wouldn't He? There is not a single commandment
against it within His Word.

The most important of all the names by which God is known is the
word represented by the Hebrew letters *yud-heh-vav-heh* (הוהי), reading from right to left. In English, הוהי is transliterated as YHWH or JHVH,
and is usually articulated as "Yahweh" (*YAH-way*), Yahveh (*YAH vey*), or
Jehovah (*Ja-HO-vah*).[253] That designation is used in the Old Testament
almost seven thousand times. This precise arrangement of Hebrew letters
is called the Tetragrammaton.[254]

The name YHWH is deeply related to the Hebrew root verb *heh-yud-
heh* ("to be"), and reflects the fact that God's existence is eternal. This is
why, when God first speaks His name to Moses, He reveals Himself as "I
Am" or "I Will Be What I Will Be."[255]

Too Holy?

Among the Orthodox Jews, the Tetragrammaton is often referred to as
"the Ineffable Name." It is frequently taught that, from time immemo-
rial, the Jews refused to pronounce YHWH because it is too holy to

utter aloud, lest it might be unintentionally taken in vain. As a result, many Orthodox Jews, and even some Messianic congregations, vocalize YHWH as *Ha Shem*—"the Name." Often, they even write the name of God as "G-d." This is done to avoid causing someone to speak His name, or to even see it in print.[256]

In reality, however, that practice had its roots in the Second Temple period, around the fifth century BC. Yet, even then, the understanding of its forbidden nature was invoked in an almost superstitious manner rather than in a strictly legalistic and all-inclusive one. According to most reliable historical sources, the practice of *never* pronouncing YHWH did not take a firm grip upon the Jewish people until the destruction of the Temple in AD 70 and throughout the years beyond. Even Israel's *Haaretz* verifies: "**When the Temple in Jerusalem was destroyed** in 70 C.E. by Rome, to punish the Jews for their latest rebellion, there was **no longer any context in which the uttering of God's name was permissible.**"[257] (Emphasis added)

The Biblical Truth

The biblical truth is that Yahweh specifically instructs His people to proclaim His name! He even tells them to sing His name and chant praises to His Name.[258] Not a single verse of Scripture forbids speaking God's name. That practice was extrabiblically devised by the rabbinical class of Judaism.

In fact, Zephaniah 3:9 foretells of the days of *God's judgment,* at which the proper use of the one true name of YHWH will be eternally set right: "For then **I will restore to the peoples a pure language,** That they all **may call on the name of the LORD [YHWH], To serve Him with one accord**" (KJV, emphasis added).[259]

The declaration of Zephaniah 3:9 is set up by the lengthy verse preceding it. Incredibly, in so doing, Zephaniah 3:8 makes use of *all twenty-seven letters* of the Hebrew alphabet, including the soffit forms—the only verse in the Bible to do so![260] And with that *purifying of the languages* of all the peoples will finally come the proper pronunciation and use of God's Name—YHWH.

Observe the following, as iterated in several prominent sources of Jewish history:

Nothing in the Torah prohibits a person from pronouncing the Name of God. Indeed, it is evident from scripture that **God's Name was pronounced routinely.** Many common Hebrew names contain "Yah" or "Yahu," part of God's four-letter Name. The Name was pronounced **as part of daily services in the Temple.**

The Mishnah confirms that there was **no prohibition against pronouncing The Name in ancient times.** In fact, the Mishnah **recommends using God's Name** as a routine greeting to a fellow Jew. Berakhot 9:5.

However, **by the time of the Talmud** [compiled between the 2nd and 5th centuries AD], **it was the custom to use substitute Names for God.** Instead of pronouncing the four-letter Name, we usually substitute the Name "Adonai," or simply say "Ha-Shem" (lit. The Name).

With the Temple destroyed and **the prohibition on pronouncing The Name outside of the Temple,** pronunciation of the Name fell into disuse.[261] (Emphasis added)

In fact, we now know it was a Jewish practice before and after the New Testament period to write out YHWH, in Hebrew, right into the Greek text of Scripture. In several examples of scholarly research, we find the following:

The New International Dictionary of New Testament Theology states:

Recent textual discoveries cast doubt on the idea that the compilers of the LXX [Septuagint] translated the Tetragrammaton

YHVH by [the Greek] *kyrios.* **The oldest LXX MSS (fragments) now available to us have the Tetragrammaton written in Hebrew characters in the Greek text.** This custom was retained by later Jewish translators of the Old Testament in the first centuries A.D.[262] (Emphasis added)

The Anchor Bible Dictionary further affirms:

There is evidence that the Tetragrammaton, the Divine Name, Yahweh, appeared in some or all of the OT quotations in the NT when the NT documents were first penned.[263] (Emphasis added)

The Connection

Rabbi Zev Porat explains that the ancient practice of applying Hebrew pictograms to each Hebrew letter, along with its corresponding meaning, was also strongly discouraged about the same time the Temple was destroyed and during the dispersion of the earliest New Testament documents. Also during this period, the widespread practice of not pronouncing the Tetragrammaton was beginning to bloom.[264]

Why was this period so important? As we have discovered, the most probable reason was directly related to the fact that the pictographic name of Yeshua is represented by the *aleph* and the *tav*—"the one true God" (*aleph*) "upon the cross" (*tav*).

This truth is further punctuated when we consider the *aleph-tav* YHWH was used to describe the very essence of His being when God declared: "I am YHWH, the first and the last—the *Aleph-Tav*—your Redeemer."

"I, the LORD—**the first and the last**—I am He. …For I myself will help you," declares the LORD, **your Redeemer**, the Holy One of Israel. (Isaiah 41:4, 14, BEREAN STUDY BIBLE; emphasis added)

To His Glory

Of course Yahweh *wants* us to speak His name! Why wouldn't He? His name is His glory. His name is our salvation. He is Yeshua. Immanuel. God with us. Yahweh. Adonai. He is our Redeemer. He is the *Aleph-Tav*, *El Shaddai*, and the First and the Last! He wants us to sing His name, praise His name, proclaim His name…and, perhaps most importantly, He wants us to honor and cherish His name.

His name saves, heals, delivers, protects, and frees us from the bondage of our sin. His name is the embodiment of all truth. And in the revealed mysteries of that truth we find our Creator…in all of His intricate glory and splendor. Sometimes, we even find His name *in code*…in the most wonderful ways, and in the most stunning places.

I'm convinced those nuggets of treasure are placed there for God's people to find and then reveal to the world. They must especially be revealed to the Jewish people of these last-days generations.

46

THE MYSTERY OF YHWH

Let them praise the name of the LORD: *for his name alone is excellent;*
his glory [is] above the earth and heaven.
~PSALM 148:13, KJV

As we've already noted, the Hebrew letters representing the name of God are יהוה. Whenever these four letters are found in English translations of the Bible, they are often represented with the word "LORD"—in all caps. However, the ancient pictographic representations of these letters also link directly to the person of Yeshua/Jesus.

For our study, and in the interest of holding to the most reliable and strictest protocols available, we'll appeal to two modern and widely acknowledged Hebrew language sites, Chabad.org and Hebrew Today, as our sources for making those awe-inspiring connections.

Chabad.org is a decidedly Orthodox site described as "the flagship website of the *Chabad-Lubavitch Hasidic*[265] movement. It was one of the first Jewish Internet sites and the first and largest virtual congregation. Chabad.org has a Jewish knowledge base which includes over 100,000 articles of information ranging from basic Judaism to Hasidic philosophy taught from the Chabad point of view."[266]

Hebrew Today, as noted in an earlier chapter, is described as a professional Hebrew language institution of instruction used by teachers in Israel's schools and in various media publication services.[267]

Letter Meanings

By using these websites and their definitions of the ancient letter meanings of the three letters that make up the four-letter Tetragrammaton, we discover the following:

1. **The *yud*** (or *yod*) means "a hand."[268] Chabad.org says: "The *Yud* can represent "A Jew, A *Yad*—a hand—which is an allusion to G-d, for we say that G-d took us out of Egypt with a mighty hand."[269]

2. **The *vav/waw*,**[270] according to Hebrew Today, means "a 'hook,' 'spear,' or 'tent peg' in Hebrew, therefore the name and shape of the letter are *directly connected to this meaning*."[271]

As a point of interest, Chabad.org gives the *vav* an even richer understanding of its meaning, especially as it would tie to the significance of the name YHWH:

> While the design of the vav looks like a hook, the word vav actually means "hook." A hook is something that holds two things together. Furthermore, the vav attached to a verb converts that verb from either the past to the future tense, or **from the future to the past tense.** For example, the word hoiya in Hebrew **means "it was."** The word v'hoiya means "it will be."** By merely attaching the vav [the spike or the nail], **the past is transformed into the future.**[272] (Emphasis added)

The word *vav*, then, without stretching the meaning whatsoever, brings up a picture of some sort of a fastener, or something that pins one object to another—as in a tent peg driven into the earth to hold a tent in place. One can also visualize something along the lines of a spike, nail, or other type of sharpened stake. All are synonyms of "peg"[273]—perhaps like a *hand* that is spiked, pegged, staked, or forcefully "hooked" to a beam of wood, or even like a spear thrust into a person's body? And, once that "attachment" is made *through the Aleph-Tav*, the past turns into the future! Each of these images precisely fits the Hebrew Today and Chabad.org definitions that have been anciently assigned to the *vav.*

3. **The *heh*.** The fifth letter of the Hebrew alphabet is the letter *heh,* which is used twice in the divine Tetragrammaton. In using this letter twice, especially in light of its ideographic meaning, it appears that YHWH is directing our deepest attention to the matter.

Once again, we'll appeal to Chabad.org, whose teachers say the letter *heh* means: "Here [it] is, to be disturbed, or Behold!"[274]

Now, think of what lies before us within those confirmed letter meanings that is acknowledged among a large number of conventional Jewish people to this day.[275]

What's in a Name?

The following is what we can legitimately end up with as we string together the current-day usage of the letter meanings of YHWH:

Behold [or "Here is!"] the hand of God Himself—in Jewish flesh!

Behold [or "Here is!"] the nail—or the spike, stake, hook, or peg!

Behold [or "Here is!"] the spear!

Behold [or "Here is!"] the One who was from the "past" but now is in the "future"—the First and the Last—tied together by the hands, nails, and spear, and appearing in Jewish flesh.

These letters could even be put in the following form, using the second definition of *heh*—"to be disturbed"—that Chabad.org teaches: "Behold! Does this "disturb" you? Here it is! The hand, the nail, and the spear! The First and the Last!"

There's no doubt: This revelation is indeed "disturbing," and at the same time, it is humbling—especially to the Jewish person who has never seen it. How astoundingly impossible—humanly speaking—is it, that this code is found in the *letter meaning* of the name of God Himself?

There's really no valid argument against this truth. The holy name of God can genuinely be represented as portraying an accurate picture of Yeshua's sacrificial work on the cross. And the earliest archeological evidence we currently possess concerning the Hebrews' use of the name YHWH dates it to be more than three thousand years old.[276]

Certainly, neither the ancient Jews nor modern Orthodox Jews intended to reveal cryptic images of the crucifixion of Yeshua/Jesus in the very letters of the name of YHWH. Yet, *there it is,* coded for thousands of years within the name, which makes the following insight from Judaism 101 even more astounding:

> In Jewish thought, a name is not merely an arbitrary designation, a random combination of sounds. **The name conveys the nature and essence of the thing named.** It represents the history and reputation of the being named.[277] (Emphasis added)

It is true—the name YHWH does emphatically convey the nature and essence of God's being. The letter identification of YHWH, as we've just defined it, also squares perfectly with what we've discovered in chapters past when the name "Jesus" is substituted in Old Testament Scriptures wherever the word "salvation" (*Yeshua*) is used.

> Then **all mankind will know** that I, the Lord, **am your Jesus** ["salvation"—*Yeshua*], **your Redeemer**, and the **Mighty One of Jacob**. (Isaiah 49:26, emphasis added)

Indeed. "Then all mankind will know…I am Yeshua!" And now, because of the technological explosion of the last days, as Daniel clearly prophesied, it's happening. *All the world* is now seeing it.

Every time we share this eternal truth throughout the world, using the technology we hold in our hands, we also are a part of that prophecy coming to life.

It was about *us*!

47

THEY WILL LOOK UPON ME

His very name, as they have known it for thousands of years, literally points to Yeshua as Messiah and LORD.

n light of the revelation we've just laid forth regarding the name YHWH, consider the following passages:

- Then saith [Jesus] to Thomas, Reach hither thy finger, and **behold my hands;** and reach hither thy hand, and **thrust it into my side** [where the spear was plunged!]: and be not faithless, but believing. (John 20:27, KJV, emphasis added)
- **They pierce my hands and my feet.** All my bones are on display; people stare and gloat over me. They divide my clothes among them and cast lots for my garment. (Psalm 22:16–18, emphasis added)
- **But he was pierced** for our transgressions, he was crushed for our iniquities; the punishment that brought us peace was on him, and **by his wounds we are healed.** (Isaiah 53:5, emphasis added)

- These things happened so that the scripture would be fulfilled: "Not one of his bones will be broken," and, as another scripture says, **"They will look on the one they have pierced."** (John 19:36–37, emphasis added)
- Look, he is coming with the clouds, and every eye will see him, **even those who pierced him**; and all the peoples of the earth will mourn because of him. (Revelation 1:7, emphasis added)
- Instead, **one of the soldiers pierced Jesus' side with a spear**, bringing a sudden flow of blood and water. (John 19:34, emphasis added)

Considering everything we've discovered about the letter meanings of YHWH, we certainly don't want to forget about the next declaration from Heaven's throne, as revealed by the prophet Zechariah. It's almost as though YHWH is telling us exactly what we just learned about the letter meanings of His eternal name!

And I [YHWH] **will pour out on the house of David and the inhabitants of Jerusalem a spirit of grace and supplication. They will look on me,** [YHWH] **the one they have pierced,** and they will **mourn for him** [*Yeshua*] as one mourns for an **only child**, and **grieve bitterly** for him **as one grieves for a firstborn son.** (Zechariah 12:10, emphasis added)

Don't forget, Chabad.org also attests that the *yud* can represent a Jewish person as well. Think about that in light of the Scripture revelations. When God put on flesh in the person of Yeshua, He put on Jewish flesh. When Yeshua went to the cross, it was His Jewish hands that were nailed to it. It was His Jewish side that was pierced with the spear. Everything these two Modern Hebrew language sites claim about the letters of YHWH relate back to Yeshua! The *picture story* these four letters tell can't get any more striking.

A Witness

Messianic Rabbi Zev Porat says:

What we have been doing at Messiah of Israel Ministries, with a greater urgency than ever, is to take these kinds of revelations directly to the Jewish people—so they can see these things with their own eyes. When they see them for the very first time, they are absolutely stunned. They simply can't believe it. Some of them even get angry that the rabbis have hidden this information. They actually feel betrayed.

I believe that by revealing these connections, the attempt of the rabbis to hide the truth will ultimately backfire on them. The Jewish people love the history of their ancestors. They love learning about the origins of our ancient language. When they discover that an important part of that history has been effectively eliminated, or purposely concealed, they become very upset. They are ready to listen. They know that there must be a reason for the concealment.

Zev concluded:

With today's technological advancements in spreading information to the entire planet within minutes, there's no way that the truth of these discoveries can be contained any longer. The more this evidence gets out, the more the Jewish people will understand, and for example, that Rabbi Kaduri's Yeshua note was not far-fetched at all. They will understand that it was not some sort of trick. Rabbi Kaduri's note actually revealed the eternal truth; *Yeshua is Messiah!* And that truth has been there since the beginning—hidden in the name of YHWH![278]

The Word Became Flesh

Consider the implications of this profound unveiling. The ancient pictograms and their accompanying meanings that God originally put in the minds of the earliest Hebrew people would later testify to the most complete meaning of God's holy name. Surely, the primeval Hebrews had no clue as to how those symbols would one day, in the distant future, declare the gospel message. It was as if those primitive letters and words had actually turned into a physical reality and *became flesh*.

This is why a first-century Jewish man by the name of John, an original follower of *Yeshua Ha' Mashiach*, penned the following divinely inspired words:

> **In the beginning was the Word**, and the Word was with God, and **the Word was God**. He was with God in the beginning. Through him all things were made; without him nothing was made that has been made....
>
> **The Word became flesh** and **made his dwelling among us.** We have seen his glory, the glory of the one and only Son, who came from the Father, full of grace and truth. (John 1:1–3, 14, emphasis added)

The Word "that became flesh" is none other than the holy name that pictographically translates to "Behold the hand, behold the nail."

Don't forget that, after His resurrection, Jesus used that phrase to prove He had indeed arisen. Remember Cleopas and his friend, James, in the opening chapters? That narrative was based upon the words of Luke 24:13–45. In the scene when Jesus instantly appeared in the Upper Room in Jerusalem where the disciples were hiding, he said to them:

> Behold my hands and my feet, that it is I myself: handle me, and see. (Luke 24:39, KJV)

That Living Word had become flesh in Yeshua—through whom the world can now *see* Yahweh and His mighty act of salvation and resurrection. This is what many Jewish people today are coming to understand. Yeshua/Jesus is indeed Messiah. He is "God with us." He is the heavenly "sign" upon whom they have long been waiting.

> Therefore **the Lord Himself shall give you a sign**: behold, the young woman shall conceive, and bear a son, and shall call his name Immanuel ["God with us"]. (Isaiah 7:14, JPS TANAKH 1917; emphasis added)

Of course, it is also a tremendous help that the Jews' most beloved Orthodox Rabbi Yitzhak Kaduri confirmed this through his Yeshua note in 2007.

Now you understand why the Orthodox elite in Israel eventually did away with "speaking" God's name. His very name, as they have known it for thousands of years, literally points to Yeshua as Messiah and LORD.

But, there's still something else. To this day, as mentioned in an earlier chapter, when Jewish people don't wish to speak or write the name "YHWH," they use a substitute for it. But in using that replacement phrase, they are still declaring the glory of Jesus Christ, as well as His unquestionable equality with YHWH.

The revelation of that phrase is next.

48

HA-SHEM

Who is this that even the wind and waves obey Him?
~MATTHEW 8:27

The Hebrew *Mishnah*,[279] dated to around AD 200, catalogs the first official use of the term *Ha-Shem.* The term, employed as a substitution
for speaking or writing the name of YHWH, *simply* means "the name."[280]

Again, Rabbi Zev Porat believes that, at least partly, this substitution
became insisted upon by the Jewish religious elite precisely because of
what we discovered in the last two chapters: The letter meaning of its
Hebrew letters, YHWH, points directly to Yeshua on the cross.

At about that time in history, either in conversation or writing, Ortho-
dox Jews began substituting the title *Ha-Shem* for the name YHWH.
However, unbeknownst to many, even that replacement word links
YHWH directly with Yeshua/Jesus!

Ha-Shem is spelled with the three letters: *heh, shin, mem*, again, reading from right to left. Those letters also reveal individual letter meanings,
as we will once again draw evidence from the two acclaimed Hebrew
sources cited in the last chapter.

We already know the letter *heh* means "here is!" or "behold!" and, we
know *shin* means "God"/*Shaddai.*"[281] Also recall that the *shin* is imprinted
on almost every mezuzah because of its ancient letter meaning.

However, up to now, we haven't examined the ideographic meaning of the *mem*. So, let's have another look at our trusted sources.

Letter Meaning of *Mem*

1. Chabad.org says: "The letter *mem* stands for [the Hebrew word] *mayim*, which means water."[282]

2. HebrewToday.com agrees with Chabad.org, but with an even richer revelation attached to it. Besides "water," Hebrew Today emphasizes the letter's prominent place in the Hebrew word for "truth," a word we've explored in chapters past.

Here is what the Hebrew Today website says:

> **Another name of G-d is—אֱמֶת (emet) which means truth.** This word starts with the first letter of the Aleph-Bet—א—and ends with the last letter—ת. This refers to all of existence and the truth in it. **The middle of the word is the letter מ which connects between the different worlds of creation, as we mentioned earlier.**
>
> Another word that starts and ends with the letter מ is the word מַיִם ["water"]. In the story of the Creation, the text mentions that G-d separated the waters above the firmament and below it. The first **mem** [final form, open] **represents the waters** above the firmament and the second mem [original form, closed] the waters below the firmament. Therefore **this letter** [mem] **is connected to the element of water.**[283] (Emphasis added)

The Message of *Ha-Shem*

Taking the three Hebrew letters that make the phrase "the name" (*ha-shem*) and applying their confirmed ideographic identifications, we can arrive at the meaning: "Behold the Almighty God on the water!"

Heh—"Behold!"

Shin—"God"/*El Shaddai*—"God Almighty"

Mem—(On the) "water"

Of course, we immediately think of Yeshua/Jesus walking on the water and calming a storm, as recorded in several places in the New Testament. On one of those occasions, the disciples exclaimed, "Who is this that even the wind and the waves obey Him?"

Jesus Walks on the Water

Later that night, the boat was in the middle of the lake, and he was alone on land. He saw the disciples straining at the oars, because the wind was against them. **Shortly before dawn he went out to them, walking on the lake.** He was about to pass by them, but when **they saw him walking on the lake,** they thought he was a ghost. They cried out, because they all saw him and were terrified. Immediately he spoke to them and said, "Take courage! It is I. Don't be afraid." **Then he climbed into the boat with them, and the wind died down.** They were completely amazed. (Mark 6:45–51, emphasis added)

Jesus Calms the Storm

Then he got into the boat and his disciples followed him. Suddenly a furious storm came up on the lake, so that the waves swept over the boat. But Jesus was sleeping. The disciples went and woke him, saying **"Lord, save us! We're going to drown!"** He replied, "You of little faith, why are you so afraid?" Then **he got up and rebuked the winds and the waves, and it was completely calm.** The men were amazed and asked, **"What kind of man is this? Even the winds and the waves obey him!"** (Matthew 8:23–27, emphasis added)

Old Testament Waterworks?

Few believers in Yeshua would have a problem remembering those accounts in the New Testament. However, an important question of context at this point would be: Does the Old Testament contain any passage that specifically declares YHWH "walks on water" or "calms the wind and waters"? Actually, there are several, and they are striking.

The first Old Testament passage we'll look at comes from the book of Job, one of the most ancient pieces of prose known to the world.[284] It is also the oldest of all the books in the Bible. Yet, a statement in Job basically says: "You want to know who the Lord Almighty is? He is the one and only...who can walk on water!"

> **Who shakes the earth** under heaven from its foundations, and its pillars totter. Who commands the sun, and it rises not; and he seals up the stars. **Who alone** has stretched out the heavens, and **walks on the sea as on firm ground**? (Brenton Septuagint Translation, Job 9:6–8; emphasis added)

Now look at the words of Psalm 77 and Psalm 107. Notice how they read very similarly to the experience of the disciples, when Jesus calmed the wind and the waves on Lake Galilee.

- **The waters saw you**, O God, the waters saw you and writhed; the very depths were convulsed. The clouds poured down water, the skies resounded with thunder; your arrows flashed back and forth. **Your thunder was heard in the whirlwind**, your lightning lit up the world; the earth trembled and quaked. **Your path led through the sea, your way through the mighty waters, though your footprints were not seen**. (Psalm 77:16–19, emphasis added)
- **They saw the works of the Lord, his wonderful deeds in the deep**. For he **spoke and stirred up a tempest that lifted high the waves**. They mounted up to the heavens and went down to the depths;

in their peril their courage melted away. They **reeled and staggered like drunkards;** they were at their wits' end. Then they **cried out to the Lord in their trouble,** and he brought them out of their distress. **He stilled the storm to a whisper; the waves of the sea were hushed. They were glad when it grew calm,** and he guided them to their desired haven. (Psalm 107:24–30, emphasis added)

But, there's yet another passage to examine, one that, in my opinion, is the most majestic of all. It comes out of a three thousand-year-old portion of Scripture found in the book of Proverbs.

Who has **gone up to heaven and come down?** Whose **hands have gathered up the wind?** Who has **wrapped up the waters** in a cloak? Who has **established all the ends of the earth? What is his name,** and what is the **name of his son?** Surely you know! (Proverbs 30:4, emphasis added)

Once again, we find ourselves looking at something seemingly unbelievable. Yet, it's right there, straight out of the Word of God and directly corresponding to the ancient Hebrew letter meanings of the word *Ha-Shem*—the Name.

"Behold, El Shaddai on the water!"

This is why Jesus admonished His disciples during those stormy occasions on the Sea of Galilee with these words: "**You of little faith, why are you so afraid?**" and "Take courage! It is I!"

In other words, Jesus was saying, "Do you not yet understand who I am? Do you not recognize what I can do? Who else do you know that can command the winds and the waves, and they obey Him, or take up the very elements themselves in His hands? Who else do you know that is able, with only a word, to multiply loaves of bread and fish to feed the gathering throngs, and have baskets left over? I'll tell you who! It is only El Shaddai, God Almighty, Yahweh Himself who can do such things! Now you know who I am. I am God in the flesh, God with you!"

Perhaps now we can more fully appreciate how, on the night in the Upper Room when Philip asked Jesus for a supernatural manifestation, Yeshua's answer was not such a strange or harsh one after all.

Philip said, "Lord, show us the Father and that will be enough for us." Jesus answered: "Don't you know me, Philip, even after I have been among you such a long time? Anyone who has seen me has seen the Father. How can you say, 'Show us the Father'? Don't you believe that I am in the Father, and that the Father is in me?" (John 14:8–10)

Next, let's take a closer look at that "name above all names"— the name of Yeshua.

49

THE MYSTERY OF YESHUA

Through the mouth of Yeshua, YHWH will speak to us.

Considering everything we've learned about the name of YHWH and the Hebrew ideographs attached to those letters, we can now unravel another splendid revelation. Let's have a look at each Hebrew letter used in the name "Yeshua." Reading from right to left, the letters are represented like this: יֵשׁוּעַ

Yud-shin-vav-ayin

We've already verified the meanings of all of these letters except one, so I'll simply list each one with the appropriate Hebrew meaning attached. Then we'll look in more detail at the letter we've not yet discussed—the *ayin*.

Yud—This represents the "hand" as well as a Jewish person. It is also in the name "YHWH."

Shin—This represents the name of God/*El Shaddai*. It is the letter emblazoned upon almost every Hebrew mezuzah on the planet.

Vav/waw—This represents a hook, peg, nail, spear, or spike and carries the connotation of fastening one thing to another. This letter is also in the name "YHWH."

Ayin—This is the sixteenth letter of the Hebrew alphabet. According to Chabad.org, it has two meanings: "eyes" and "salvation."[285]

On the same website we find the following fuller definition of the letter:

> Ayin **means eyes,** as it states: in [Isaiah 30:20] "And **your eyes shall see your Teacher** (i.e., G-d)." Another verse reads: "And the **glory of G-d shall be revealed and all flesh shall see together that the mouth of G-d speaks**" [Isaiah 40:5, 52:10]. Furthermore, ayin also **stands for salvation.**[286] (Emphasis added)

That last sentence is especially revealing since we know what the word for "salvation" is in Hebrew. Adhering to the conventions of discovery we've been employing, we uncover yet another Hebrew letter that leads to several amazing revelations. The message of *ayin* alone, especially as it's found in the name *Yeshua,* could be understood as something like: "The whole world will see God Himself, and He will be our Teacher, and our Salvation (Jesus/*Yeshua*). Through the mouth of Jesus, YHWH will speak to us."

The Isaiah 52 Connection

In Isaiah 52:10—referenced by Chabad.org's description of the a*yin*—is another verse that sets up the crucifixion scene of Isaiah 53. Notice the emphasis placed on "sight" and "seeing" God's salvation. This too, as we've just discovered, is the exact idea of the a*yin.*

> The LORD **will lay bare** his holy arm **in the sight of all the nations,** and all the **ends of the earth will see the Jesus** [*Yeshua*-salvation] of our God. (Isaiah 52:10, emphasis added)

In the next illustration, have a look at the striking Hebrew word analysis for Isaiah 52:10.

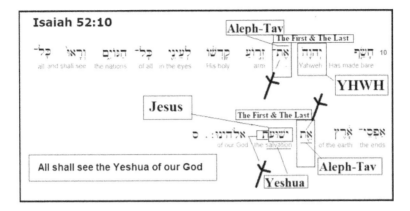

Several of the most prominent and striking word pictures of Genesis 1:1 are also represented in Isaiah 52:10, including the three crosses and the presence of *aleph-tav* twice. In addition, the names *Yahweh* and *Yeshua* are present in the same surface text.

Perhaps the truths declared by the letter *ayin* alone will also bring new light to the first few verses of the New Testament book of Hebrews:

> **In the past God spoke** to our ancestors through the prophets at many times and in various ways, but **in these last days [God] has spoken to us by his Son**, whom he appointed heir of all things, and **through whom also he made the universe. The Son is the radiance of God's glory and the exact representation of his being**, sustaining all things by his powerful word. (Hebrews 1:1–3, emphasis added)

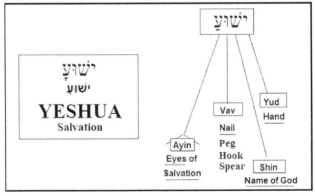

50

THREE CRUCIFIXIONS

For what I received I passed on to you as of first importance:
that Christ died for our sins according to the Scriptures.
~1 Corinthians 15:3 (Berean Study Bible)

There are many prophecies in the Old Testament concerning the First Coming of Jesus. They portray certain elements about His life, His ministry, His miracles, His sacrificial death, His resurrection, and His coming again, as well as the birth of the Church, the spreading of the gospel, and the Tribulation of the last days.

However, only *three passages* in the Old Testament prophetically speak of the clearly portrayed crucifixion of Yeshua, and in graphic terms (Psalm 22, Isaiah 53, and Zechariah 12). Each includes the word "pierce" to describe what happens to the Christ of God, nailed to the *tav-*"cross."[287] In those passages, we find additional seemingly coded revelations, each exalting Yeshua in the midst of the prophecies.

Isaiah

The prophet Isaiah, in a vision, was taken to the scene of the life, ministry, persecution, beating, crucifixion, burial with criminals, and resurrection of Jesus Christ (Isaiah 53). Isaiah wrote this prophecy seven hundred years before it came to pass.

Earlier we examined the monumentous findings in Isaiah 53: the crosses, the *aleph-tav*, the word "truth" that commences with *aleph-tav*, and even the ELS code *Yeshua Shemi*, "Jesus is my name."

But the two essential passages in Isaiah that *lead up to* Isaiah 53 actually set the stage for the crucifixion and the resurrection that the words of chapter 53 so vividly display. Most modern Christians know the passages as an integral part of the traditional Christmas account.

Isaiah 7:14: The Sign of the Virgin

> Therefore the Lord himself **will give you a sign**: The virgin will conceive and give birth to a son, and will call him Immanuel. (Emphasis added)[288]

The fulfillment of this prophecy opens the New Testament. It's on the first page of the first chapter of the first book—Matthew 1: 22–23.

> All this took place to fulfill what the Lord had said through the prophet: "The virgin will conceive and give birth to a son, and they will call him Immanuel" (which means "God with us").

See in the illustration below what we find in that portentous declaration of Isaiah that was given seven centuries prior to its fulfillment.

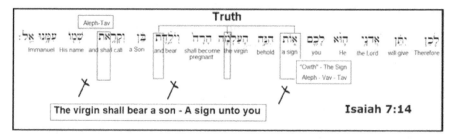

There's the pattern yet again: three crosses, the *aleph-tav*, the word "truth" (*emeth*), and even the Hebrew word "sign" (*owth*) from which the word "truth" emanates.

But there's still more. Something similar occurs in Isaiah 9:6–7, the well-known passage that illuminates the eventual fulfillment of Isaiah 7:14.

Isaiah 9: The Sign of the Savior

For to us a child is born, to us a son is given, and the government will be on his shoulders. And he will be called Wonderful Counselor, Mighty God, Everlasting Father, and Prince of Peace. Of the greatness of his government and peace there will be no end. He will reign on David's throne and over his kingdom, establishing and upholding it with justice and righteousness from that time on and forever. The zeal of the LORD Almighty will accomplish this. (Isaiah 9:6-7)

See below what we find in that verse: three crosses, the word "truth," and the *aleph-tav*, just like in Genesis 1:1.

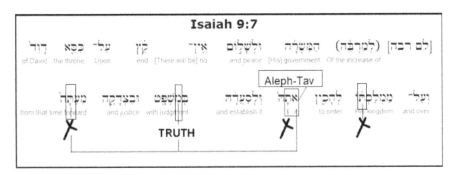

Don't forget, in the original Paleo-Hebrew text, those cross signs would have been visible to the earliest readers, yet their significance would be undisclosed for hundreds of years. Both Isaiah 7:14 and 9:7 follow a pattern of that in Genesis 1:1.

Now, let's see what we discover in the crucifixion passages of Zechariah.

51

THE PROPHET PRIEST

It's as if God wants to be certain we don't miss the identification
of who we are looking at when we see this One who is pierced.

Zechariah is one of more than thirty so-named men in the Old Testament. The name means "Yahweh has remembered."[289]

We don't know as much about Zechariah as we do about many of the other prophets, except that he was a priest as well as a prophet and was a contemporary of Zerubbabel[290] and the prophet Haggai. Zechariah's ministry was among those who had returned from the Babylonian exile as they were in the early stages of resettling the land. In spite of the limits of what Scripture says about him, we do know that this *prophet-priest* lays forth one of the most concise prophecies in Scripture concerning the crucifixion of Jesus.[291] He also told of a vision of the "piercing" of Yeshua, but with an added dimension of spectacular revelation. Here again is that mournful declaration of Yahweh Himself.

> They will look on me, **the one they have pierced**, and they will **mourn for him** as one mourns for **an only child**, and **grieve bitterly** for him **as one grieves for a firstborn son.** (Zechariah 12:10, emphasis added)

Here's what we find involving the most controversial declaration in that verse: "They will look upon me."

Yet again we see a Genesis 1:1 pattern: two Hebrew words on either side of the *aleph-tav* and a cross in the middle. It's as if God wants to be certain we don't miss the identification of the one who is pierced. *Simply astounding.* Yet there's more.

Zechariah 13 declares that "on that day"—the day Yahweh/Yeshua is on the cross being "pierced"—a "fountain will be opened." That fountain provides for the cleansing of sin.

> On that day a fountain will be opened to the house of David and the inhabitants of Jerusalem, to cleanse them from sin and impurity. (Zechariah 13:1)

Here's the graphic breakdown for that passage:

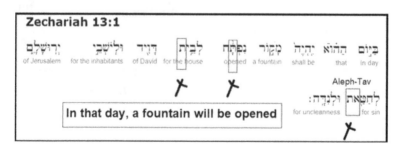

Even Zechariah 9, which foretells Yeshua's triumphal entry into Jerusalem on the back of a donkey, displays a noteworthy graphic—once again closely following the pattern of the other Yeshua passages and Genesis 1:1.

Of course, the prophecy of Zechariah 9:9 commences the Passion Week of Yeshua, when He's on His way to Golgotha's cross.

However, of the three crucifixion prophecies of the Old Testament, the next one we will look at is probably the most intimate of them all. It is the prophecy from which Jesus quoted as He hung on the cross, spikes in His hands and feet, suspended between earth's vile evil and Heaven's divine throne of redemption.

52

THE PSALMIST KING

They pierce my hands and my feet. All my bones are on display;
people stare and gloat over me. They divide my clothes
among them and cast lots for my garment.
~PSALM 22:16–18

King David is another prophet who was taken in a vision to the foot of the cross of Jesus. David obviously witnessed the piercing of Messiah's hands and feet because he described it in such vivid detail. He heard the words of mocking spoken on the day of the crucifixion, and he saw the soldiers gambling for Jesus' clothing, right under His feet.

Psalm 22 was written about a thousand years before the crucifixion. But what sets this psalm apart from every other Yeshua crucifixion passage is that it is the one Jesus quoted from the cross on that dreadful day. He began with the first verse, "My God, my God, why have you forsaken me?"

Shocking Discovery

Rabbi Zev Porat first showed me this next scriptural treasure. When we were looking at the passage together, he said, "Right there in the Hebrew word that means "from helping me" is the name of Jesus! It's *Yeshua*! It's spelled out perfectly!

Zev was correct. The first verse of Psalm 22, the words Yeshua quoted
while on the cross, has His name in it! This chapter in the Psalms directly
testifies of the grisly details of His crucifixion.

A little farther into Psalm 22, we find in verse 15 that God Himself
laid Yeshua in the "dust of death" on that cross. We find, yet again, *three
crosses*.

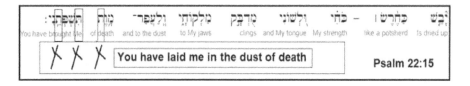

Then, in verses 16–17, where the prophecy speaks of piercing the
hands and feet of Yeshua and of the fact that He could "count all His
bones" while hanging on the cross, we find two more crosses, one for each
declaration of what's happening to Him there.

There we have it. The only three passages in the Old Testament that
speak of Yeshua's piercing on Calvary's cross are also the passages that
match up with the letter meanings directly associated with the names
Yahweh and *Yeshua*. Both names, already explored, speak of His pierced

hands, nails, a spear, and Heaven's *saving sacrifice* for humanity. They also speak of Golgotha and the crucifixion of *Yeshua Ha Mashiach*. And they dramatically reverberate the first passage of Genesis, "In the beginning…," which is also echoed by 1 Peter and Revelation.

- All inhabitants of the earth will worship the beast—all whose names have not been written in the Lamb's book of life, the Lamb who was slain from the creation of the world. (Revelation 13:8)
- He was chosen before the creation of the world, but was revealed in these last times for your sake. (1 Peter 1:20)

Shifting Gears

So far, we have primarily examined what the Word of God says either in the surface texts of the English language or of the Hebrew, and we've even inspected a couple of important ELS codes that seem to be supernaturally located in stunning locations within the biblical text. We've also unveiled and scrutinized Hebrew letter images located within significant Yeshua texts, especially noting the similarity between them and the same images found in Genesis 1:1. I think by now we can agree we've uncovered a number of rich treasures and amazing pieces of evidence along the way.

Next, we will take a brief plunge into several areas of the natural realm.

PART IX

CREATION

For since the creation of the world God's invisible qualities—his eternal power and divine nature—have been clearly seen, being understood from what has been made, so that people are without excuse.

~ROMANS 1:20

I WILL PUT MY NAME THERE

*But you shall seek the LORD at the place which the LORD your
God will choose from all your tribes, to establish His Name
there for His dwelling, and there you shall come.*
~DEUTERONOMY 12:5

In an earlier chapter, I mentioned Uri Mendel, the Israeli guide my wife
and I became friends with while on a tour of the Holy Land. Sometime
after that tour, Uri visited us in our home in Florida, where I showed
him the word "computer" in Daniel 12:4. The following event happened
while we were on that tour. This is what helped cement our friendship
and eventually brought Uri to see us a few years later.

The Confession

In early 1997, my wife, Pam, and I, as part of a large international tour
group, stood on the Mount of Olives gazing upon the Holy City of God.

We were at the spot of the Jerusalem overlook known in Israel as
Mitzpe Gandhi. Our tour guide held up a map of the Old City of Jerusalem for all to see, pointing out some of the locations we would visit within
the city walls.

At an appropriate moment in his presentation, I asked Uri if I could show him something amazing. We had already become very good friends, and he graciously obliged.

I took my index finger and slowly began to trace the three significant valleys that were an integral part of the Jerusalem landscape. One of them, the Kidron Valley, flanks the eastern side of the Old City. It was the valley through which Jesus and His disciples crossed, having traversed the Brook Kidron in order to get to the Garden of Gethsemane.

I continued moving my finger down the Kidron Valley until it came just south of the city, then eventually connected to the Hinnom Valley. That valley traverses the far western side of the city and was the ancient garbage dump area in Jesus' time. The connection of those two valleys form a rough "U" shape that surrounds the greater part of the Old City.

From there, I slowly moved my finger back down the Hinnom Valley until it reached the bottom of the "U." From that point, I took my finger and began to slowly move it up the Tyropoeon Valley. This valley travels almost due north, beginning at the bottom of the "U," with a slight crook to the left as it nears the top of its route. As a result of my finger movements, I had traced out an image that looked similar to the letter "W" in the English language.

As I began to trace the path of the Tyropoeon Valley, Uri's face broke into a broad grin. The revelation was coming to light in front of him.

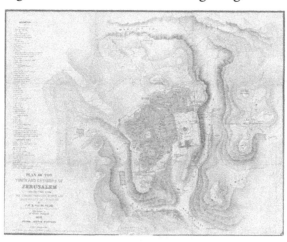

"What do you see?" I asked him.

"Oh my!" he exclaimed. "The valleys outline the shape of a *shin*. It is the Hebrew letter that stands for the name of God—*El Shaddai*. The *name of God* is on our city—just like it's on the mezuzahs on the doorposts of our homes and businesses! It's literally there *on* Jerusalem!"

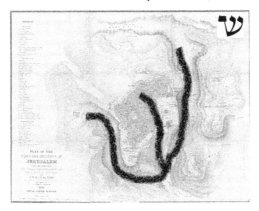

"Yes!" I said. "And it's always been there, at least from the very first days after Noah's Flood. Perhaps it's been there even from the days of the Garden of Eden itself."

"One thing is certain," I continued, "this city surely is the place where God has put His name—and in many different ways."

"I have never seen this before," Uri said. "I've seen it on the mezuzahs, of course, but not here. I can't believe what I'm seeing! From now on, I will show this to everyone!"

> But you will cross the Jordan and settle in the land the Lord your God is giving you as an inheritance…
>
> Then to **the place** the Lord your God will choose as a **dwelling for his Name**—there you are to bring everything I command you. (Deuteronomy 12:10–11, emphasis added)

I believe the presence of the letter *shin* carved out by the valleys and rocks of Jerusalem indicates the place where God literally put His name.

He carved it in the rocks.

54

OF HILLS AND VALLEYS

My name will remain in Jerusalem forever.
~2 CHRONICLES 33:4

The valleys of Jerusalem are not the only way we see God's name upon the city. The mountains themselves also tell a story pointing to His name.

Jerusalem, also called the "City of David," contains three prominent mountains:

- Mount Zion (The Western Hill—sometimes used symbolically in a wider sense for the city of Jerusalem itself, or even the entire land of Israel)
- Mount Moriah (Upper Eastern Hill—the location of the Temple Mount)
- Mount Ophel (Lower Eastern Hill—the old City of David; probably where the wilderness tabernacle was restored by David before Solomon built the Temple on Moriah)[292]

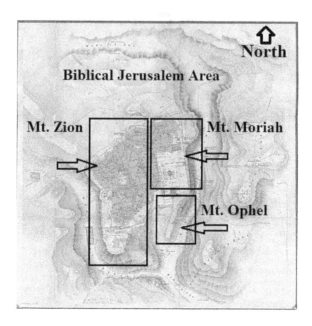

Ophel

The following passage from 2 Chronicles includes one of the five times Ophel is mentioned by name in the Scriptures.[293]

> Jotham rebuilt the Upper Gate of the temple of the Lord and did extensive work on the wall at the hill of Ophel. (2 Chronicles 27:3)

The Hebrew word *ophel* means "the hill of: stronghold, fortress, or the tower of strength."[294]

Throughout the Old Testament we find affirmation that Elohim Himself is known as our rock, our fortress, our high tower, and our place of strength. Therefore, the person of Yahweh, our Heavenly Father, is represented by the underlying concept of the word *ophel*.

Zion

The term "Zion" is found dozens of times in the Bible, from 2 Samuel to the book of Revelation. Its meaning is deeply spiritual and is used with several nuances of significance. For example, "Zion" can refer to anything from the specific hilltop found in Jerusalem to the city of Jerusalem or, in its fullest spiritual sense, to Heaven itself.[295]

The root verb of Zion (*sawa*) means "to command" or "to charge." The masculine form of the noun (*siyun*) means "signpost" or "monument," while the feminine form (*miswa*) means "commandment." When the feminine form is preceded by the article "the," Zion then means "the full code of the law."[296]

Moriah

As powerfully as this name's significance relates to the entire biblical message, it is found only twice in all of Scripture.

Moriah was where Abraham offered up his only son, Isaac, to the Lord.

> Then God said, "Take your son, your only son, Isaac, whom you love, and go **to the region of Moriah**. Sacrifice him there as a burnt offering on one of the mountains I will tell you about." (Genesis 22:2, emphasis added)

Moriah was also where Solomon was led by the Lord to build the Temple.

> Then Solomon began to build the temple of the Lord **in Jerusalem on Mount Moriah**, where the Lord had appeared to his father David. (2 Chronicles 3:1, emphasis added)

Not only is the word "Moriah" used as the proper noun for the location of a specific mountaintop, it also comes from the root of two Hebrew words that together mean "to be seen of Yahweh."[297]

The root verb of "Moriah" means "to see" or "to look at." It can also mean "to intently consider." Additionally, the many scriptural references to the Lord or an angel "appearing" upon the earth use this same verb. In this context, the verb form of "Moriah" is used in the sense of "becoming visible or understandable."[298]

In other words, "Moriah" often means "God sees" or "to see God."

The Mountains Declare

The implications of what we have learned thus far are astounding. As the tracing of the valleys that surround and bisect the city of Jerusalem literally declare the name of God, so do the mountaintops of the city.

Mt. Ophel can represent the biblical characterization of God the Father; God is our strong tower, our fortress, and our strength (Psalms 18:2; 46:7, 11).

Mt. Zion can easily characterize the Holy Spirit of God, who is the mark or the monument signifying that we belong to the Lord (Ephesians 1:13). And the Holy Spirit is the one Yahweh uses to write the commands of God's Law and Word upon our heart (Hebrews 8:10; 10:16; 2 Corinthians 3:3; Romans 2:15).

Mt. Moriah is obviously the very place where Abraham "saw God," and, at the same time, was "seen of God." Abraham proclaimed that, at this place, "God will provide himself a lamb." And "In the mount of the LORD it shall be seen" (Genesis 22:14, KJV).

Moriah is also where the Temple was finally erected by King Solomon. There, the people of God "met" with Him; they "saw Him" and He "saw them."

But, most importantly, it was very near Moriah, just outside the gates of Jerusalem, within sight of the Temple, and *on* the Mount of Olives where Jesus was crucified.[299] And it was on Golgotha's hill, through the eyes of Jesus, where we were "seen of God." It was also on that cross, in the person of Jesus Christ, that the world "saw God" (Zechariah 12:10).

Think of it! One mountain, comprising three different "hills" or "heads"—Ophel, Zion, and Moriah. One place—actually three places, *the three that are the one.* All three speak something significant about the name of God, and all three make up the city of Jerusalem.

Surely the ancient Hebrews would not have dreamed of giving even a veiled reference to what we know as the concept of the Trinity by using those names. That thought is not even a human possibility. Yet, apparently, the Holy Spirit put it upon the hearts of ancient humans to give the mountain heads, upon which the City of God was built, those significant names, the very names by which they are known to this day.

Though these amazing connections could not have been planned in the minds of mortal men, they obviously *were* planned at the throne of God.

Silence Them!

On the first day of the last week of Jesus' life, He rode into Jerusalem upon the back of a donkey's colt, fulfilling yet another prophecy concerning the coming of the True Messiah.[300]

Before that week was over, in the place where Elohim had put His name, Jesus would fulfill many more messianic prophecies. The people lined the streets by the thousands. They shouted words of praise and worship. They declared Jesus to be the King who was finally among them, the One who would come "in the name of the Lord"—a distinctly messianic identification. They waved palm branches and laid their cloaks on the road in the path of the donkey. In other words, they gave Him the reception of an arriving sovereign.

> As [Jesus] went along, people spread their cloaks on the road. When he came near the place where the road goes down the Mount of Olives, the whole crowd of disciples began joyfully to praise God in loud voices for all the miracles they had seen:
>
> "Blessed is the king who comes in the name of the Lord!" "Peace in heaven and glory in the highest!"

Some of the Pharisees in the crowd said to Jesus, "Teacher, rebuke your disciples!"

"I tell you," he replied, "If they keep quiet, the stones will cry out." (Luke 19:36–40)

In years past, I thought seriously about why Jesus used what seemed to be hyperbole in His response to the Pharisees. *How could the stones actually cry out?*

Now we know it wasn't hyperbole, because the stones had indeed been crying out for thousands upon thousands of years, carved in the valleys and mountains—and in the rocks that form them. Yahweh told His people, over a thousand years before Jesus arrived there on the back of a donkey: "This very place is where I have put my name."

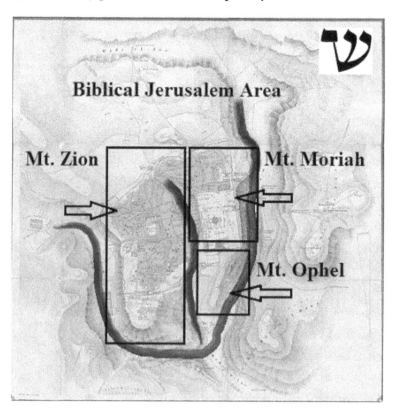

55

A MATTER OF THE HEART

And there His name will stand, until the Aleph-Tav/Yeshua returns.

There is yet another amazing place where the name of God is represented in the *shin*. It's in the human heart! It's "written" there… perfectly.

> You will seek me and find me when you **seek me with all your heart.** (Jeremiah 29:13, emphasis added)

> The Lord does not look at the things people look at. People look at the outward appearance, but **the Lord looks at the heart.**" (1 Samuel 16:7, emphasis added)

> I have **hidden your word in my heart** that I might not sin against you. (Psalm 119:11, emphasis added)

> "This is the covenant I will make with the people of Israel after that time," declares the LORD. "**I will put my law** in their minds and **write it on their hearts.** I will be their God, and they will be my people. (Jeremiah 31:33, emphasis added)

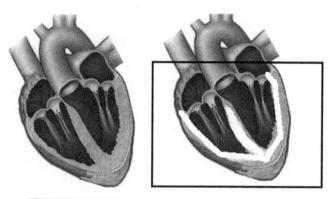

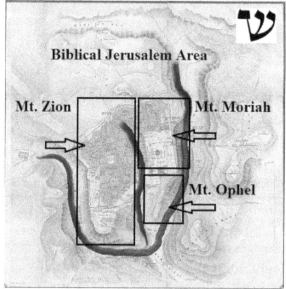

- And the peace of God, which transcends all understanding, will **guard your hearts** and your minds in Christ Jesus. (Philippians 4:7, emphasis added)
- Peace I leave with you; my peace I give you. I do not give to you as the world gives. **Do not let your hearts be troubled** and do not be afraid. (John 14:27, emphasis added)
- Above all else, **guard your heart**, for it is the wellspring of life. (Proverbs 4:23, emphasis added)
- The word is near you; it is in your mouth **and in your heart.** (Romans 10:8, emphasis added)

To this day, in that singular letter *shin*, His name is still there in the valleys of Jerusalem. The three-fold glory of His name is also represented in the mountains that are embraced by that *shin*.

And, of all places, it's also emblazoned upon our own hearts—and there His name will stand, until the Aleph-Tav/Yeshua returns.

56

THE BOOK OF LIFE

DNA produces both life and language, and it "speaks" and operates from a language of its own, and from within itself.

The Human Genome Project (HGP) launched in 1990 was a mammoth research effort that became an international undertaking and eventually spanned thirteen years of intensive study filled with ups and downs and costing more than $3 billion to complete. This astonishing pursuit of human triumph was marked by a White House celebration in June 2000. In that same year, the *New York Times* alone published 108 articles related to the HGP.[301]

The result of the effort was the structuring and recording of the precise order of the three billion letters in the human genome, amounting to $1 spent on the structuring of each of the letters! The publication of the first draft of the report was released in February 2001, and it was completed in April 2003.[302]

The National Human Genome Research Institute described the project like this:

The Human Genome Project (HGP) was one of the great feats of exploration in history. Rather than an outward exploration of the planet or the cosmos, the HGP was an inward voyage of discovery led by an international team of researchers looking to sequence and map all of the genes—together known as the genome—of members of our species, Homo sapiens.

Beginning on October 1, 1990 and completed in April 2003, the HGP gave us the ability, for the first time, to read **nature's complete genetic blueprint for building a human being.**[303] (Emphasis added)

Today, scientists sometimes refer to this biological ordering of the genetic code of human beings as "The Book of Life."[304]

 On June 26, 2000, Francis Collins, director of the National Human Genome Research Institute, announced the completion of the first draft in a major media event at the White House. In that announcement he stated, "'Today, we celebrate the revelation of the first draft of **the human book of life'** and declared that this breakthrough lets humans for the first time read 'our own instruction book'"[305] (emphasis added).

It's interesting that Collins would compare the DNA code to a "book." Books, without exception, have to be written by an intelligent designer in order to produce a meaningful and functioning arrangement of the words.

It's also interesting that he would compare DNA to an "instruction book." Imagine—a *book* that also gives and enables the carrying out of *instructions*. But, of course, in the secular worldview, that book supposedly occurred by a cosmic happenstance, and without intelligent input. *Not hardly*—not by following scientific method protocol. That assertion is statistically and scientifically impossible.

Perhaps the label of the "Book of Life" calls to mind Psalm 139:13–17, a piece of poetic Hebrew praise and worship that is now almost three thousand years old:

For you created my inmost being;
You knit me together in my mother's womb.

I praise you because **I am fearfully and wonderfully made;**
Your works are wonderful,
I know that full well.
My frame was not hidden from you
When I was made in the secret place,
When I was woven together in the depths of the earth.[306]
Your eyes saw my unformed body;
All the days ordained for me were written in your book
Before one of them came to be.
How precious to me are your thoughts, God!
How vast is the sum of them! (Emphasis added)

Complex Code

Also consider this. Your DNA is unique; it's different from anyone else's DNA in the world, and it is exclusive to anyone who came before you throughout history. Its distinctive code knows your past and plots out your potential future, including who you originated from as well as who you might create as your own gender-specific reproductive cells join those of another human being. The conceptualization of the human DNA code, besides the "Book of Life" moniker, is often compared to a computer language, even by biological scientists. The similarities between the two are indeed uncanny.[307]

However, our DNA code is far more complex than a binary code, which is based on 0 and 1, as is our current computer coding. Rather, our DNA information-exchange process is based on a quaternary nucleotide biological sequencing code that scientists have labeled "ATCG." These four nucleotide bases in our DNA code are adenine (A), cytosine (C), guanine (G), and thymine (T).

These DNA bases form specific pairs (A with T, and G with C) that, when arranged in certain combinations, determine every piece of information about who we are. That information is transmitted to all of the 37 trillion cells throughout our body, cells the information implanted within our DNA actually created. The same DNA info exchange process continues to transmit instructions to our cells for our entire life.

DNA coding produces both life and *language*. That process "speaks" and operates by employing a language all its own. All the while, the information necessary to make this happen appears to emerge solely from *within* itself. In this sense, DNA possesses a form of intelligence—an intelligence that obviously received its original input code from *outside* of itself. A huge number of acclaimed scientists acknowledge that this information had to be inserted *on purpose*.

Following are just a few experts from among more than a thousand on record stating that.[308]

Dr. Yvonne Boldt, PhD, microbiology, University of Minnesota:

> **When Darwinian proponents claim there is no controversy regarding the cohesiveness of the scientific evidence** for evolution as creator, they are merely **expressing a heartfelt desire…. There is a growing contingent of scientists who have found the evidence for Darwinian evolution wanting,** and who are ready and willing to debate Darwinists on scientific grounds.[309] (Emphasis added)

Dr. Marcos Eberlin, member of the Brazilian Academy of Sciences and founder of the Thomson Mass Spectrometry Laboratory:

> As a (bio)chemist **I became most skeptical** about Darwinism **when I was confronted with the extreme intricacy of the genetic code** and its many **most intelligent strategies to code,** decode and protect its information, such as the U x T and ribose x deoxyribose exchanges for the DNA/RNA pair and **the translation of its 4-base language to the 20AA language of life that absolutely relies on a diversity of exquisite molecular machines** made by the products of such translation forming a chicken-and-egg dilemma that evolution has no chance at all to answer.[310] (Emphasis added)

Dr. Stanley Salthe, Professor Emeritus, Brooklyn College of the City University of New York:

Darwinian evolutionary theory was my field of specialization in biology. Among other things, **I wrote a textbook on the subject thirty years ago.** Meanwhile, however **I have become an apostate from Darwinian Theory** and have described it as part of **modernism's origination myth.**[311] (Emphasis added)

An Illustration

Think of it like this. What if a meteorite splashed into the ocean and caused a gigantic tsunami to crash along the shore across miles of coastland beachfronts? What would you think if, after the tsunami had washed back out to sea, line upon line of beautiful prose—poems, lyrics, and narratives—were left behind along that stretch of beach? And, what if each of those lines contained perfect grammar and faultless sentence structure, and was filled with life-changing meaning and awe-inspiring communiques? What if the messages also included specific instructions for building intricate buildings and machines?

"Crazy," you say? "This could *never* happen, not even in a *googleplexian* years," you say?[312] Well, I agree! Any other sane person would agree as well. It just cannot happen.

However, the latest biological science has shown us the code in our DNA is far more complex than the hypothetical, impossible, accidental beach-writing scenario because, as beautiful as that beach code might appear, it cannot think, reproduce, dream, create, express emotion, feel pain or pleasure, or "plan" to do anything else. It has no "life" within. It just lies there, displaying a beautifully complex and meaningful message, but only until another wave washes it all away.

Yet, we are told to "trust the science" and believe an organically written and continually active writing and rewriting of that biological code of three billion letters combined itself perfectly for the purpose of making you, *uniquely you.* And it supposedly happened by a mere cosmic happenstance. The entire process of what makes you the living being that you are was allegedly brought about with no intelligent input and no preconceived ultimate purpose *at all.* Three words describe this staggering proposition: *Not a chance.*

So now the question ultimately becomes: If DNA truly is the coded language we've discovered it to be, and one that literally makes things come to life...*then who is the speaker?* And what sort of speaker can merely utter a coded biological language—with that very utterance having the capability of instantaneously producing living beings?

Where's the Signature?

Scientifically speaking, we can assert that all of life truly is a biological *code*—a living, communicating, intelligent code. One would think that, if Yahweh actually is the Creator of such an amazingly intricate and securely encrypted cypher, a process responsible for every living thing known to humanity, then surely He might also have left His "signature" upon it *somewhere.* Maybe just a bread crumb or two? Why wouldn't He? As we've demonstrated many times, He certainly seems to delight in such revelations!

Next, you'll meet the acclaimed Hebrew chemist and professor who believes he has actually found that evidence.

57

THE DIVINE WATERMARK

Then I asked the million-dollar question, listen carefully,
I asked the software, "When does the bridge appear?"
~Dr. Israel Rubenstein

D r. Israel Rubinstein, professor of chemistry with the Department of Materials and Interfaces at the Weizmann Institute of Science in Rehovot, Israel, holds a PhD in chemistry from Tel Aviv University.[313] In a video presentation, Dr. Rubinstein unveiled a stunning piece of information he claims to have discovered in 1986, when, if you remember, there was no Internet, no worldwide video-posting platforms, and no other practical means for globally distributing his findings, especially to the general populace. So, for the longest time, most of the world was unaware of his research.

But now, Dr. Rubinstein's presentation has been made available to the entire planet—hearkening back to the fulfillment of the prophecy we studied in Daniel 12:4. Following is the transcript from that presentation, which premiered on a YouTube channel on June 23, 2021, but with an unknown origin date.[314] Dr. Rubinstein is speaking to a live but mostly unseen audience (presumably his students) while he is seated behind his desk.

Okay, listen carefully. In the year 1986, when most of you hadn't been born yet, I was already a doctor and a scientist in the Weizmann Institute of Science. I researched the DNA mainly of mice, monkeys, and Humans…18,000 tissues of liver, kidneys, muscles and even a human eye, I inspected them under a microscope. For your information, the optic microscope can magnify up to 10,000 times.

The digital microscope, on the other hand, can enlarge up to 1 million times! You really enter inside the cell. A digital microscope is not the regular one you are familiar with. It's basically a huge computer, and you are looking through a screen and communicating with the software. Is that clear to everyone? This is science, not religion!

So I communicated with this software, and I asked the software, "What is the force that holds the DNA attached?" The software responded that sometimes there is a sulphuric bridge [disulfide bonds], which makes sure the DNA stays attached.[315]

Then I asked the million-dollar question. Listen carefully, I asked the software, "When does the bridge appear?" The software answer was that there are four nucleic acids which are the basis of the DNA chain: A, T, C & G. These are the acids which make up the DNA chain; that's a scientific fact! And the sulphuric bridge appears in the following manner: every 10 acids there was a bridge, every 5 acids a bridge, every 6 acids a bridge… and again every 5 acids were a bridge. [Number sequence: 10-5-6-5]

I was shocked! A sulphuric bridge that keeps the DNA attached? I was amazed!

Who can tell me the meaning of 10-5-6-5? [Dr. Rubinstein is looking at the students in his class for an answer; unintelligible responses are heard from the unseen audience.]

This is the numerical digit of Y-H-W-H! Our Heavenly Father is in our DNA!

Like a Rembrandt with a signature at the bottom of His artwork, God tells us, "I made you"!

Our Heavenly Father signed His name in every cell of our body!

I think I discovered God![316] (Emphasis added)

Of course, I don't claim to be an expert in biological science, DNA structuring, or disulfide bridges within the DNA bonding processes. But Dr. Rubinstein *is* an expert in all of this, and more. His résumé lists his "areas of activities" as: "Supramolecular chemistry; self-assembly; nano-structured metal films; localized Plasmon; optical sensors; electrochemistry; thin films; nanoparticles; template synthesis." His bio also states he has received eleven prestigious academic awards since 1971. In addition, he has written scores of articles published by scholarly journals in a multitude of scientific fields.[317]

Therefore, since I've also scoured the Internet for months without finding a single scientifically verified refutation of his claim, I have to trust that he has spoken accurately in the video.

With that in mind, let me remind you of an important scriptural declaration written two thousand years ago:

All things were created through Him and for Him. He is before all things, and in Him all things hold together. (Colossians 1:16–17)

Also, consider the following: More than likely, only a Hebrew, one familiar with the Hebrew letter numbering system, could have readily recognized this coded signature upon our DNA. Dr. Rubenstein, of course, is a Jew who *did* see it. God revealed the truth to him at such a time in history and in such a manner that it would be given to *us* by way of a global communication and information system that is now archived and watched by the world—24/7. And, Dr. Rubenstein discovered it by using a *computer*. Imagine that.

The Magnitude of the Matter

The numerical code Dr. Rubenstein is talking about comes from the Hebrew alphabet. As stated in an earlier chapter, employing a numbering system for each letter is a characteristic of the Hebrew alphabet. (It is also true of several other alphabets, and has been so for thousands of years.) This is not a process of mere divination or numerology; *it is historical fact.*

1	2	3	4	5	6	7	8	9	10	11	12	13	14	15	16	17	18	19	20	21	22
א	ב	ג	ד	ה	ו	ז	ח	ט	י	כ	ל	מ	נ	ס	ע	פ	צ	ק	ר	ש	ת
1	2	3	4	5	6	7	8	9	10	20	30	40	50	60	70	80	90	100	200	300	400

The numeric code for the name YHWH is easily verified. We've seen these letters many times before—*yud, heh, vav, heh*—the name of God, the Tetragrammaton. The numbers correspond exactly with each of those letters in the Hebrew alphabet. The sequence is 10 (*yud*), 5 (*heh*), 6 (*vav/waw*), and 5 (*heh*)—10-5-6-5, YHWH, just as Dr. Rubenstein said.

I ask yet again: What are the chances? I would imagine they are practically zero, wouldn't you?

God's Trademark

Think of what we have here. We are talking about the *name of Yahweh*—the divine name that has been in use among the Hebrew people for thousands of years, the name found more than seven thousand times in the Old Testament. It is a name with a deeply profound *meaning,* as we discovered just a few chapters earlier, connecting directly with the crucifixion of Yeshua.

Now we discover from a PhD chemistry professor in Israel that the ancient and widely known numeric code of the name "YHWH" just happens to also be the numeric code with which our DNA molecule connects a disulfide bridge to the nucleotides. That disulfide bridge just happens to hold together the DNA structure of our body's cells.[318]

Dr. Rubenstein, of course, didn't necessarily "discover" God, but it certainly appears he may have discovered our Creator's signature. That signature exists in every cell of our body—all thirty-seven trillion of them!

That coded signature of YHWH is like a watermark, God's watermark, stamped all over our body. In this way, YHWH has ensured that, in the last-days generation, when this discovery was made public—*by computer* (Daniel 12:4)—no one could take credit for the creation of *us* except Him! Not Satan, not the silly evolutionists, not the arrogant scientists who continually try to manipulate and alter the building blocks of life. No one can lay claim to the original development of DNA except for YHWH, our Creator.

He is:

The Beginning and the End.

The First and the Last.

The *Aleph* and the *Tav*.

The Word that became flesh.

Our God…who is our Yeshua!

Part X

THE REVEALING

Jesus did many other things as well. If every one of them were written down, I suppose that even the whole world would not have room for the books that would be written.

~JOHN 21:25

Among the mature, however, we speak a message of wisdom—but not the wisdom of this age or of the rulers of this age, who are coming to nothing. No, we speak of the mysterious and hidden wisdom of God, which He destined for our glory before time began. None of the rulers of this age understood it. For if they had, they would not have crucified the Lord of glory.

~1 CORINTHIANS 2:6–8

58

THE DOUBTER

Even the religious and government officials spoke of the
matter as though it were the evidence-laden truth.

Almost a week had passed and Thomas was still in hiding.

He had long been firmly convinced that mostly bad things happen on cloudy days. Today was a cloudy day in Jerusalem. The last several had been as well. Accordingly, thus far, nothing had gone as he thought it would. Now, he had more questions running through his mind than ever before.

Did Yeshua lie to us? Had the Teacher been mistaken about what the Father would do for Him? Would He really come back from the dead? Really? Thomas always had reservations about those claims. They seemed impossible promises to fulfill. *Had Yeshua simply meant His words metaphorically? Who knows? Most likely; how could they have been anything else?*

He isn't here now. That's all Thomas knew. Yeshua had been crucified. Buried. And now His body was missing, and after several days, it was still nowhere to be found.

Yeshua was almost always speaking in riddles and elaborate stories. The people loved His tales, but sometimes those parables and their mysteriously symbolic words were hard to decipher. Why couldn't He just say what they meant? *We were, after all, His most trusted—the Twelve. Why couldn't He speak to us in plain language and explain His exact plans? Why did He have to talk of a crucifixion, a resurrection, building mansions in Heaven, and coming back to take us to be with Him? Why couldn't we have just gone to wherever He was going—right then?*

Have I and the other disciples been duped? It is surely beginning to shape up that way. *Had the entire thing merely been the ruse of a sincere, but disturbed man? That prospect is seeming more likely with each passing day. But...how could He have worked those miracles? Ah...those miracles. That is a tough thing to deny. I have seen them with my own eyes...*

But miracles are one thing, continual promises of a *resurrection*, especially after a brutal and preplanned death...well, that is something else altogether!

Perhaps I and the other disciples have been blinded by false hopes of a messianic overthrow of the Roman shackles of oppression. How wonderful that would have been! Yet, Yeshua had never really made that specific claim. Not in those words...had He? Thomas couldn't remember, but he was pretty sure He hadn't.

He simply couldn't think straight right now, and he knew it. His memory was still playing tricks on him. His head hadn't stopped spinning since the news came from the women that Yeshua's body was missing. He had always been a fidgety person, even since childhood. Now he was especially restless as he paced back and forth like a nervous cat, deep in thought.

And another thing, he pondered. *Had Judas hung himself for no reason? What about that?*

Obviously, unknown to the rest of us at the time, even Judas had begun to doubt Yeshua's grandiose claims. After all, Judas was the most trusted one among us, wasn't he? He was in charge of the money bag! He was the sole distributor of our funds. He kept us fed and clothed.

How could the rest of us have known Judas was conspiring with the religious authorities against Yeshua? Did Judas know something the rest of us didn't? Maybe he truly was the smart one among us. He was the logical one, without argument. He certainly was the math intellect among us. Maybe he had it all figured out long before the rest of us.

And, what about all those promises…a coming Kingdom? Ruling and reigning…with us Twelve by His side. The restoration of all things. Making everything new. Judgment against the ungodly and wicked. Had all those promises been mere delusions as well? Come to think of it, how could he and the rest of us even entertain the idea that Yeshua could somehow overthrow the entire Roman governmental system and take away its throne of power? Not an army on the planet had been able to do so. How could we have been so naïve to think Yeshua and a gang of fisherman could do it?

It was true enough, Yeshua's body was indeed missing from the tomb. But the Roman guards had already made their official report, which was spreading like wildfire throughout the city. The news criers had run with it. *Surely they wouldn't lie about such an important official matter. However, they actually claimed that we—Yeshua's disciples—had come during the night and secreted His body away. What an out and out lie!*

I was with them, Thomas reminisced, *all night long. I was one of them! We didn't go on a body-snatching raid—none of us! And even if we did, how could we overtake the armed Roman soldiers guarding the tomb under the seal of Rome? Has anyone even bothered to address that detail? The so-called news is phony; it is a lie!*

But many of the people were more than ready to believe the lie—and they were even more eager to spread the fabricated report throughout Jerusalem and wherever else it could be told. Even the religious and government officials spoke of the accusation as though it were the evidence-laden truth. What a crazy, evil world.

Thomas then remembered their last Passover meal together less than a week ago. It was the night that turned out to be just before the day of His crucifixion. *How could we have known that would be our last time alone with Him—our very last meal with Him?*

Yeshua had just finished washing their feet before the evening meal, then He had warned of a coming betrayal from within their own ranks.

A little while later, He had matter-of-factly dismissed Judas from the room. Judas had quietly complied, as though his exit was simply a routine errand. *We all thought Judas was sent out to buy some more supplies for the evening festivities,* Thomas recalled.[319]

Then, of all things, Yeshua told Peter, "I tell you the truth, before the rooster crows in the morning, you will have disowned me three times." *Was Peter to be the traitor?* They had wondered but dared not believe.

Well, one thing's for certain, Thomas thought, *Yeshua sure got that one right. Peter* did *deny Him—three different times. But, that would have been a fairly easy prediction for almost any of us to make. Peter is always shooting off his mouth, speaking whatever pops into his mind. Everybody knows that! Always looking out for himself…at least that's what some of us think about him. Bless him, Lord."*

But, come to think of it, on that night, I, myself, also questioned Yeshua… publicly. Yeshua had proclaimed, "I am going away. But I will come back and take you to where I'm going, and you know the way to where I am going."[320] *That's when I had challenged, "Lord, we don't know where you are going, so how can we know the way?"*

Yeshua's response had been, "Thomas, I am the way and the truth and the life. No one comes to the Father except through me. Surely you know this by now."

But I wasn't the only one confused by that evening's pronouncements. Even Philip had chimed in, wanting more proof of what Yeshua was claiming: "Lord, show us the Father, and that will be enough for us. Then we'll know. Then we'll be certain of all you're telling us!"

Yeshua had answered Philip, "Have I been with you for so long, and you still don't know who I am? If you've seen me, you've seen the Father."

It had all sounded good—even emotionally satisfying—at least for the rest of that night. But now He is gone. Dead. The body is missing…and I am one of the ones being blamed for its disappearance!

Thomas had heard the reports of Yeshua's supposed appearance to a group of disciples almost a week ago, while they were gathered in secret lodging in the heart of the city. But he doubted if any of those reports were true. *How could they have seen Him? What are they up to, making such a wild claim?*

He mumbled aloud to nobody but himself, *"Hmph!* I won't believe any of it unless I see where the nails were driven into His hands and the scar from where His side was pierced with the thrust of that soldier's spear!"

But here I am now, he thought. *I'm hiding in Jerusalem. Slinking around in the shadows, my hood pulled over my head, hoping no one recognizes me. I can't keep this up forever.*

The crowds that had swelled the city during the feasts were beginning to dramatically diminish. Staying hidden away would soon become much more difficult.

Thomas was hungry. He hadn't eaten much for days. He gathered up his meager belongings, tossing everything he owned into a small travel bag. During those three years with Yeshua, he had learned how to be ready to travel at a moment's notice.

He headed to the market, hood pulled low.

59

THE DEMAND

I'll need to see the scars in His hands and put my fingers in them.

Thomas couldn't believe he had run into some of the other disciples so quickly. But there stood Nathanael and Philip right before him. They had also come to the market; they had baskets of fruit, vegetables, and bread to show for it. His mouth watered just looking at the food.

"Thomas!" Nathanael greeted him discreetly. He recognized Thomas' one and only cloak and the unique way he held himself as he walked. They were still being careful not to draw attention in public, but spotting Thomas wasn't a problem for those who knew him intimately. "It's good to see you again, my brother!"

Philip grabbed Thomas, embraced him, slapped him on the back, and quietly whispered in his ear, furtively looking around as he spoke. "Thomas, you really must come back with us. *We have seen Yeshua!* Peter saw Him as well. Then He came to all of us, last Sunday evening. We've spoken with Him. We've seen and touched the scars in His hands, His side. It's true!"

Thomas' eyes widened. He shook his head ever so slightly, indicating his thoughtful consideration of everything Philip was telling him.

Philip continued, "Cleopas and James have seen Him too, even before us—and then once more on that same night—while they were with us!

Those two are *still* with us, Thomas. They came to us in the night, all the way from Emmaus! They had been with Him for hours and had eaten with Him. *Please, Thomas!* Will you come, too?"

Thomas didn't give an indication one way or the other.

Nathanael cut in, his voice quivering, "Do you think we are lying? Do you think we are delusional, Thomas? We're not!"

"Philip, Nathanael," Thomas said, "slow down just a moment. Look. I love you both deeply. But I'm not so sure about all these resurrected Messiah 'sightings'. First, Mary Magdalene. Then you tell me about Cleopas and James...then Peter. And now, Yeshua meets with all of you—*in secret*? It doesn't make sense. Why does He not just show Himself to the world, if it's really Him? And why has He not appeared to me? Why has He not appeared to the ones who crucified Him? I know that's the first place I'd go!"

"My dear brother," Philip said. "So many questions. So many doubts."

He pulled Thomas close again and whispered, "Please come to where we're meeting. It's the same place you already know about. Soon, He'll answer all your questions Himself. We wouldn't lie to you about this. We're not delusional. We have seen Him, talked to Him, eaten with Him! What do you say? Come back with us now. We've got food and drink. We can sort things out together. We've been praying for you, my brother. We miss you! In fact, Thomas, Yeshua even asked us about you. He asked us to bring you to Him. It was the last thing He said before he vanished from our presence." Thomas was moved. That last announcement was something he needed to hear. His swelling eyes betrayed his attempt to hide the fact.

"I'll come then," he said as he swallowed hard, holding back his emotions.

After he had composed himself, Thomas still had to lay down the rules. Always so exacting. Always the organized one.

"Thank you so much for your concern, especially your prayers, and even the kindness you've shown me in this moment," he said. "But you must understand...I simply won't believe it's Him until I can look into

His eyes, see His face in full. And, most importantly, I'll need to see the scars in His hands and put my fingers on them. And the scar in His side. I'll have to examine the wounds for myself. I'll not be going into this blindly. I'll want some real proof, some real answers. Something tangible. No more parables and strange stories. And another thing—"

"—listen to me, Thomas!" Nathanael interjected. "I understand. I support you fully. But we mustn't discuss the matter any further here. Not in the market, my friend; there are simply too many prying eyes and listening ears. Forgive my mistrust, but I think we are already being scrutinized." He smiled at Thomas, then looked over his shoulder at someone behind them in the crowd. "You know what I mean, brother?"

"Let's go then," Thomas agreed. "Apparently your prayers have been answered. *Here I am*. So, let's go!" Thomas chuckled as he said the words. It felt good to laugh again. It had been a while since he'd been able to do so. The three friends and brothers, fellow disciples of Yeshua, eased out of the marketplace and set out for the downtown hideaway. Nathanael couldn't help but notice Thomas eyeing the food. With a huge grin, he handed their doubting friend a piece of fruit and a chunk of fresh bread. Thomas devoured it as they departed the market. He continued to ponder all that his friends had been telling him. But, he couldn't have come close to imagining what he was soon to experience.

60

THE PROOF

It wasn't the most pleasant way to live.
But at least they were together.

t was Sunday evening again. It had been exactly one week since the disciples claimed Yeshua had visited them in this very place, and it had been at just about this same time of day.

As they were finishing up the evening meal, they agreed to engage in a time of worship. They would sing from the Psalms, then go back through some of the Scriptures Yeshua had illuminated while with them last week. Cleopas and James were still unfolding the mysteries Yeshua had shown them that day on the road to Emmaus. So, they also wanted to give the two men time to share even more of those incredible disclosures.

At least that's what they had planned to do. But something much better was about to happen…again.

Matthew had just gone across the room to make certain the door was secure, the locking shaft resting tightly in its iron cradle. He pulled back the corner of the heavy woven curtain and peeked outside the window near the door. Earlier, a ruckus in the streets below had unnerved the disciples a bit. But not now. Nothing unusual was going on, just the regular sounds of life.

This is how they'd been existing for a week now. On edge…continually. It wasn't the most pleasant way to live, but at least they were together. They planned on living like this until the furor of the missing body died down. That could be days…maybe weeks. It didn't matter. They would do what they had to do.

The disciples—both men and women—were sitting on cushions on the floor facing Matthew, who was still standing before them at the front of their living quarters. Peter and John were punching each other in the arm, acting like a couple of kids, enjoying the moment as memories of better days flooded their minds. The others were bawling with laughter at the antics of the two biggest "children" among them.

It was finally time to get the evening of worship underway. Matthew peeked out the window again, ever the careful one. He had just turned back to report that the streets below appeared normal, ready to lead as cantor in the opening song. But, instead of speaking, Matthew froze.

He stood, slack-jawed, eyes focused in the direction of the wall on the other side of the room. The rest of those gathered were oblivious to Yeshua's presence as He stood against that wall behind them. Yeshua, looking straight at Matthew and grinning from ear to ear, quickly raised His finger to His closed lips and motioned for Matthew to be silent.

Matthew, stoic by nature, was easily able to fool the others by not letting on who had joined the group. Matthew withdrew his gaze from Yeshua while the others adjusted themselves, nestling into their mats, ready to begin the service as Matthew prepared to lead the first song of worship.

That's when Yeshua spoke.

"Shalom! Baruch Hashem Adonai!"[321]

The place erupted into a circus of scurrying disciples who were thrilled, laughing, and chattering amid their uncontainable excitement. Leaping from their cushions, they surrounded Yeshua and smothered Him with massive bear hugs and emotional greetings.

Matthew howled with delight—something he rarely did. But this was different. This was a moment of pure celebration and joy watching his brothers react to the sudden presence of Yeshua.

Thomas, still seated and in shock, was now the one whose mouth was hanging open. He slowly rose to his feet amidst the growing disarray of spontaneous celebration. He stood gawking, skeptical, sizing up the situation. The sounds of celebration congealed into a mass of indiscernible human noise. It was like he was underwater, looking up through the surface at seemingly melted-looking faces and hearing the muffled sounds of life above.

He studied Yeshua's face and stance. He traced out in his mind every detail of what he remembered about Yeshua's features: His nose, mouth, eyes, forehead, general shape, and size. Everything was as he remembered it, except—He was not bruised or battered, nor did He have flesh hanging from His flogging and crucifixion-destroyed visage. He looked younger, fresher, more alive than ever! And, the spikes and spear... *Wait a minute! That's it! What about...?*

As soon as those thoughts rippled through Thomas' mind, Yeshua stopped. He held up His hand to restore order, then He turned and gazed into Thomas' face. *Those eyes!* Thomas had seen that look before. But, he still had to know. *What about the nails, the—*

"Thomas!" Yeshua called out to him. "Come here, my friend." Yeshua began rolling up His sleeves and loosening the sash around His outer garment. "You need to see the evidence, don't you?"

Thomas almost lost his composure, at least what was left of it. *How does Yeshua know what I was going to ask?*

"Thomas, put your finger here. Behold my hands! Reach out your hand and put it here to my side. Put your fingers and hand into the place of the wound. Stop doubting, Thomas, and *believe*, my friend. I have kept every promise I've ever made to you—and I'll never stop keeping them."

Thomas' hands trembled. He seemed unable to make them stop shaking as he touched the wounds. They were real. It was Him! The injuries were there—grotesque-looking, still healing, but genuine.

His legs buckled. He fell to the floor, then quickly rose, but only to his knees. "My Adonai and my Elohim!" Thomas wept at Yeshua's feet. Yeshua knelt beside him and cradled His arms around him, pulling Thomas closer. Thomas was heaving great sobs. He was embarrassed at his sudden burst of emotion, but he simply couldn't help it. He was consumed by the *Presence*. The personification of *Love* before him. Yeshua lovingly stroked the hair on Thomas' head, calming him.

Yeshua pulled Thomas even closer and whispered in the sobbing man's ear. "Blessed are those Thomas, who have not seen, nor will they ever see what you've just beheld...yet, they will still believe."

Thomas, still sobbing, lifted his head and looked into Yeshua's eyes. "Thank you, Adonai. *Thank you!*" Yeshua nodded His approval.

Thomas fell back into the arms of His Creator, his Friend.

61

THE DISCLOSURE

*Beginning with Moses and all the Prophets, He explained to
them what was said in all the Scriptures concerning Himself.*
~LUKE 24:53

After a time, those gathered had arranged themselves on the floor
around Yeshua. He was going to teach them again. The atmosphere
was heavy with anticipation. They didn't know it then, but what they were
about to hear would change them, and the world…forever.[322]

Yeshua took a deep breath and began. "My brothers and sisters,
my friends, what I will tell you tonight, I want you to remember, and
remember it well. These are eternally important matters." He looked
around the room. They shook their heads to acknowledge the gravity of
His Words.

"And," He continued, "I want you to share all of this with the world
of your day, for the rest of your lives. Preach it, teach it, and write it. The
Holy Spirit will anoint you. He'll give you the words to say. Your words
will eventually be preached to the generations of every age, from this day
forth, until the end. But it is given for you *first*, beginning tonight." Yeshua
rearranged Himself on the mat and continued.

"Matthew, John, and Peter—when the time is right, and you'll know
when it is to be done, I want you to write all these things down, as well as

the things you've already seen. The *called-out ones* will need this record in the days to come, especially in the future ages."

The disciples sat enthralled. His revelations of the deepest mysteries of God's Word, hidden through the ages, now being divulged to them were magnificent, and humbling.

An hour had passed, yet it seemed like half that time. Yeshua reached out to take the cup of water on the floor beside Him and lifted it to His mouth. He closed His eyes as He savored the cool liquid. How well He remembered this pleasure, one that just a short time ago, while He had been on the cross, had been cruelly withheld from Him. The torture of that seemingly small denial had been indescribable.

The disciples had not stirred, awaiting His next words.

He resumed His teaching. "Certainly, you remember the night when I spoke to the wind and the waves, and they obeyed." The disciples shook their heads "yes."

"Likewise, you remember the time when I came to you walking on the water!" Again, they agreed to the vivid memory. How could they ever forget such things? They would speak of them for the rest of their lives!

"Those were done so that you would know. *Only God* can walk upon the waves of the sea. Search that truth where Job declares '*He alone* stretches out the heavens and treads on the waves of the sea.'[323]

"*Only God* can speak and calm the wind and the waves! Consult the psalmist, who wrote, 'He stilled the storm to a whisper; the waves of the sea were hushed.' Now you can speak this truth, preach it, and teach it without shame or hesitation. It was veiled, throughout history, before you were even born!

"Now, consider my name—*Yeshua*. You'll remember, it was given from Heaven's throne through the angel Gabriel. It was given to Mary, and to Joseph as well. This is the name by which they were to call me. *Why?*

"Search it out for yourself. Find every instance of my name in the Word of God, the Law of Moses, the prophets, and the Psalms. Pay close attention to how it is paired with the name of Yahweh, and with Heaven's plan of redemption.

"Observe how it is intricately connected with the throne of God and the eternal promises given to God's people. See how *Yeshua* is linked to the Kingdom reign that is to come. From now on, read the Scriptures in that way—once again, you'll see it was veiled, yet written for all to see throughout all the ages. There it was, and you are now living it.

"But there's still more. Go back and look at Isaiah's prophecies about me. Born of a virgin. Pierced, beaten beyond recognition, silent before my accusers, mocked, reviled, despised, and rejected. Yet, it was long foretold that, 'After he has suffered, he will see the light of life and be satisfied.' The suffering, the humiliation, the rejection, the crucifixion, even the resurrection...they were there all along! *All of them*, and more![324]

"Behold, and remember, David's vision of me on the cross. The psalm of David begins, 'My God, my God, why have you forsaken me?' and goes on to say, 'They have pierced my hands and feet.'[325]

"You witnessed with your own eyes the fulfillment of that day. My revilers were screaming out the same mocking words found in that prophecy. You heard them with your own ears, 'He trusts in the Lord...let the Lord rescue him. Let the Lord deliver him, since he delights in him.'[326]

"They weren't even aware of what they were doing or saying! My bones were out of joint, my clothing was being gambled over, right beneath me! And David saw it all. I arranged for him to experience it himself a thousand years before it would come to pass! Yet, *you* were actually there!

"Furthermore, I spoke that first verse of David's vision of Golgotha to call attention to what was coming to life right before everyone there that day, for everyone who had eyes to see. Now...go back and look at it again. Buried within the words and letters of the first words of that passage is my name—*Yeshua*. It's right there. It always has been.

"Go back through the prophecy again...ponder every word. Look at the images there—the actual letters join together to deliver their message. As I've always told you, 'Not one stroke, not one dot, not one letter from my Word will pass away'! You will be shocked by what you will find there. Show it to others. Teach it to the church that is soon to be born. Teach it now, and teach it until I return.

"In the very same way, consider the prophet Zechariah. Find the place in the scroll where the Lord says, 'I will pour out on the house of David and the inhabitants of Jerusalem a spirit of grace and supplication. They will look upon me, the one they have pierced, and they will mourn for him as one mourns for an only child, and grieve bitterly for him as one grieves for a firstborn son.'[327]

"And right after that, when the Lord declares, 'On that day a fountain will be opened to the house of David and the inhabitants of Jerusalem, to cleanse them from sin and impurity." Now you know. It was Me all along! That fountain is My sacrifice, My blood—the blood of the true Lamb of God.

"Of all the prophecies about Me in the scrolls of Moses, the Psalms, and the Prophets—precisely *three* mention *the piercing* of My hands and feet. *Three.* Now you have seen the fulfillment of the three…with your own eyes.

"Shall I go on?" Yeshua stopped talking to ask.

"Yes!" His listeners answered. "Please continue! Don't stop now, Lord! This is glorious!"

"I will tell you of many more mysteries of the ages yet to come, but still veiled in the Word of God. Additional prophecies will soon be given to the world, many more, and they will be given through you, after the Holy Spirit is given, just as I have promised!

"In years to come, one of you here today will be caught up to Paradise, right into the throne room of YHWH. You will be shown the distant future, and the coming of the Son of Man in all His splendor. You will see the details of the restitution of all things. You will see the days of Daniel's prophecy—when men will 'run to and fro over the face of the earth, and knowledge will explode over the entire planet'!

"And you will write it all down. Your writing will never fade or perish, all the way to the end.

"To the rest of you, I say this: Do not envy the man upon whom this responsibility will be bestowed. Because the deliverance of that prophecy will be accomplished through a great price that he must pay for his faithfulness, a great sacrifice wrought upon him through an evil world system. But he will be faithful to the end. His life will be spared. And he will live for many years later, as a witness to the believers, to tell what he is shown.

"The things he will be shown will eventually unfold before the eyes of future generations. Those people will be the ones chosen in their day, in the same way you have been chosen in your day. This is how My Kingdom work will move forward until the very end.

"Behold, I tell you the truth. To those who overcome, I will give the eternal life for which their soul has always longed."

Yeshua looked at His disciples with an expression of fatherly kindness. "I'm afraid I've given you more in one evening than you can bear, but I have much more to tell you. However, before I go to My Father, I will disclose even more mysteries to you in the weeks ahead. But tonight… you need to rest. It's been a long day."

He rose from His seat, pleasantly glancing at each one of them, and stood. As the disciples pondered these things and began to discuss them among themselves, there was a slight shiver in the atmosphere around them. It was like the soft flapping of a bedsheet in a gentle spring breeze. The men and women looked around the room, searching for the source of the sound. As they looked, they sensed just a few more shudders, then a flash of brilliant light, and Yeshua was gone.

But they would see Him again.

⚮

Yeshua would be among His children for a total of forty days after His resurrection. During that time, and on one occasion alone, He would appear to more than five hundred of his followers at once.[328]

He would also be atop the Mount of Olives, a large crowd of His disciples at His side, as He ascended into Heaven, again slipping into another dimension right before their eyes.

But before all of those things would happen, and sometime after the Upper Room experience, when Thomas was finally satisfied with the evidence he sought, Yeshua would meet with them again—on a beach, around a campfire.[329] And, once again, He would reveal astounding mysteries. Because that's what He loves to do when He is among His children.

And on that occasion, He would, again, eat His favorite meal with them.

Fish.

62

THE QUESTION

For presently we see through a glass in obscurity;
but then, face to face. Presently, I know in part;
but then I will know fully, even as I have been fully known.
~1 CORINTHIANS 13:12; BEREAN'S LITERAL BIBLE

Think about this mind-bending proposition. What if the world we're presently living in—the one in which we go about our daily lives, carry out business endeavors, and form and maintain relationships, is not the genuine one? What if this life is only a murky, fallen, dirty shadow of the truly ineffable *divine life*—the life meant for us from the beginning?

What if another kind of life does exist, just behind an indiscernible veil, a dimensional shift that's operating in a presently unseen and indescribable realm of physical reality? A physical existence where death is virtually impossible, where misery and disease are nonexistent. Where there is only *life*, as it was meant to be from the beginning. What if that were so?

What if, before this moment, you had missed the Heaven-declared and absolute promise of such a thing? What if you had previously been unwilling to think outside the sphere of *only the known,* refusing to believe in something better and ineffably different?

Now we understand why the Bible declares that no one will enter the dimension called Heaven, or Paradise, without first going through Jesus

Christic.[330] He is the only *way*. He alone is *the door*. No one but Jesus is *the gate*. No one else holds *the keys*!

In other words, Jesus is *the only portal* to that dimension, or any other realm that exists anywhere. And only He has the power to physically transform us into a glorified state, fit for the new life of every dimension He has created for us.

He alone is Yahweh, *who is our Yeshua*. Only He set everything in motion and lovingly thought of us when He did it. He alone lowered Himself to exist in mere human flesh for the sole purpose of safely delivering us back into His arms, back into His first creation, back into Paradise...back home, where we belong.

He did all this and so much more to demonstrate the unbounded magnitude of His love for us. He did it for the purpose of showing us the way, the truth, and the real life—the alternate, but very physical reality that awaits us in His Paradise—the place just through the dimensional divide, a realm that exists all around. A realm from which the disciples saw Him cross back and forth on a number of occasions. The same realm He promised to the repentant thief on the cross when He announced, "I tell you the truth. Today, you will be with me in Paradise!" It is a realm the Word of God repeatedly discloses to us, from its opening pages to its last.

Yeshua not only divulges glimpses of the depths of that reality to us through the pages of Scripture, but also through the contextual protocols of simply exploring His gloriously magnificent name.

At the beginning of this book, I quoted the following text from the *Pulpit Commentary*. I believe it succinctly sums up the central theme of the journey we've taken and its importance. Have a look at it again. This time, now that we've completed our journey together, truly savor its words of truth.

The name of God is uniformly treated in Scripture as something very different from a mere arrangement of letters or an arbitrary vocal sound. The name of God was not of man, nor from man, but of his own direct revelation. Like the "word" of God, it cannot be dissociated from God himself.[331]

~Dr. H. D. M Spence-Jones

No matter how we approach the matter—whether by using intricate computer programs, ELS codes, exploring the depths of quantum physics, delving into ancient Hebrew letter meanings and their illustrations, studying the latest archeological finds, standing on the Mount of Olives and looking down upon the hills and valleys that encircle His name around His Holy City, or peering through the most powerful and computerized microscopes the world has ever known and seeing Yahweh's name encoded upon our own DNA—we can't escape the truth. *He's here. He's there. He's everywhere!* The presence of His name is inescapable.

He is our life. He's our next breath. He is the Creator of the ground we stand upon. He is the "stuff" of our very makeup. He is the glue that holds us together. He is the next beat of our heart. He is our Creator, our Heavenly Father…and our Savior.

He is Yeshua. The Pierced One. The Resurrected One. The One whom the Scripture declares from the opening verse to the last. He is the *Aleph* and the *Tav*, *Alpha* and *Omega*, the First and the Last. And He is the One who is coming again to rule and reign for eternity—and those who love Him will reign with Him, at His side.

This is why He came to us in the first place—to assure us that something much bigger exists outside our strictly earthbound and very temporary reality. He ultimately wants us to live in that dimension of Paradise with Him. He wants to restore us to the glory our primordial ancestors once held in Eden, before the Fall.[332] He reaches down into our lowly existence, inside a desperately fallen world, and offers to pull us out and transform us into His likeness.[333]

The truth is, many who call themselves believers in Yeshua are on their own Emmaus Road journey of fear and doubt. Some are even playing the part of the Doubting Thomas of today's church, needing more evidence before they fully believe that God is really in absolute control of everything that's happening in the world.

However, because of our Creator's loving activity in our world and in our own lives, occasionally, many of us get to experience a peek into those divine truths, into those unseen realms, and even a little beyond. They are sacred glimpses of the eternal nature of all God has made and all He has in store for us. They are revelations of biblical insight that shore up our faith, increase our courage, and equip us to be the ambassadors He has called us to be. When those foretastes are revealed to us, our lives are rarely ever the same.

> **The Lord has made known to us the mystery of his will** according to his good pleasure, which he purposed in Christ, **to be put into effect when the times reach their fulfillment—to bring unity to all things in heaven and on earth under Christ.** When you believed, **you were marked in him with a seal,** the promised Holy Spirit, who is **a deposit guaranteeing our inheritance until the redemption of those who are God's possession—to the praise of his glory.** (Ephesians 1:9-10, 13–14; emphasis added)

The kind of things we've seen brought to light throughout these pages are only a small part of the overall last-days unsealing foretold by Daniel, and also spoken out of the mouth of Jesus Himself. These are revelations given most specifically for our generation.

The revealing is happening now, all over the world, in a magnitude that's not been known before our time. And, I believe there are many more divine disclosures yet to unfold.

Through our journey together, we've come about as close as we can get, within our limited world, to seeing something of the bigger picture of life. Now we've seen with our own eyes a large sampling of *what's actually there.*

Like Joseph and Mary discovering themselves in the Scriptures or the disciples sitting at the feet of Jesus during His forty days among them after the resurrection, listening to Him teach deep revelations about Himself in the Old Testament Scriptures. Now, like them, because of the things we've learned, we are also and forevermore without excuse. We have a deeper understanding of what life, death, and eternity are *really about*...more than any who've come before us.

Thank you for taking this excursion of discovery with me. It has been a joy to share it with you. If you've found it to be a revelation to your own mind and spirit, please share it with others.

Now...may the one who calms the wind and waves by His uplifted hand, and by the thunder of His voice, and through His very presence, bless you and keep you.

Always.

☙❧

"To you," Jesus replied, "has been entrusted the secret truth concerning the Kingdom of God; but to those others outside your number all this is spoken in figurative language; that 'they may look and look but not see, and listen and listen but not understand, lest perchance they should return and be pardoned.'"

~MARK 4:11–12; WEYMOUTH NEW TESTAMENT

The word is near you; it is in your mouth and in your heart," that is, the message concerning faith that we proclaim: If you declare with your mouth, "Jesus is Lord," and believe in your heart that God raised him from the dead, you will be saved.

For it is with your heart that you believe and are justified, and it is with your mouth that you profess your faith and are saved.

As Scripture says, "Anyone who believes in him will never be put to shame," for "everyone who calls on the name of the Lord will be saved."

~Romans 10:8–11, 13

ABOUT THE AUTHOR

Carl Gallups has been the senior pastor of Hickory Hammock Church in Milton, Florida, since 1987.

He is a graduate of the Florida Law Enforcement Officer Academy, Florida State University (BSC in Criminology), and New Orleans Baptist Theological Seminary (MDiv in Theology), and has served on the board of regents at the University of Mobile in Mobile, Alabama, since 2000.

He is a former decorated Florida law enforcement officer, having served under three sheriffs with two county sheriff's offices, and has also worked in an administrative capacity in the Central Office of the Florida Department of Corrections in Tallahassee.

Pastor Gallups is also a critically acclaimed, Amazon Top 60 bestselling author, an internationally known talk-radio host 2002–2022, heard on several Gulf Coast radio stations, and a regular guest on numerous television and radio programs. He is a frequent guest speaker at national prophecy and Bible conferences. He has preached the gospel of Jesus Christ on three continents and in four nations, including Peru and Israel, and all over the United States—including Hawaii and Alaska. He has also preached, on several occasions, in the Canadian provinces of British Colombia, Alberta, and Ontario.

Pastor Gallups lives in Milton, Florida, with his beloved wife, Pam. You can find more information about him at www.carlgallups.com.

Carl's life promise Scripture is Romans 8:28, 31:

And we know that in all things God works for the good of those who love him, who have been called according to his purpose.... What, then, shall we say in response to these things? If God is for us, who can be against us?

Appendix 1
Proto-Sinaitic Script Compared to Modern Hebrew Script

HEBREW ALPHABET				
Proto-Sinaitic		Bible Script Paleo-Hebrew		
Letter Name	Early	Middle	Late	Modern
Aleph	⏗	✝	א	א
Beyt	𐤁	𐤁	𐤁	ב
Gimel	𐤂	𐤂	𐤂	ג
Dalet	⊓	⊲	⊓	ד
Hey	⟊	⟌	⊓	ה
Vav	⟊	⟊	⟊	ו
Zayin	⟊	工	⟊	ז
Chet	⊟	⊞	⊓	ח
Tet	⊗	⊗	⊘	⊓
Yud	⟊	⟊	⟊	׳
Kaph	𐤊	⟊	⟊	כ ך
Lamed	⟊	⟊	⟊	ל
Mem	∿	⟊	⟊	מ ם
Nun	⟊	⟊	⟊	נ ן
Samech	◀	⟊	⊘	ס
Ayin	⟊	◯	⟊	ע
Pey	⟊	⟊	⟊	פ ף
Tsade	⟊	⟊	⟊	צ ץ
Quph	⟊	⟊	⟊	ק
Resh	⟊	⟊	⟊	ר
Shin	⊔	W	⟊	ש
Tav	✝	✗	⟊	ת

321

Appendix 2
Proto-Sinaitic Script with Pictures and Meanings

Symbol Letter		PICTURE	MEANING
𐤀	El	Ox head	Strong, Power, Leader
𐤁	Bet	Tent floorplan	Family, House, In
𐤂	Gam	Foot	Gather, Walk
𐤃	Dal	Door	Move, Hang, Entrance
𐤄	Hey	Man with arms raised	Look, Reveal, Breath
𐤅	Waw	Tent peg	Add, Secure, Hook, Nail
𐤆	Zan	Mattock	Food, Cut, Nourish
𐤇	Hhet	Tent wall	Outside, Divide, Half
𐤈	Tet	Basket	Surround, Contain, Mud
𐤉	Yad	Arm and closed hand	Work, Throw, Worship
𐤊	Kaph	Open palm	Bend, Open, Allow, Tame
𐤋	Lam	Shepherd Staff	Teach, Yoke, To, Bind
𐤌	Mem	Water	Chaos, Mighty, Blood
𐤍	Nun	Seed	Continue, Heir, Son
𐤎	Sin	Thorn	Grab, Hate, Protect
𐤏	Ghah	Eye	Watch, Know, Shade
𐤐	Pey	Mouth	Blow, Scatter, Edge
𐤑	Tsad	Trail	Journey, chase, hunt
𐤒	Quph	Sun on the horizon	Condense, Circle, Time
𐤓	Resh	Head of a man	First, Top, Beginning
𐤔	Shin	Two front teeth	Sharp, Press, Eat, Two
𐤕	Taw	Crossed sticks	Mark, Sign, Signal, Monument

Appendix 3
Modern Square Script with Numerical Values Assigned

Decimal	Hebrew	Letter	Decimal	Hebrew	Letter	Decimal	Hebrew	Letter
1	Aleph	א	10	Yod	י	100	Kof	ק
2	Bet	ב	20	Kaf	כ	200	Resh	ר
3	Gimel	ג	30	Lamed	ל	300	Shin	ש
4	Dalet	ד	40	Mem	מ	400	Tav	ת
5	He	ה	50	Nun	נ	500	Kaf (final)	ך
6	Vav	ו	60	Samekh	ס	600	Mem (final)	ם
7	Zayin	ז	70	Ayin	ע	700	Nun (final)	ן
8	Het	ח	80	Pe	פ	800	Pe (final)	ף
9	Tet	ט	90	Tsadi	צ	900	Tsadi (final)	ץ

Appendix 4
Paleo-Hebrew—Original Script of the Hebrew Scriptures

The Paleo-Hebrew alphabet's main differences from the Phoenician script were "**a curving to the left of the downstrokes in the 'long-legged' letter-signs**....the consistent use of a Waw/Vav with a concave top, [and an] **x or cross-shaped Taw/Tav.**"[334]

Until the First Temple was destroyed by the Babylonians in 586 BC, the **paleo-Hebrew script** was **the only alphabet** used by the Israelites.[335]

Name	Paleo-Hebrew	Block	Name	Paleo-Hebrew	Block
Aleph	𐤀	א	Lamedh	𐤋	ל
Beth	𐤁	ב	Mem	𐤌	מ, ם
Gimel	𐤂	ג	Nun	𐤍	נ, ן
Daleth	𐤃	ד	Samekh	𐤎	ס
He	𐤄	ה	Ayin	𐤏	ע
Waw	𐤅	ו	Pe	𐤐	פ, ף
Zayin	𐤆	ז	Tsade	𐤑	צ, ץ
Heth	𐤇	ח	Qoph	𐤒	ק
Teth	𐤈	ט	Resh	𐤓	ר
Yodh	𐤉	י	Shin	𐤔	ש
Kaph	𐤊	כ, ך	Taw	𐤕	ת

Note the Tav/Taw of the original biblical script.
It is an "x" with a downward extended leftward slope...the shape of a "cross."

Taw	𐤕

The original text of the Hebrew scriptures would have represented the Aleph-Tav like this: 𐤀𐤕

NOTES

1. Numbers 6:7, Pulpit Commentary, Biblehub.com, https://biblehub.com/commentaries/numbers/6-27.htm.
Henry Donald Maurice Spence-Jones, with a doctor of divinity from Cambridge University, was the vicar and rural dean of St. Pancras, London, and the principal of Gloucester Theological College. He authored the entire *Pulpit Commentary* collection, still widely used by biblical scholars today. Wikipedia. "Pulpit Commentary," accessed 4/2/22, https://en.wikipedia.org/wiki/Pulpit_Commentary.

2. For an excellent study of ancient Emmaus see: David N. Bivin, "A Farewell to the Emmaus Road," Jerusalem Perspective, 1/13/17, https://www.jerusalemperspective.com/16208.

3. This narrative is based on the biblical text of Luke 24. Some liberty has been taken with the actual discussion, and even the name of one of the two travelers to Emmaus, since the Scripture only mentions one by name—Cleopas. Even though parts of the narrative are fictional, the overall story strictly adheres to the biblical truths and sound doctrine of Luke 24.

4. James. This is my fictional name for Cleopas' friend, who is unnamed by the Scriptures, although Cleopas is named. See the commentary that follows.
From *Meyer's New Testament Commentary*: "From the fact of his not being named, there is neither to be concluded a greater nor a less degree of knowledge regarding him...although Nathanael, Bartholomew, Peter, or another Simon, Luke himself, and even, conjecturally, the younger James, as having made the journey with his father Alpheus—have been guessed."

5. Ibid. For an excellent study of ancient Emmaus, see: David N. Bivin, "A Farewell to the Emmaus Road." For additional study, also see the commentary entries at: https://biblehub.com/commentaries/luke/24-13.htm.

6. How far did people walk in Jesus' day? "The standard mode of transport was usually by foot with an estimated mileage of around 20 miles a day, but citizens also rode on oxen, donkeys and camels.... According to The New Testament, the principal locations for the ministry undertaken by Jesus were Galilee and Judea, with activities also taking place in surrounding areas such as Peres and Samaria. Christian texts refer to Jesus walking 3,125 miles during his ministry. Taking into account that a determined person, on a mission, could make the trip from Judea to Galilee (150 – 200 km) on foot in six days, it is possible that an experienced walker with knowledge of the terrain could venture far greater distances.... Over Jesus' lifetime, a conservative estimate of the number of miles he may have walked is put at around 21,525 miles, almost the equivalent of walking around the entire world."
See: History.com.uk. "The Lost Years of Jesus: The Mystery of Christ's Missing 18 Years," accessed 4/23/22, https://www.history.co.uk/articles/the-lost-years-of-jesus-what-was-he-doing-in-those-missing-18-years.

7. Kingsley A. Glover, "The Dress of the Master," *University of Chicago Press Journal, the Biblical World*, Vol. 15, No. 5 (May, 1900), pp. 347–357 esp. p. 350), https://www.jstor.org/stable/pdf/3136935.pdf.

8. *Barnes' Notes on the Bible:* "They seem to have given up all for lost, and to have come to the conclusion that Jesus was not the Messiah, though they naturally conversed about it, and there were many things which they could not explain. Their Master had been crucified contrary to their expectation, their hopes dashed, their anticipation disappointed, and they were now returning in sadness, and very naturally conversed, in the way, of the things which had happened in Jerusalem." See https://biblehub.com/commentaries/luke/24-14.htm.

9. Luke 8:2–3; Mark 16.

10. Isaiah 48:6–7.

11. Daniel 2:21–22.

12. Daniel 12:4.

13. Of course, Scripture does not include the detail I've inserted here. But, it would not be outside the scope of biblical accuracy if the Lord had decided to leave a small revelation of Himself for the innkeeper. It certainly would have been within His nature to do such a thing. In effect, I have

Jesus leaving His "calling card," evidencing that His disciples had told the innkeeper the truth.

14. *Ellicott's Commentary for English Readers*: "They rose up the same hour.—as it was towards evening when they had arrived at Emmaus, and its distance from Jerusalem was about eight miles, they must have reached the chamber where the Eleven were assembled after nightfall. If we identify this gathering with that of John 20:19, there were but ten Apostles present, Thomas being absent."

15. Ephesians 3:10.

16. *Tanakh:* Hebrew for what we call the Old Testament.

17. *Benson Commentary:* "And between thy seed—All carnal and wicked men, who, in reference to this text, are called the children and seed of Satan; and her seed—That is, her offspring, first and principally CHRIST, who, with respect to this promise, is termed, by way of eminence, her seed, (see Galatians 3:16; Galatians 3:19,) whose alone work it is to bruise the serpent's head, to destroy the policy and power of the devil. But also, secondly, all the members of Christ, all believers and holy men, are here intended, who are the seed of Christ and the implacable enemies of the devil and his works, and who overcome him by Christ's merit and power." See: https://biblehub.com/commentaries/genesis/3-15.htm.

18. Isaiah 7:14. There is no doubt this prophecy is about Jesus' virgin birth through the womb of Mary and the importance of His designation as God in the flesh as our Savior. Matthew 1:13 bears out this truth in the very first page of the New Testament.

19. I have chosen not to reference this website, or article, in this book. I don't wish to disparage anyone, if at all possible. However, I could not let this true account go unused. It makes for a perfect teaching example of one of the things missing in today's "institutionalized" church. I can assure you every word of my characterization of that piece is factual.

20. Galatians 4:4.

21. Dr. James Tabor: "The Book of Daniel is the apocalyptic book of the Hebrew Bible. Its sister book would be the Book of Revelation." Quoted by: PBS Frontline, "The Book of Daniel," pbs.org, accessed 2/17/22. https://www.pbs.org/wgbh/pages/frontline/shows/apocalypse/explanation/

bdaniel.html#:~:text=The%20Book%20of%20Daniel%20is%20
the%20apocalyptic%20book%20of%20the,us%20from%20the%20
Babylonian%20exile.

22. Moody Bible Institute of Chicago, "Daniel the Key to Prophetic
Revelation" (1971), accessed 2/26/22, https://bible.org/book/export/
html/6551.

23. Moody Bible Institute of Chicago: "Christ Himself in Matthew 24:15
predicted the abomination of desolation of Daniel 12:11 as future, not
past. Prophecies of the book of Revelation written late in the first century
also anticipate as future the fulfillment of parallel prophecies in Daniel. For
example, Revelation 13 parallels the final stage of Daniel's fourth empire.
This could not, therefore, refer to events fulfilled in the second century
B.C. [Daniel's own time]." See: Moody Bible Institute: "Daniel. The Key to
Prophetic Revelation," accessed 2/26/22 (written 1971), https://bible.org/
book/export/html/6551.

24. The word for "book" or "scroll" in Daniel 12 is the Hebrew word
sepher. In English translations, it can be written as either "book" or "scroll."
That word is now used among the Hebrew-speaking people for the modern
word for "book." See: https://biblehub.com/hebrew/5612.htm.

25. *Everett's Study Notes on the Holy Scriptures*, "Daniel 12," Studylight.
org, https://www.studylight.org/commentaries/eng/ghe/daniel-12.
html#verse-1-13.

26. Dr. Gary Everett received his master of divinity (1992) and doctor of
ministry (2015) degrees from Southwestern Baptist Theological Seminary.
He served as pastor for five years and taught in Bible College for ten years.
Since 1997, he has worked as the station manager of Lighthouse Television,
located in Kampala, Uganda, an affiliate of Trinity Broadcasting Network.
https://www.studylight.org/commentaries/eng/ghe.html.

27. Daniel 12:4, *Everett's Study Notes on the Holy Scriptures*, Studylight.org,
https://www.studylight.org/commentaries/eng/ghe/daniel-12.html.

28. The only other place in the Bible, before Revelation 5, wherein a scroll
is sealed, is in Daniel chapter 12. In Daniel 8 and 9, the prophet is told to
"seal up the vision" until the last days. However, concerning the passage
in Daniel 12, commentators G. K. Beale and D. A. Carson say, "Daniel

12:8–9 implies the future unsealing of the book in a latter-day period." There's only one place in the future where a scroll is unsealed. It's found in Revelation 5 and 6.

G. K. Beale, *The Book of Revelation: A Commentary on the Greek Text, New International Greek Testament Commentary* (Grand Rapids, MI; Carlisle, Cumbria: Eerdmans; Paternoster Press, 1999) p. 347

See also: G. K. Beale and D. A. Carson (eds), *Commentary on the New Testament Use of the Old Testament*, (Grand Rapids: Baker, 2007), p. 1101.

29. Dr. Phillip G. Kayser: "This written revelation [Revelation 5] has already been closed up and sealed (5:2–5; 6:1f.) And parallels Daniel's scroll being closed up and sealed (Daniel 12:4, 9; cf. the sealing up of all vision and prophet in Dan. 9:24 before 70 AD [v. 27])."

See: Dr. Phillip G. Kayser. "The Identity of the Scroll. Revelation 5," Biblical Blueprints, accessed2/22/22https://kaysercommentary.com/ Sermons/New%20Testament/Revelation/Revelation%205/Revelation%20 5_1.md.

30. Most scholars agree that the "time of the end" actually began with the arrival of God in the flesh, in the person of Jesus Christ. It began at the crucifixion and resurrection, the birth of the Church, the preaching of the Gospel—and all that would come after it. There will, of course, arrive a more specific "time of the end" at the coming of the "Day of the Lord." That time, even the very day and hour of it, is still shrouded in obscurity at the throne of God concerning the mystery of its ultimate fulfillment. That "day" is quickly approaching.

31. Beale, *The Book of Revelation: A Commentary on the Greek Text*: "The idea of sealing and opening books in connection with end-time happenings is found in the OT only in Daniel 12 and 7…. Revelation 5 portrays a vision of inaugurated fulfillment of OT prophecy. The metaphor of seals can be found outside Daniel elsewhere in the OT and Jewish apocalyptic, but the seals in Rev. 5:1ff come from Dan. 12:4, 9."

See: Beale, *The Book of Revelation: A Commentary on the Greek Text*, pp. 339, 347.

32. *Torah Class—Rediscovering the Bible:* "So essentially Revelation chapter 5 is a fulfillment of Daniel 12:4; although we must acknowledge that it

is only a partial fulfillment because even though the contents are being revealed to John, the actions the content describes have yet to happen." See: Torah Class. "Lesson 13. Revelation 5," Accessed 2/24/22, https://www.torahclass.com/bible-studies/new-testament-studies/1917-new-testament-revelation/2956-lesson-13-revelation-5.

Expositor's Greek Testament (regarding Revelation 5:1): "The sealing is really a Danielic touch, added to denote the mystery and obscurity of the future." See also the commentary entries for *Benson Commentary* and the *Cambridge Bible Commentary for Schools and Colleges* at the same web address: https://biblehub.com/commentaries/revelation/5-1.htm.

33. Rev. Dr. Gregory K. Beale (PhD, Cambridge, & ThM, Dallas Theological Seminary) holds the J. Gresham Machen chair of New Testament and is research professor of New Testament and biblical interpretation at Westminster Theological Seminary.

34. Beale, *Book of Revelation,* p. 347.

35. Revelation 13:13.

36. For examples, see Matthew 24:14; Revelation 13:7, 11–18; 14:9, 11; 15:2; 16:2; 19:20; 20:4.

37. See the United Nations document: "United Nations Strategy for Legal Identity for All: Concept note developed by the United Nations Legal Identity Expert Group." Especially see the subsections (16, 19, 37a–b) titled, "Population register, Implementation—General Norms, Digital Identity, and Biometrics." https://unstats.un.org/legal-identity-agenda/documents/UN-Strategy-for-LIA.pdf.

38. Ryan Whitwam, "Clearview Plans Facial Recognition Database That Knows Every Person on Earth." Extreme Tech, 2/18/22, https://www.extremetech.com/extreme/331819-clearview-plans-facial-recognition-database-that-knows-every-person-on-earth.

See also https://www.washingtonpost.com/technology/2022/02/16/clearview-expansion-facial-recognition.

39. Ibid.

40. "The Power of Digital Intermediaries: Insight Report," World Economic Forum, February 2022 Edition, Accessed 3/6/22, https://www3.weforum.org/docs/WEF_Advancing_towards_Digital_Agency_2022.pdf. Also see: "Quick Synopsis of the WEF Publication" by The Blaze: "The

World Economic Forum recently published a new 46-page report detailing its Orwellian plan to control pretty much everything in your life. The report, called Advancing Digital Agency: The Power of Data Intermediaries describes a digital ID system that would collect personal data about your online behavior, purchase history, network usage, medical history, travel history, energy uses, health stats, and more. This data would then be used to determine who could open bank accounts, conduct financial transactions, access insurance, health care treatment, book trips, cross borders, and more." See: Staff, Blaze TV. "World Economic Forum Unveils New 'Digital ID' Plan—and It's TERRIFYING: 'Nothing is beyond the realm of possibilities'" The Blaze, 3/3/22, https://www.theblaze.com/amp/wef-digital-id-plan-2656835686?fr=operanews.

41. *Coffman's Commentaries on the Bible:* "The really destructive heresy regarding this chapter is the error of seeing nothing in it except the conclusion of the persecutions under Antiochus Epiphanes. Keil pointed out that the critical application of the first few verses of Daniel 12 to the times of Antiochus could be true and correct, 'Only if the premises from which it is drawn were allowed.' These premises were confidently contradicted by Keil…it absolutely imperative to understand that in this chapter the focus of the prophecy moves to the climax of the Messianic kingdom itself in the Final Judgment and Second Advent of Jesus Christ," https://www.studylight.org/commentaries/eng/bcc/daniel-12.html.

42. See my book, *The Summoning* (Crane, MO: Defender, 2021) for a detailed explanation, rife with startling biblical truth, of how we are indeed living in one of the Bible's most "guaranteed" signs of the last days.

43. Max Roser and Hannah Ritchie, "Technological Progress," Accessed 2/20/22, https://ourworldindata.org/technological-progress.

44. For example, The CERN Hadron Collider: ""The Large Hadron Collider (LHC) is the world's largest and most powerful particle accelerator. It first started up on 10 September 2008, and remains the latest addition to CERN's accelerator complex. The LHC consists of a 27-kilometre ring of superconducting magnets with a number of accelerating structures to boost the energy of the particles along the way," Accessed 2/20/22, https://home.cern/science/accelerators/large-hadron-collider.

Also see: "Extra Dimensions, Gravitons, and tiny Black Holes,"

CERN, accessed 2/20/22, https://home.cern/science/physics/
extra-dimensions-gravitons-and-tiny-black-holes.
45. That number was 4.5 billion people in 2019.
"ICAO / Annual Report 2019 / The World of Air Transport in 2019,"
accessed 2/24/22, https://www.icao.int/annual-report-2019/Pages/the-
world-of-air-transport-in-2019.aspx.
46. Peter Dockrill, "NASA Finally Makes Contact with Voyager 2 after
Longest Radio Silence in 30 Years," Live Science, 11/5/20, https://www.
livescience.com/nasa-makes-contact-voyager-2-long-radio-silence.html.
47. Science Daily. "Big Data, for Better or Worse: 90% of World's Data
Generated over Last Two Years," 5/22/13, https://www.sciencedaily.com/
releases/2013/05/130522085217.htm.
48. An exabyte is equal to one billion gigabytes. A zettabyte is one thousand
times larger than an exabyte and is 2 to the 70th power bytes, also expressed
as 10^{21} (1,000,000,000,000,000,000,000 bytes).
See also: "Exabyte—An extraordinarily large unit of digital data, one
Exabyte (EB) is equal to 1,000 Petabytes or one billion gigabytes (GB).
Some technologists have estimated that all the words ever spoken by
mankind would be equal to five Exabytes," https://www.teradata.com/
Glossary/What-is-an-Exabyte#:~:text=An%20extraordinarily%20large%20
unit%20of,be%20equal%20to%20five%20Exabytes.
49. Seed Scientific. "How Much Data Is Created Every Day?" 10/28/21,
https://seedscientific.com/how-much-data-is-created-every-day.
50. A 2006 analysis put it this way: "The fastest increasing quantity on
this planet is the amount of information we are generating. It is (and has
been) expanding faster than anything else we create or can measure.…
Information is accumulating faster than any material or artifact in this
world, faster than any by-product of our activities.

…Two economists at UC Berkeley calculated our total global information
production for one year… [Hal] Varian and [Peter] Lyman estimate that
the total production of new information in 2000 reached 1.5 exabytes.
They explain that is about 37,000 times as much information as is in the
entire holdings Library of Congress. For one year! Three years later the
annual total yielded 3.5 exabytes. That yields a 66% rate of growth in
information per year."

See: "The Speed of Information," The Technium, accessed 2/28/22, http://www.kk.org/thetechnium/archives/2006/02/the_speed_of_in.php.

51. This piece was written in 2013 by Industry Tap: "Buckminster Fuller created the 'Knowledge Doubling Curve'; he noticed that until 1900 human knowledge doubled approximately every century. By the end of World War II knowledge was doubling every 25 years. Today things are not as simple as different types of knowledge have different rates of growth. For example, nanotechnology knowledge is doubling every two years and clinical knowledge every 18 months. But on average human knowledge is doubling every 13 months. According to IBM, the build out of the 'internet of things' will lead to the doubling of knowledge every 12 hours." See: David Shilling, "Knowledge Doubling Every 12 Months, Soon to be Every 12 Hours," 4/19/13, https://www.industrytap.com/knowledge-doubling-every-12-months-soon-to-be-every-12-hours/3950. For example: "In summary, the idea of technology increasing as a sign of the end times is a popular one, but is also often exaggerated. Daniel 12:4 simply speaks of an increase in knowledge, offering no additional details. We are only promised knowledge will be increased in the final days, without any predictions regarding today's technologies," (emphasis added); https://www.compellingtruth.org/Bible-technology.html.

52. GotQuestions.org, "Does the Bible say that an increase in technology is a sign of the end times?" Accessed 2/17/22, https://www.gotquestions.org/Bible-technology.html.

53. As one reads the article, we quickly discover that their main purpose is to discredit Daniel 12:4 as a verse that genuinely speaks of technology advancement in the last days.

54. GotQuestion.org, "Does the Bible say that an increase in technology is a sign of the end times?"

55. I wish to make clear that I respect the overall scholarship of that biblical commentary site, as evidenced by the fact that I have often quoted their studies on other topics in a number of my books (this one included). However, I believe their specific analysis regarding technology advancements of the last days to be incorrect. You'll soon see why.

56. Matthew 24:14.

1. *Dr. Constable's Expository Notes:* "Jesus proceeded to give His disciples

a general picture of conditions just before He will return to end the present age and inaugurate His kingdom." https://www.studylight.org/commentaries/eng/dcc/matthew-24.html#verse-1-3.

2. *Gaebelein's Annotated Bible:* "The end of which the Lord speaks... will be the visible manifestation of the Son of Man in power and in glory out of the opened heavens. The glorified church, the Lamb's wife, comes forth with Him in that visible manifestation." https://www.studylight.org/commentaries/eng/gab/matthew-24.html#verse-1-51.

57. 1. *Meyer's New Testament Commentary:* "[Jesus' declaration] must not be limited to the Roman Empire (Luke 2:1), but should be taken quite generally: over the whole habitable globe," https://biblehub.com/commentaries/matthew/24-14.htm.

2. *Expositor's Greek Testament:* "Matthew 24:14 asserts the same thing with regard to the preaching of the gospel of the kingdom: time for preaching it in the whole world, o all nations, before the end. ... Jesus wished to ensure that all Israel should hear the gospel before the end came; therefore He emphasized the shortness of the time. Here He wishes to impress on the disciples that the end will not be for a good while; therefore He emphasizes the amount of preaching that can be done," https://biblehub.com/commentaries/matthew/24-14.htm.

58. 1. *The Pulpit Commentary* (on Matthew 24:14): "The truth is that the gospel will be everywhere offered, but not everywhere received. And then, when all these signs ... shall have appeared, shall the end come, primarily of Jerusalem, secondarily of this world or this age." https://biblehub.com/commentaries/matthew/24-14.htm.

2. *Ellicott's Commentary on the Entire Bible* (on Matthew 28:20): "Even unto the end of the world.—Literally, of the age. The phrase is the same as that in Matthew 13:39-40; Matthew 13:49; Matthew 24:13-14. In Hebrews 9:26 it is used of the time of the appearance of Christ in the flesh, as the beginning of the last age of the world." https://biblehub.com/commentaries/matthew/28-20.htm.

3. *Bridgeway Bible Commentary (on Matthew 24:21):* "When Jesus spoke of the destruction of the temple, his disciples immediately connected this with the return of the Messiah and the end of the age. They asked him what significant events would occur before these final great events

(Matthew 24:1-3; Luke 21:5-7).... The end would not come till the gospel had spread throughout the world, and this goal would be reached only after much opposition.... Jesus did not return at the fall of Jerusalem, nor immediately after. It seems, then, that his prophecy still awaits its greater fulfilment. If that is so, there could be a repeat of conditions such as those during the destruction of Jerusalem in AD 70, but on a wider scale and with greater intensity. The powers of nature on earth and in space will be thrown into confusion, nations will be in turmoil, and people everywhere will be filled with fear. The present age will come to an end as Jesus returns in power and glory to save his own and judge his enemies (Matthew 24:29-31; Luke 21:25-28). https://www.studylight.org/commentary/matthew/24-21.html.

59. John F. Walvoord, president, Dallas Theological Seminary; editor, *Bibliotheca Sacra*: "Having completed in Matthew 24:4–14 the itemization of the nine signs which will be fulfilled in the present age in general and which will be especially characteristic of the end of the age, Christ now gives specific signs, answering the disciples' original question. They had asked for the sign of the end of the age and of His coming into His kingdom," "Signs of the End of the Age," accessed 2/24/22, https://bible.org/seriespage/3-signs-end-age.

60. Matthew 24:14. Examples of this more contextual understanding: *Meyer's New Testament Commentary:* "[Unto all the world] must not be limited to the Roman empire (Luke 2:1), but should be taken quite generally: over the whole habitable globe, a sense which is alone in keeping with Jesus' consciousness of His Messianic mission, and with the [to all nations] which follows." https://biblehub.com/commentaries/matthew/24-14.htm.

61. The gospel of the Kingdom is the very same thing as the gospel of Jesus Christ—the message of eternal salvation. *Pulpit Commentary:* "Verse 14. This gospel of the kingdom. The good news of the coming of Messiah's kingdom—what we call in short, 'the gospel'— 'that God was in Christ reconciling the world unto himself,'" (2 Corinthians 5:19).

62. Commentary on Matthew 24:14. *Coffman's Commentary on the Scriptures*" "[That] phenomenon [of the

global preaching of the gospel] will also occur before the second event, the end of the world. The end of the age is mentioned in the Great Commission (Matthew 28:20) and vividly described by the apostle Peter in 2 Peter 3:1–8. In retrospect, how bold was the prophecy of Christ! That the gospel of a man who had absolutely none of the worldly advantages of power and prestige, who never wrote a book, who owned no property, who was rejected by the powerful leaders of his nation, who never traveled far from home, whose chosen followers were humble and obscure men, who was born in a stable, and at last humiliated and crucified between two thieves—that the gospel of THAT MAN should last thirty years must have seemed an impossibility to those who set him at naught; but not only did it happen, it is still happening, and in the WHOLE WORLD, nearly two thousand years after the prophecy was made. There is no HUMAN explanation of such a fact." https://www.studylight.org/commentaries/eng/bcc/matthew-24.html.

63. Maps at the Library of Congress. "Maps That Changed Our World." Accessed 2/22/22, https://www.loc.gov/ghe/cascade/index.html?appid=ddf9 824ff56b4fb6a0f3e11515716738&bookmark=1854.

64. Commentary on Matthew 24:14, *Coffman's Commentary on the Scriptures*: "[That] phenomenon [of the global preaching of the gospel] will also occur before the second event, the end of the world."

65. Compound prophecy: The biblical principle of a *compound prophecy* interpretation is well known among scholars and serious students of God's Word. A compound prophecy is one that starts off talking about the prophet's own days, but then, almost on a dime, it morphs into a prophecy of Jesus Christ, or the person of Satan, or even the ultimate time of the end. Just a few examples of some compound prophecies of this nature are Psalm 22, Isaiah 14, and Ezekiel 28. One of the most dramatically certain instances of a compound prophecy is found in Habakkuk 1. The next few verses of Habakkuk 2 then proceed to declare that what we've just read has a double meaning, one of which concerns the time of the end! There are many other examples as well. In most cases, however, they are not as easy to discern as the one in Habakkuk. Therefore, one has to be intimately familiar with this style of prophetic writing, or else its intended meaning can quickly be lost on the researcher.

See: Dr. Lehman Strauss, "Bible Prophecy (A Principle of Prophetic Interpretation; Isaiah's Prophecies; Micah's Prophecies)," Bible.org. Accessed 11/4/17. https://bible.org/article/bible-prophecy.

Example statement of Dr. Strauss on the compound nature of Genesis 3:15: "What we now desire to emphasize in the Edenic prophecy in Genesis 3:15…. We have already stated that this verse contains a compound prophecy combining both the first and second appearances of Christ on earth."

66. For an example of how this "shifting" of time context works, consider the book of Habakkuk. In the first chapter, the prophet is talking to the people of his day. He gives them the prophetic oracle from the Lord. There certainly is meaning in it for their generation. But then, in chapter 2, Habakkuk is given these words: "Then the Lord replied: 'Write down the revelation and make it plain on tablets so that a herald may run with it. For the revelation awaits an appointed time; it speaks of the end and will not prove false.'" (Habakkuk 2:2–3)

See *Pulpit Commentary* on Habakkuk 2:2–3: "The prophecy personified yearns for its fulfilment in 'the end,' not merely at the destruction of the literal Babylon, but in the time of the end—the last time, the Messianic age, when the world power, typified by Babylon, should be overthrown," https://biblehub.com/commentaries/habakkuk/2-3.htm.

67. Following are several of the contrasting Bible versions of this passage that can be found at https://biblehub.com/daniel/12-4.htm.

1. *Good News Translation*: "He said to me, 'And now, Daniel, close the book and put a seal on it until the end of the world. Meanwhile, many people will waste their efforts trying to understand what is happening.'"

2. *New American Bible*: "As for you, Daniel, keep secret the message and seal the book until the end time; many shall wander aimlessly and evil shall increase."

3. *Amplified Bible*: "But as for you, Daniel, conceal these words and seal up the scroll until the end of time. Many will go back and forth and search anxiously [through the scroll], and knowledge [of the purpose of God as revealed by His prophets] will [greatly] increase."

68. 1. *Coffman's Commentaries on the Bible*: "The really destructive heresy regarding this chapter is the error of seeing nothing in it except the

conclusion of the persecutions under Antiochus Epiphanes. Keil pointed out that the critical application of the first few verses of Daniel 12 to the times of Antiochus could be true and correct, 'Only if the premises from which it is drawn were allowed.' These premises were confidently contradicted by Keil; and, as we found in our studies of the last paragraph of Daniel 11, there is no reference whatever in those verses to Antiochus. That impressive gap between undeniable references to Antiochus earlier in chapter eleven, prior to Daniel 11:36, and the introduction of the resurrection of the dead in the first three verses of this chapter, make it absolutely imperative to understand that in this chapter the focus of the prophecy moves to the climax of the Messianic kingdom itself in the Final Judgment and Second Advent of Jesus Christ.... In this connection, Albert Barnes declared that: 'The full meaning of the language (Daniel 12:1–3) is not met by the events of the times of the Maccabees. The passage looks forward and onward to a higher and more important event than any that occurred in the times of Antiochus.'" https://www.studylight.org/commentaries/eng/bcc/daniel-12.html.

2. See also: C. F. Keil, *Commentary on the Old Testament, Daniel* (Grand Rapids: Eerdmans), p.475.

3. See also: Albert Barnes, *Barnes' Notes, Daniel* (Grand Rapids: Baker Book), p. 263.

69. See Daniel 7, 8, 9, 10 and 11. A number of scholars believe chapter 10 is a definitive compound prophecy. That is, it begins by speaking of the rise of the days of Antiochus Epiphanes of the soon-coming Greek Empire, but then morphs into an image and prophecy of the last-days Antichrist himself.

For example, see *Everett's Study Notes on the Holy Scriptures:* "Many scholars suggest that Daniel 11:36–45 refers to the antichrist figure that will arise during the Tribulation Period, whom Paul calls the Son of Perdition. Within this context, the king of the North would refer to Gog and his army that surrounds Jerusalem during the Battle of Armageddon, as described in Ezekiel 38–39." https://www.studylight.org/commentaries/eng/ghe/daniel-12.html#verse-1-13.

70. The Time of the End (Daniel 12) Not Antiochus Epiphanes:

1. *Keil and Delitzsch Biblical Commentary on the Old Testament:* "[The

conclusion that many make] would be indisputable if the premises from which it is drawn, that (at that time) is the time of Antiochus, were well founded. All attempts of [thus] believing interpreters … appear on close inspection to be untenable." https://biblehub.com/commentaries/daniel/12-1.htm.

2. *Pulpit Commentary:* "To the time of the end. The end is not the end of the persecution of the days of Antiochus - that is already past; we have now reached the consummation of all things. Many shall run to and fro, and knowledge shall be increased. This is to be looked upon as a description of the last time, when circumstance shall remove the seal from the book." Daniel 12:4. "Commentaries," Biblehub.com, https://biblehub.com/commentaries/daniel/12-4.htm.

3. *Gill's Exposition of the Entire Bible:* "And seal the book, even to the time of the end; till the time comes appointed for the fulfilment of it, which shows that it reached to times at a great distance; that till these times were come, or near, it would be as a sealed book, and yet the accomplishment of it would be sure and certain." Daniel 12:4. "Commentaries," Biblehub.com, https://biblehub.com/commentaries/daniel/12-4.htm.

4. Dr. Constable's Expository Notes: "By sealing it, Daniel would certify that what stood written was exactly what God had revealed to him and had promised would happen (cf. Revelation 22:18-19)…. Daniel was to preserve this revelation until the end of time…. What God had revealed to him concerned the far distant future…. As time passed and knowledge increased, they would understand these things better than Daniel could." https://www.studylight.org/commentaries/eng/dcc/daniel-12.html.

5. *Gaebelein's Annotated Bible:* "And at that time. What time? The time of the end, the time of trouble such as never was before; the same time to which our Lord refers in Matthew 24:21." https://www.studylight.org/commentaries/eng/gab/daniel-12.html#verse-1-13.

6. *Coffman's Commentary on the Scriptures* (Daniel 12): "One of the favorite dictums of Bible enemies is that we should look for what was 'probably in the mind of the prophet' to understand and interpret his words; but the Holy Scriptures in this passage offer the complete denial of such a [wayward] ruling, which, alas, influences much of the so-called

'interpreting' of the ancient prophecies.... Here Daniel freely admitted that
he did not understand the words which the holy one spoke unto him and
which he wrote down and sealed. He asked for information about what the
words meant, but the holy one refused to enlighten him further, saying, 'Go
thy way, the words are shut up and sealed till the time of the end.'"
The prophecies of knowledge being increased and men going "to and fro"
could never have been fully understood by any person living prior to the
twentieth century! In this connection, one should read 1 Peter 1:10–12,
where this phenomenon of the prophets not understanding their own
prophecies is specifically stated. https://www.studylight.org/commentaries/
eng/bcc/daniel-12.html#verse-1.

71. Daniel 12:13. "Barnes' Notes on the Bible," Biblehub.com, https://
biblehub.com/commentaries/daniel/12-13.htm.

72. See Matthew 5:14–16.

73. Daniel 12:3, "Jamieson-Fausset-Brown Bible Commentary," Biblehub.
com, https://biblehub.com/commentaries/daniel/12-3.htm.

74. Commentary examples:

1. *Matthew Poole's Commentary:* "Here the faithful are called wise, i. e.
to salvation, and so these two members include teachers, and disciples
that are truly taught the way of salvation, i.e. such as are taught of God
to learn Christ as the truth is in Jesus, John 6:45 Ephesians 4:21. They
that teach true justification by the righteousness of Christ." Daniel 12:3,
"Commentaries," Biblehub.com, https://biblehub.com/commentaries/
daniel/12-3.htm.

2. *Gill's Exposition of the Entire Bible:* "And they that turn many to
righteousness as the stars forever and ever; or, 'that justify many'; that
teach the doctrine of a sinner's free justification by the righteousness of
Christ; that lead and direct souls sensible of sin, and of the weakness of
their own righteousness, to the righteousness of Christ, as being that only
which justifies before God." Daniel 12:3, "Commentaries," Biblehub.com,
https://biblehub.com/commentaries/daniel/12-3.htm.

3. *Benson Commentary:* "Daniel 12:3. They that be wise—Namely, that
are wise unto salvation through faith in Christ, that are truly godly and
righteous, shall shine as the brightness of the firmament—Shall be clothed
with glory and immortality; shall have bodies conformed to Christ's

glorious body; shall shine forth, says Jesus, as the sun in the kingdom of their Father, Matthew 13:43; and especially those shall be thus glorious who are wise to win souls.… Turn to righteousness—literally, 'justify,' that is, convert many to justification through Christ (Jas 5:20)." Daniel 12:3. "Benson's Commentary on the Entire Bible," Biblehub.com, https://biblehub.com/commentaries/daniel/12-3.htm.

75. Hartman, *Prophecy Interpreted*, 147–177. Gundry, *Use of OT in Matthew*, 46–55. Vetne, *The Influence and Use of Daniel in the Synoptic Gospels*, 152–219. Theophilos, *Abomination in Matt. 24:15*, 154–156. Ford, *Abomination in Eschatology*, 130–131.

76. Will be delivered. The Hebrew word for "delivered" means to "slip away, be saved, and rescued." https://biblehub.com/hebrew/4422.htm.

1. *Hole's Old and New Testament Commentary* (Daniel 12:1): "This time of great trouble is evidently the time our Lord referred to in His prophetic discourse as the 'great tribulation'," (Matthew 24:21). https://www.studylight.org/commentaries/eng/fbh/daniel-12.html#verse-1-13.

2. *Coffman's Commentary on the Bible* (Daniel 12:1): "Fortunately, this verse is crystal clear in its meaning, thanks to the direct comment of Jesus Christ himself regarding what is here prophesied [Matthew 24:21]," https://www.studylight.org/commentaries/eng/bcc/daniel-12.html#verse-1.

3. *Trapp's Complete Commentary* (Daniel 12:1): "Ver. 1. And at that time,] i.e., In the last days, and toward the end of the world; for in this chapter seemeth to he set forth the state of the Church in the last times, that it shall be most afflicted; yet she shall be fully delivered by Christ's second coming to judgment," https://www.studylight.org/commentaries/eng/jtc/daniel-12.html#verse-1.

77. Matthew 24:29–31.

78. Daniel 12. "Coffman's Commentaries on the Bible," Studylight.org, https://www.studylight.org/commentaries/eng/bcc/daniel-12.html#verse-1.

79. National Human Genome Research Center. "The Human Genome Project." Accessed 2/24/22. https://www.genome.gov/human-genome-project#:~:text=The%20Human%20Genome%20Project%20was,of%20the%20entire%20human%20genome.&text=In%202003%2C%20an%20accurate%20and,than%20the%20original%20estimated%20budget.

80. Hebrew 7227. *Rab.* Biblehub.com, https://biblehub.com/hebrew/7227. htm.

81. Hebrew 7751. *Shuwt.* Biblehub.com, https://biblehub.com/ hebrew/7751.htm.

82. Hebrew 7235. *Rabah.* Biblehub.com, https://biblehub.com/ hebrew/7235.htm.

83. Daniel 12. "Bell's Commentary on the Bible" Studylight.org, https:// www.studylight.org/commentaries/eng/cbb/daniel-12.html#verse-1-13.

84. Lode Star Solutions. "How Fast Is Knowledge Doubling?" Accessed 2/22/22, 2022, "https://lodestarsolutions.com/ keeping-up-with-the-surge-of-information-and-human-knowledge.

85. "By 330 BC, Aristotle coined the Greek term *technologia* and split scientific knowledge into three parts: theoretical science, practical science, and productive science (technology). According to Luna (1994), the earliest use of the word technology in the United States was found in a Harvard University course on the 'application of the Sciences to the Useful Arts' in 1816. The 1832 Encyclopedia Americana defined technology as principles, processes, and nomenclatures." See: San Jose State University in San Jose, CA. "Introduction History of Technology." Accessed 2/22/22, https://www. sjsu.edu/people/patricia.backer/history/introduction.htm.

86. Jürgen Klein, (2012), "Francis Bacon," in Edward N. Zalta (ed.), *The Stanford Encyclopedia of Philosophy* (Winter 2016 ed.), Metaphysics Research Lab, Klein, Jürgen (2012), https://plato.stanford.edu/archives/ win2016/entries/francis-bacon.

87. Daniel 12:4. "Cambridge Bible for Schools and Colleges," Biblehub. com, https://biblehub.com/commentaries/daniel/12-4.htm.

88. (Bacon, 1605, bk. 2, p. 15–15v), as referenced in: Cahiers François Viète. "At the end of the days": Francis Bacon, Daniel 12:4, and the possibility of science, 2019, p.27. https://www.academia.edu/40710926/_ At_the_end_of_the_days_Francis_Bacon_Daniel_12_4_and_the_ possibility_of_science.

89. See the abstract of the initial study of ELS and its established, peer-reviewed scientific and statistical boundaries, as published in: "Statistical Science" 1994, Vol. 9, No. 3, 429–438.

Doron Witztum, Eliyahu Rips, and Yoav Rosenberg. "Equidistant Letter

Sequences in the Book of Genesis: II. The Relation to the Text: Key words and phrases. Genesis, Equidistant letter sequences, Strings of letters, Cylindrical representations, Statistical analysis." Accessed 3/3/22, https://www.math.toronto.edu/~drorbn/Codes/Nations/WRR2/index.html. "ABSTRACT. It has been noted that when the Book of Genesis is written as two-dimensional arrays, equidistant letter sequences spelling words often appear in close proximity with portions of the text which have related meaning. Quantitative tools for measuring this phenomenon are developed. Randomization analysis is done for three samples. For one of them the effect is significant at the level of .000000004."

90. The origins of searching the Bible for the so-called ELS codes actually began in the Middle Ages. So this is certainly not a new speculation. Unbeknownst to many, even Sir Isaac Newton (1642–1747) also spent a sizeable portion of his life seeking for what he considered to be hidden *Bible codes*. Throughout history, many Jewish and Christian scholars have attempted to find hidden or coded messages within the Bible's text. One of the first to describe an ELS in the Bible was the thirteenth-century Rabbi Bachya ben Asher when he discovered a four-letter code relating to the beginning of the Hebrew calendar. See: https://www.linkedin.com/pulse/torah-codes-bible-cardinal-thomas-h-cavin/?trk=read_related_article-card_title.

To this day, Issaac Newton is referred to as the father of modern science. Newton's thinking and discoveries revolutionized our understanding of our world and our existence. He was well accomplished in several important scientific fields, including astronomy, physics, and mathematics. Newton gave the world new theories on gravity, planetary motion, and optics. With the publication of *Philosophiae Naturalis Principia Mathematica* in 1687, he even laid down the groundwork for modern physics. See: Mead, Wendy. "7 Fascinating Facts about Sir Isaac Newton," Biography.com, 5-20-20, https://www.biography.com/news/isaac-newton-biography-facts#:~:text=Sometimes%20called%20the%20father%20of, gravity%2C%20planetary%20motion%20and%20optics.

Newton also placed a great deal of emphasis upon the interpretation of the Book of Revelation, writing generously upon its deep and hidden mysteries, and authored several manuscripts detailing his interpretations

of those mysteries. Newton, Isaac (5 April 2007). "The First Book
Concerning the Language of the Prophets," The Newton Project.
Archived from the original on November 8, 2007.https://web.archive.
org/web/20071108210637/http://www.newtonproject.sussex.ac.uk/texts/
viewtext.php?id=THEM00005&mode=normalized.

91. As a matter of academic integrity of my work in this book, I
have included the link to a lengthy, but easy-to-read publication of
the arguments *against* the overall use of ELS. The article, written by
commentator Don Stewart at the online *Blue Letter Bible* study library,
is found at the link below. As you probably would guess, I disagree with
several of Mr. Stewart's assertions. And, I will set forth my concerns as we
move forward in our study. See: Stewart, Don. "Is There a Secret Code in
Scripture That Proves Its Divine Authority? (The Bible Code) https://www.
blueletterbible.org/Comm/stewart_don/faq/false-views-scripture/question9-
is-there-a-secret-code-in-scripture.cfm.

92. If that ELS code couldn't find the next letter at the proper skip, then
the program would return to the first "c" in the passage and start over with
another skip parameter. The next in line would be a 21-letter skip, and
so on until it found "carl," with each letter appearing at the exact same
skip. Of course, there's always the greater possibility that it would not find
my name at any skip distance whatsoever! The proper use of ELS is very
demanding, as you can see. And those precise demands are exactly why we
must take a closer and studied look when the ELS actually does return a
significant "find" using the proper scientific protocols of discovery.

93. For the purpose of this example, I'm limiting it to only a horizontal
search of the text. However, the official ELS program can also search
vertically and diagonally, as well as forwards and backwards in word
spelling.

94. The Ongoing ELS Research. "The 'great rabbis experiment' was
published in 1994 in the peer-reviewed journal Statistical Science, in the
context of a 'challenging puzzle.' Harold Gans, former Senior Cryptologic
Mathematician for the United States National Security Agency, conducted
another experiment in 1997 where the names of the famous rabbis were
matched against the places of their births and deaths. The results were once
again found to be significant. Bible codes soon became popular due to the

book *The Bible Code* by American journalist Michael Drosnin in 1997, and became a best-seller in many countries. In 2002, Drosnin published another book on the same subject, called *Bible Code II: The Countdown*. Other published books mentioning the Bible Codes include: *The Torah Codes* by Ezra Barany, and *Paranormal Puzzle* by John Griffin II. The main researcher today, Richard Ruff, is based in Australia and has conducted a seminar in Baja California, Mexico. He provides lessons on researching the Torah Codes from Australia." https://www.linkedin.com/pulse/torah-codes-bible-cardinal-thomas-h-cavin/?trk=read_related_article-card_title.

95. Objections to ELS Code: "Many will say that a similar Equidistant Letter Sequence (ELS) code can be found in numerous books with enough words, such as War & Peace or Moby Dick, which may be true in some capacity. However, the major differences between the possibility of these or any other work of literature to have comparable results are minuscule, to say the least. Here are two simple facts of the Torah Code:

"1. No other ELS code can reproduce the insurmountable odds against random occurrence (sometimes 1 in over a million) found in many Torah Code discoveries.

"2. No other ELS contains relatable and relevant terms, with such close proximity to the primary search terms of the most profound discoveries in the Torah Code.

"The most important and world-changing discovery yet, one that all other Torah Code researchers fear the results of, is the identity of the Messiah, who is confirmed in over a thousand Torah Code tables. Still more are found every day."https://www.linkedin.com/pulse/torah-codes-bible-cardinal-thomas-h-cavin/?trk=read_related_article-card_title.

96. Uri Mendel is not his real name. I'm using this randomly chosen name to protect his identity and privacy. The conversation was witnessed by several people in my home. This name represents no one that I know personally, or have ever heard of. All the other facts about the man are true.

97. Michael Drosnin, *The Bible Code*, A Touchstone Book, (NY: Simon & Shuster, 1997, 1998), pp 13–14.

98. Steven Kurutz, "Michael Drosnin, Who Found Clues in the Bible, Is Dead at 74," New York Times, 6/21/20, https://www.bostonglobe.com/

metro/obituaries/2020/06/21/michael-drosnin-who-found-clues-bible-dead/9US5vAD3NrDvhjJyy6MHDJ/story.html.

99. Drosnin, *Bible Code*, p. 99.

100. Drosnin, *Bible Code*, pp. 13–14.

101. Prof. Eliyahu Rips, "Public Statement by Dr. Eliyahu Rips, Professor of Mathematics, Hebrew University, Jerusalem, Israel," as republished online by Torah-Code.org, Jerusalem, Israel, 6/3/97.
Read Dr. Rips' rebuttal here: http://www.torah-code.org/controversy/rips_statement.pdf.

102. "Quantum mechanics, the basic mathematical framework that underpins it all, which was first developed in the modern quantum mechanics was born in 1925 by Niels Bohr, Werner Heisenberg, Erwin Schrödinger, and others."
David A. Edwards, (1979). "The Mathematical Foundations of Quantum Mechanics," Synthese. Springer Science and Business Media LLC. 42 (1): 1–70.
David A. Edwards, (1981). "Mathematical Foundations of Quantum Field Theory: Fermions, Gauge Fields, and Supersymmetry Part I: Lattice Field Theories," *International Journal of Theoretical Physics*. Springer Science and Business Media LLC. 20 (7): 503–517.

103. The word "quanta"—or its singular, "quantum"—is Latin for "how much." It is where we get our words "quantity" and "quantitative," for example.

104. Martin Gardner and John Archibald Wheeler, "Quantum Theory and Quack Theory," *New York Review*, 5/17, 79, https://www.nybooks.com/articles/1979/05/17/quantum-theory-and-quack-theory.

105. Matter: For a thing to be considered matter, it has to have a measurable degree of mass and it has to take up space. For example, some "things" like gravity and electromagnetism truly do exist. But these are best described as "forces." They have no measurable degree of mass, nor do they occupy quantities of measurable space.

106. "The Atom Builder Guide to Elementary Particles." Accessed 3/12/22. https://www.pbs.org/wgbh/aso/tryit/atom/elempartp.html#:~:text=Atoms%20are%20constructed%20of%20two,make%20up%20an%20atom's%20nucleus.

See also: Britannica. "Subatomic Particle," accessed 3/11/22, https://www.britannica.com/science/subatomic-particle.

107. "More than 200 subatomic particles have been detected—most of them highly unstable, existing for less than a millionth of a second—as a result of collisions produced in cosmic ray reactions or particle accelerator experiments." Britannica. "Subatomic Particle." Accessed 3/11/22, https://www.britannica.com/science/subatomic-particle.

108. Lawrence M. Krauss. https://www.brainyquote.com/quotes/lawrence_m_krauss_526729?src=t_quantum_mechanics.

109. Richard Webb, "Quantum Physics: Our Best Basic Picture of How Particles Interact to Make the World," New Scientist. Accessed 3/11/22, https://www.newscientist.com/definition/quantum-physics/#ixzz7NBER4pzG.

110. Matt Hunter, "The Quantum Computing Era Is Here. Why It Matters—And How It May Change Our World," *Forbes,* 1/16/20. https://www.forbes.com/sites/ibm/2020/01/16/the-quantum-computing-era-is-here-why-it-mattersand-how-it-may-change-our-world/?sh=3f0184545c2b.

111. Physics World, "Quantum Research Update: Quantum computer is smallest ever, claim physicists," physicsworld.com, 7/7/21, https://physicsworld.com/a/quantum-computer-is-smallest-ever-claim-physicists.
See also: Brooke Singman, "Biden to Sign Executive Order, national security memo to advance quantum technologies: Biden admin pushes to 'protect against this quantum computing threat tomorrow,'" Fox News, 5/4/22, https://www.foxnews.com/politics/biden-executive-order-national-security-memo-quantum-technologies.

112. Electromagnetism is the study of the electromagnetic force, one of the four fundamental forces of nature. The electromagnetic force pushes or pulls anything that has an electric charge, like electrons and protons. It includes the electric force, which pushes all charged particles, and the magnetic force, which only pushes moving charges…. Electromagnetic radiation is thought to be both a particle and a wave. This is because it sometimes acts like a particle and sometimes acts like a wave. To make things easier we can think of an electromagnetic wave as a stream of photons. A photon is an elementary particle, meaning that it cannot be

broken down into smaller particles. It is the particle that light is made up of. Photons also make up all other types of electromagnetic radiation such as gamma rays, X-rays, and UV rays.

For a layman's explanation, see: https://simple.wikipedia.org/wiki/Electromagnetism.

113. Oregon State, Science Dept. "What Keeps the Nucleus Together?" accessed 3/10/22, http://sites.science.oregonstate.edu/chemistry/courses/ch121-3s/ch121/Answers%20to%20interesting%20questions/What%20Keeps%20the%20Nucleus%20Together.pdf.

114. University of Chicago, "Electromagnetic Force." Accessed 3/10/22, https://ecuip.lib.uchicago.edu/multiwavelength-astronomy/astrophysics/05.html.

115. The Paradox: Is light really matter? (my answer):

1. Generally speaking, many physicists assert that it would be better to define light as "a force of energy" rather than as actual matter. Light is electromagnetic radiation. The purist definition of matter is anything that has mass and takes up space. Light has neither of these properties. However, the energy force of light does indeed solidify the atomic elements and hold them together so that matter can be formed. In this regard, light and matter are practically inseparable. Light is more of a form of energy, not necessarily a pure form of matter. Matter is made up of atoms, held together by the energy of light (photons).

For more study, see: "Is Light Matter?" (answer 3), University of California Santa Barbara (UCSB), 1/20/04, http://scienceline.ucsb.edu/getkey.php?key=512#:~:text=Light%20is%20a%20form%20of,Light%20is%20actually%20electromagnetic%20radiation.

2. *Nova Science*: $E = mc2$. It's the world's most famous equation, but what does it really mean? 'Energy equals mass times the speed of light squared.' On the most basic level, the equation says that energy and mass (matter) are interchangeable; they are different forms of the same thing. Under the right conditions, energy can become mass, and vice versa. We humans don't see them that way—how can a beam of light and a walnut, say, be different forms of the same thing?—but Nature does." "Einstein's Big Idea," PBS.org. Accessed 3/12/22, https://www.pbs.org/wgbh/nova/einstein/lrk-hand-

emc2expl.html#:~:text=%22Energy%20equals%20mass%20times%20 the,become%20mass%2C%20and%20vice%20versa.

116. Ibid., PBS' *Nova Science*.

117. Brian Koberlein, "How Are Energy and Matter the Same?" Universetoday.com, 11/26/12, https://www.universetoday.com/116615/ how-are-energy-and-matter-the-same.

Following is a peer review assessment of Koberlein's article, in the comment section:

Roto (avatar name)

November 27, 2014, 1:50 AM

Nice article Brian. As a physicist, I like seeing mind expanding articles to encourage young people to think about things they may not have. I would add that relativistic mass, and the inertia resulting therefrom, is quite different from rest mass and inertia resulting from that. They are in fact independent and additive. Also, I think mentioning Einstein's theory of [General Relativity] is great and it certainly links space and time to mass and energy.

For a much more detailed expose of the concept of "frozen light" see the following:

Dr. John D. Norton, "Chasing a Beam of Light: Einstein's Most Famous Thought Experiment," Department of History and Philosophy of Science, University of Pittsburgh. Accessed 3/13/022, https://sites.pitt. edu/~jdnorton/Goodies/Chasing_the_light.

118. Hebrews 11:3, "Ellicott's Commentary for English Readers," Biblehub.com, https://biblehub.com/commentaries/hebrews/11-3.htm. Also see: *Cambridge Bible for Schools and Colleges*. "A somewhat harsh way of expressing that 'the visible world did not derive its existence from anything [physically perceptible].' In other words, the clause denies the pre-existence of matter. It says that the world was made out of nothing.... showing that [creation's] first object must be a Divine and Infinite Creator." https://biblehub.com/commentaries/hebrews/11-3.htm.

119. Rajat Kumar Pradhan, "Is It Possible to View any Sub-atomic Particles Like Electron, Proton, or Neutron?" Accessed 3/11/22. https://www. researchgate.net/post/Is_it_possible_to_view_any_sub-atomic_particles_

like_electron_proton_or_neutron/52fa267ed4c1182c728b45bd/citation/
download.

120. Matthew 5:14–16.

121. Colossians 1:17, "Ellicott's Commentary for English Readers,"
Biblehub.com, https://biblehub.com/commentaries/colossians/1-17.htm.

122. Colossians 1:17, "Meyer's New Testament Commentary," Biblehub.
com, https://biblehub.com/commentaries/colossians/1-17.htm.

123. Colossians 1:17, "Jamieson-Fausset-Brown Bible Commentary,"
Biblehub.com, https://biblehub.com/commentaries/colossians/1-17.htm.

124. See Job 38:1–7. Also see my books, *Gods and Thrones*, *Gods of the
Final Kingdom*, and *Gods of Ground Zero* for an in-depth understanding of
what the Bible actually says about this amazing truth.

125. *Meyer's New Testament Commentary*: "Luke relates an involuntary
removal of Philip effected by the Spirit of God (νοίρυκ). Comp. 2
Corinthians 12:2; 2 Corinthians 12:4; 1 Thessalonians 4:17; Ezekiel 3:14;
1 Kings 18:12; 2 Kings 2:16. The Spirit snatched him away (comp. John
6:15), in which act not only the impulse and the impelling power, but also
the mode, is conceived of as miraculous."

126. For examples from the Old and New Testaments. see Daniel 10 and
Ephesians 6.

127. Eugene Lim, "The Theory of Parallel Universes Is Not Just Math—
It is science that can be tested," PHYS.org, 9/3/15, https://phys.org/
news/2015-09-theory-parallel-universes-maths-science.html.
Also see this: "When someone mentions 'different dimensions,' we tend to
think of things like parallel universes—alternate realities that exist parallel
to our own.… However, the reality of dimensions and how they play a role
in the ordering of our Universe is really quite different from this popular
characterization.… We are immediately aware of the three dimensions
that surround us on a daily basis—those that define the length, width, and
depth of all objects in our universes. Beyond these three visible dimensions,
scientists believe that there may be many more. In fact, the theoretical
framework of Superstring Theory posits that the universe exists in ten
different dimensions." Matt Williams, "A Universe of 10 Dimensions,"
12/11/14, phys.org, https://phys.org/news/2014-12-universe-dimensions.
html.

128. Nearly a century ago, Edwin Hubble's discovery of red-shifting of light from galaxies in all directions from our own suggested that space itself was getting bigger.… Hubble's discovery implied that the cosmos exists in more than the three dimensions we're familiar with in everyday life…. We don't see or feel more dimensions; nevertheless, theoretical physics predicts that they should exist. David Warmflash, "Three Totally Mind-bending Implications of a Multidimensional Universe," *Discover Magazine*, 12/04/14, http://blogs. discovermagazine.com/crux/2014/12/04/multidimensional-universe/#. W9uSRJNKhdg.

129. Dr. Kaku holds the Henry Semat Chair and Professorship in theoretical physics and a joint appointment at City College of New York and the Graduate Center of City University of New York.

130. Micho Kaku, "Nobel Prize Awarded to Two Quantum Physicists," *Big Think*, 10/10/12, https://bigthink.com/dr-kakus-universe/ nobel-prize-awarded-to-two-quantum-physicists.

131. CERN is the European Organization for Nuclear Research. The name CERN is derived from the acronym for the French *Conseil Européen pour la Recherche Nucléaire*, a provisional body founded in 1952 with the mandate of establishing a world-class fundamental physics research organization in Europe. https://en.wikipedia.org/wiki/CERN.

132. Ibid.

133. Adam Milton-Barker, "How CERN Plan to Use the Large Hadron Collider to Open Portals to Other Dimensions, and Possibly Already Have." Techbubble.info, 5/4/15, https://www.techbubble.info/blog/ quantum-physics/entry/how-cern-plan-to-use-the-large-hydrogen-collider-to-open-portals-to-other-dimensions.

134. Lewis Page, "'Something May Come Through' Dimensional 'Doors' at LHC," The Register, 10/6/09, https://www.theregister. co.uk/2009/11/06/lhc_dimensional_portals. This Bertolucci quote was reported all over the Internet, including through *Charisma Magazine* and *Breaking Israel News*. I am not aware of any reputable source that claims Bertolucci or CERN denies the veracity of the quote.

135. Corey S. Powell, "Scientists Are Searching for a Mirror Universe. It Could Be Sitting Right in Front of You," nbcnews.com, 6/30/2019, https://

www.nbcnews.com/mach/science/scientists-are-searching-mirror-universe-it-could-be-sitting-right-ncna1023206.

136. Juliana Kim, "The Large Hadron Collider Will Embark on a Third Run to Uncover More Cosmic Secrets," NPR, 7/5/22, https://www.npr.org/2022/07/05/1109742531/cern-large-hadron-collider.

137. Robert Lea, "Dark Matter Could Be a Cosmic Relic from Extra Dimensions," Live Science, 4/9/22, https://www.livescience.com/dark-matter-particles-from-extra-dimensions.

138. Juliana Kim, "Large Hadron Collider Will Embark on a Third Run."

139. *Talk of the Nation*, "Resetting the Theory of Time," NPR, 5/17/13, https://www.npr.org/2013/05/17/184775924/resetting-the-theory-of-time.

140. Gabriel Popkin, "Einstein's 'spooky action at a distance' Spotted in Objects almost Big Enough to See: Entangled Electronic Devices Could Help Scientists Make a Quantum Internet," Science.org, 4/25/18. https://www.science.org/content/article/einstein-s-spooky-action-distance-spotted-objects-almost-big-enough-see#:~:text=Albert%20Einstein%20colorfully%20dismissed%20quantum,to%20a%20satellite%20in%20space.

141. Karl Tate, "How Quantum Entanglement Works (Infographic)" Live Science, 4/8/13, https://www.livescience.com/28550-how-quantum-entanglement-works-infographic.html.

142. *Universitat Autonoma de Barcelona*, "Record Quantum Entanglement of Multiple Dimensions," phys.org, 3/27/14, https://phys.org/news/2014-03-quantum-entanglement-multiple-dimensions.html.

143. Micho Kaku, "4 Things That Currently Break the Speed of Light Barrier," *Big Think*, 11/9/10, https://bigthink.com/dr-kakus-universe/what-travels-faster-than-the-speed-of-light.

144. Marina Alamanou. "The Applications of Quantum Entanglement," Data Drive Investor, 6/20/29. https://www.datadriveninvestor.com/2019/06/20/quantum-entanglement.

145. "It sounds preposterous that electrons and atoms can be in many states at the same time, but this is the foundation of modern civilizations. [The theory] has been tested to 1 part in 100 billion in accuracy, making it the most successful physical theory of all time.... The idea that you can be in many places at the same time can be proven indirectly, by looking at the

properties of many atoms, but testing it on single atoms and single photons was beyond reach. Until now.

Micho Kaku, "Nobel Prize Awarded to Two Quantum Physicists," *Big Think*, 10/10/12, https://bigthink.com/dr-kakus-universe/nobel-prize-awarded-to-two-quantum-physicists.

146. Hebrews 11.

147. "They will look upon me, whom they will pierce…".

1. *Cambridge Bible for Schools and Colleges:* "The Speaker is Almighty God. …They pierced Him, literally and as the crowning act of their contumacy, in the Person of His Son upon the Cross, John 19:37. Comp. Revelation 1:7."

2. *Pulpit Commentary:* "There was a literal fulfilment of this piercing, i.e. slaying (Zechariah 13:3; Lamentations 4:9), when the Jews crucified the Messiah, him who was God and Man, and of whom, as a result of the hypostatic union, the properties of one nature are often predicated of the other. Thus St. Paul says that the Jews crucified "the Lord of glory" (1 Corinthians 2:8), and bids the Ephesian elders "feed the Church of God, which he hath purchased with his own blood," (Acts 20:28).

For the foregoing quotes from the *Cambridge* and Pulpit commentaries, see: zechariah 12:10, "Commentaries," Biblehub.com, https://biblehub.com/commentaries/zechariah/12-10.htm.

148. Zechariah 12:10

1. *Cambridge Bible for Schools and Colleges:* "The Speaker is Almighty God…. They pierced Him, literally [it was "literally" the Almighty, not metaphorically] and as the crowning act of their contumacy, in the Person [in flesh and blood] of His Son upon the Cross, John 19:37. Comp. Revelation 1:7. Zechariah 12:10. https://biblehub.com/commentaries/zechariah/12-10.htm.

2. *Pulpit Commentary:* "The Speaker is Jehovah. But there was a literal fulfilment of this piercing, i.e. slaying (Zechariah 13:3; Lamentations 4:9), when the Jews crucified the Messiah, him who was God and Man, and of whom, as a result of the hypostatic union [the union of the divine and human natures into one singular being—at one time], the properties of one nature are often predicated of the other." https://biblehub.com/commentaries/zcchariah/12-10.htm.

3. *Jamieson-Fausset-Brown Bible Commentary*: "The change of person is due to Jehovah-Messiah [Yahweh in the flesh *is* Messiah, and Messiah *is* Yahweh existing with humanity in the flesh!] speaking in His own person first, then the prophet speaking of Him…. The Hebrew word is always used of a literal piercing (so Zechariah 13:3); not of a metaphorical piercing."

4. *Gill's Exposition of the Entire Bible:* "The Messiah here prophesied of appears to be **both God and man**; a divine Person called **Jehovah**, who is **all along speaking in the context,** and in the text itself; for none else could pour out the spirit of grace and supplication; **and yet he must be man, to be pierced**; and the same is spoken of, that would do the one, and suffer the other; and therefore **must be the or God-man in one person**…. And as for the change from the first person to the third, this is **not at all unusual** in Scripture."

https://biblehub.com/commentaries/zechariah/12-10.htm.

149. James Burton Coffman (May 24, 1905–June 30, 2006) was known for his exhaustive writing and study of Old Testament and New Testament Scriptures. Throughout his life he served as a preacher, teacher, author of biblical commentaries, and community leader. Most of his career defined him as a teacher and administrator in school systems, congregational contexts, and as a military chaplain.

150. Zechariah 12:10, "Coffman Commentaries on the Bible," Studylight. org, https://www.studylight.org/commentary/zechariah/12-10.html.

151. Dr. Constable, contemporary to the writing of this book, is the founder of Dallas Seminary's Field Education department (1970) and the Center for Biblical Studies (1973), both of which he directed for many years before assuming other responsibilities. He served as senior professor of Bible exposition, Dallas Theological Seminary. https://www.logos.com/ search?filters=author-15793_Author&sortBy=Relevance&limit=30&page= 1&ownership=all&geographicAvailability=all.

152. Zechariah 12:10. "Expository Notes of Dr. Thomas Constable," Studylight.org, https://www.studylight.org/commentary/zechariah/12-10. html.

153. This apparent conundrum is called "hypostatic union" in the theological scholarship.

"At no time did Jesus ever cease to be God. Although He was made fully human, there was never a point when He abrogated His divine nature (see Luke 6:5, 8). It is equally true that, after becoming incarnate, the Son has never ceased to be human. As the apostle Paul wrote, 'For there is one God, and there is one mediator between God and men, the man Christ Jesus' (1 Timothy 2:5, emphasis added). Jesus is not half-human and half-divine. Rather, He is Theanthropos, the God-man. The Lord Jesus Christ is one eternally divine Person who will forever possess two distinct yet inseparable natures: one divine and one human."

"How Can Jesus Be Both God and Man at the Same Time?" Got Questions. A=accessed 3/18/21, https://www.gotquestions.org/Jesus-God-man.html.

154. I am certainly not suggesting that somehow God has to work through "quantum mechanics" to accomplish His miraculous works and manifestations, including the phenomenon of "prayer." What I am saying is this: If quantum physics shows us the distinct possibility of these phenomena occurring through known scientific principles, then surely, God, who created the principles of quantum physics in the first place, could also do these same things within the nature of His very being if He so desiredo.

155. The word "Jesus," as we vocalize it in today's English, comes from the Latin *Iesus*, which is a transliteration of the Greek *Iesous*, which in turn is a transliteration of the Aramaic *Yeshua*. And, the Aramaic *Yeshua* comes from the oldest Hebrew form *Yehoshua*—or, as it would be pronounced in English, *Joshua*. Our use of the Aramaic word *Yeshua* comes from the Hebrew verb *yasha*, which means "he saves" joined with the proper name *Ya*, which is short for the name *Yahweh*. Put together, Jesus' name, Yeshua, in its original languages, means "Yahweh saves" or "Yahweh is salvation" or simply "salvation."

Hebrew Streams, "The Hebrew Meaning of Jesus," Hebrew-Streams.com. Accessed 5/23/28.http://www.hebrew-streams.org/frontstuff/jesus-yeshua.html.

156. Deuteronomy 32:15, a prophecy.

Benson Commentary: "Moses here, transported in his mind to future scenes, speaks in the prophetic style, which often represents future events as actually present, or already past, to denote the certainty of the things foretold...."

As if he had said, I see the time approaching when they shall notoriously abuse the goodness of God, and behave with the utmost ingratitude toward the Author of all their mercies." https://biblehub.com/commentaries/deuteronomy/32-15.htm.

157. See: Romans 14:11; Philippians 2:10.

158. Romans 10:8–17.

159. See Revelation 1:7, 19:7, 21:2, 9, 22:17.

160. See Matthew 21:1–5. See also the *New American Standard Bible* translation of this passage: "Rejoice greatly, daughter of Zion! Shout in triumph, daughter of Jerusalem! Behold, your king is coming to you; He is righteous and endowed with salvation, [Yasha] Humble, and mounted on a donkey, Even on a colt, the foal of a donkey." https://biblehub.com/zechariah/9-9.htm.

Yasha—*NAS Exhaustive Concordance* ("savior," "endowed with salvation," "salvation"). https://biblehub.com/hebrew/3467.htm.

161. "Redeemer" is a synonym for "Savior" and "Jesus." https://thesaurus.yourdictionary.com/redeemer.

162. David Bivin, "The Amidah Prayer," CBN. Accessed 5/11/18, http://www1.cbn.com/biblestudy/the-amidah-prayer.

163. Jewish Virtual Library, "Jewish Prayers: The Amidah." Accessed 3/22/22. https://www.jewishvirtuallibrary.org/the-amidah.

164. At this point you might wonder how the Jewish people could miss a revelation as simple and obvious as the one we have been examining. Just like in the days of Jesus' earthly ministry, most of the fault lies at the feet of the Orthodox rabbis. They discourage, or even forbid their people to read and interpret the Scriptures on their own. So, the people simply recite approved liturgy, Scriptures, and rabbinical writings. They don't know, or understand, the Scriptures as deeply as most readers of this book do. Additionally, many centuries ago, the rabbis devised a way to "hide" the name Yeshua from the Jewish people—as the true Messiah. They arranged another word to be used in the place of Jesus/Yeshua. The word is *Yeshu*. They claim this is the "real" Christian Messiah. They claim that *yeshua* simply is the Hebrew word for salvation—nothing more—and that the Christians stole or co-opted that word and name.

The word *Yeshu* is actually a derogatory Hebrew acronym. Each of its letters makes up a sentence that expresses the declaration: "May His Name Forever Be Cursed." See the book, The Rabbi, the Secret Message, and the Identity of Messiah (Crane, MO: Defender, year of pub) that Messianic Rabbi Zev Porat (Tel Aviv, Israel) and I wrote. There are several in-depth chapters in that book verifying these truth, and greatly expanding upon this topic.

165. Proto-Sinaitic: "Proto-Sinaitic, the North Semitic alphabet, or Early Alphabetic, is considered the earliest trace of alphabetic writing and the common ancestor of both the Ancient South Arabian script and the Phoenician alphabet. These are the scripts that led to many modern alphabets of the world."

1. Yosef Garfinkel; Mitka R. Golub; Haggai Misgav; Saar (Ganor, May 2015), "The ʾIšbaʿal Inscription from Khirbet Qeiyafa." Bulletin of the American Schools of Oriental Research. 373 (373): 217–233.

2. "North Semitic alphabet," Encyclopedia Britannica. Accessed 2/12/22. https://www.britannica.com/topic/North-Semitic-alphabet.

3. C. Rollston (2020), "The Emergence of Alphabetic Scripts," in R. Hasselbach-Andee (ed.), A Companion to Ancient Near Eastern Languages (1st ed., pp. 65–81). Wiley.

4. "Sinaitic inscriptions | ancient writing," Encyclopedia Britannica. Accessed 3/14/22, https://www.britannica.com/topic/Sinaitic-inscriptions.

5. "Earliest Known Hebrew Text in Proto-Canaanite Script Discovered in Area Where 'David Slew Goliath'," Science Daily. 11/3/08. https://www.sciencedaily.com/releases/2008/11/081103091035.htm.

6. "Proto-Sinaitic script," Wikipedia. Accessed 3/22/22, https://en.wikipedia.org/wiki/Proto-Sinaitic_script.

166. There are, however, experts in the ancient languages of the world that believe the Hebrew alphabet may actually prove to be the oldest of all known alphabets. That would include, they claim, even those that are presently dated to have preexisted the Hebrew. Of course, those discoveries are also disputed by a bevy of other renowned experts, but it's still a fascinating possibility to consider.

Is Hebrew the oldest language? See the following:

1. Fox News. Walt Bonner, "Hebrew May Be World's Oldest Alphabet," Foxnews.com, 12/5/16, https://www.foxnews.com/science/hebrew-may-be-worlds-oldest-alphabet.

2. Bruce Bower, "Oldest Alphabet Identified as Hebrew," Science News, 11/19/16, https://www.sciencenews.org/article/oldest-alphabet-identified-hebrew.

3. *Times of India*. "[Hebrew] Oldest Language of the World," 5/13/20, https://timesofindia.indiatimes.com/readersblog/whatsup-university/oldest-language-of-the-world-19460.

167. Paleo-Hebrew:

1. Robin Ngo, "Computer Program Learning to Read Paleo-Hebrew Letters," *Biblical Archeology*, 4/30/ 15, https://www.biblicalarchaeology.org/daily/biblical-artifacts/inscriptions/computer-program-learning-to-read-paleo-hebrew-letters.

2. "Paleo-Hebrew Alphabet:"

"Palaeo-Hebrew, Proto-Hebrew or Old Hebrew, is the writing system found in Canaanite inscriptions from the region of biblical Israel and Judah. It is considered to be the script used to record the original texts of the Hebrew Bible due to its similarity to the Samaritan script, as the Talmud stated that the Hebrew ancient script was still used by the Samaritans," https://en.wikipedia.org/wiki/Paleo-Hebrew_alphabet.

3. Modern Hebrew development: "Between the 6th and the 2nd century BCE, Classical, or Square, Hebrew gradually displaced the Aramaic alphabet, which had replaced Early Hebrew in Palestine. Square Hebrew became established in the 2nd and 1st centuries BCE and developed into the Modern Hebrew alphabet over the next 1,500 years. It was apparently derived from the Aramaic alphabet rather than from Early Hebrew but was nonetheless strongly influenced by the Early Hebrew script."Accessed 2/21/22, https://www.britannica.com/topic/Hebrew-alphabet.

4. Yehuda Shurpin, "What Is the Authentic Ancient Hebrew Alphabet?: Ketav Ivri vs. Ketav Ashurit," Chabad.org. Accessed 3/13/22, https://www.chabad.org/library/article_cdo/aid/3582435/jewish/What-Is-the-Authentic-Ancient-Hebrew-Alphabet.htm.

"[The currently used Hebrew script], ketav Ashurit ("Assyrian script"), is the one we know today as the Hebrew alphabet."

168. Rabbi Aaron L. Raskin, "Ayin: The Sxteenth Letter of the Hebrew Alphabet," Chabad.org. Accessed 4/12/22, https://www.chabad.org/library/article_cdo/aid/137088/jewish/Ayen.htm.

169. Some Hebrew names have mystical-spiritual meanings: "Each letter in the Hebrew alphabet (Aleph-Bet) has both a literal and mystical [spiritual/transcendent] meaning. This means that each name has a mystical [spiritual/transcendent] significance, based on the letters which form the name," Yigal Tzadka, "The Book of Hebrew Letters," hebrewtoday.com. Accessed 5/3/22, https://hebrewtoday.com/product/the-book-of-hebrew-letters.

170. "The principal debate is between an early date, around 1850 BC, and a late date, around 1550 BC. The choice of one or the other date decides whether it is proto-Sinaitic or proto-Canaanite, and by extension locates the invention of the alphabet in Egypt or Canaan respectively." F. Simons, "Proto-Sinaitic—Progenitor of the Alphabet," Rosetta 9 (2011): 16–40, http://www.rosetta.bham.ac.uk/issue_09/simons_alphabet.pdf.

Still being found today" "From a Dec 2019 excavation in the Holy Land—a folded lead table from Mt. Ebal was discovered. This is the oldest form of Hebrew alphabet...that predated the Paleo-Hebrew—a Canaanite script. YHWH found twice in this tablet. Only the Israelites in the ancient world worshipped YHWH. Older than Dead Sea Scrolls by more than a thousand years. Fox 26, Isiah Carey, "The Hebrew Curse Tablet." Accessed 4/10/22, https://twitter.com/derekcaraway/status/1512610998032732160.

171. The ancient Semitic/Hebrew language did have *meanings* attached to each letter, and those ancient meanings are still used and studied by a number of Hebrew people today. For further study, see the following resources:

1) Michael Handelzalts, "In the Beginning: The Origins of the Hebrew Alphabet," Haaretz, 8/4/13, https://www.haaretz.com/jewish/.premium-why-hebrew-should-be-called-jewish-1.5316745. "The names of the Hebrew *letters have meaning* in the Hebrew language. That doesn't actually matter when writing or reading, but it is nice to know."

2. Dr. George W. Benthien. "The Hebrew Language And Way of Thinking," January 2013. Accessed 2/23/22, https://gbenthien.net/assets/docs/Hebrew.pdf.

3. Hebrew Alphabet Letter Meanings: Based upon the notes and understandings from studying with Kabbalist Samuel Avital. "Hebrew Alphabet Letter Meanings." Accessed 3/12/22, http://www.

walkingkabbalah.com/hebrew-alphabet-letter-meanings.
(Note: While I do not put stock in the mystical Kabbalistic practices
of Orthodox Judaism, I include this reference as attestation that the
"letter meaning" phenomenon is widely recognized even among the
most conservative Orthodox Jews and has been studied, interpreted, and
practiced for well over one thousand years. This is an important refutation
to some detractors who claim there is no such phenomenon attached to the
Hebrew alphabet, modern or ancient.)
4. Bible Lexicons: Ancient Hebrew Alphabet.
Study Light Bible Study Site: "Ancient Hebrew Alphabet." https://www.
studylight.org/lexicons/eng/hebrew/ahl_alphabet.html. © 1999–2013;
Ancient Hebrew Research Center. Old Testament Hebrew Lexical
Dictionary developed by Jeff Garrison for StudyLight.org. Copyright
1999–2022. All Rights Reserved, Jeff Garrison, Gdansk, Poland.
5. Rabbi Dan Cohn-Sherbok, "Creation Mysticism: Fashioning the World
from Letters," My Jewish Learning publication. Accessed 3/13/22, https://
www.myjewishlearning.com/article/creation-mysticism-fashioning-the-
world-from-letters. (*My Jewish Learning* was launched in 2003 and is now
a part of 70 Faces Media, the largest nonprofit, nondenominational Jewish
media organization in North America.)
6. Bruce K. Waltke; M. O'Connor (1990), *An Introduction to Biblical
Hebrew Syntax*. (Winona Lake, Indiana: Eisenbrauns) p. 83.
7. Aren M. Wilson-Wright, "On Origin of Alphabetic Writing," Radboud
University, Nijmegen. November 2019, https://bibleinterp.arizona.edu/
sites/bibleinterp.arizona.edu/files/images/On%20the%20Origin%20
of%20Alphabetic%20Writing.pdf.
172. 8. *Hebrew Today*, "The Hebrew Alphabet—The Letter
Shin (ש)." Accessed 4/8/22, https://hebrewtoday.com/alphabet/
the-letter-shin-%D7%A9/.
9. Tzvi Freeman, "KabAlefBet! The Kabbalah of every one of the letters of
the Hebrew alphabet." Accessed April 2, 2022, https://www.chabad.org/
multimedia/video_cdo/aid/829340/jewish/KabAlefBet.htm.
This site details the modern interpretations of the ancient Hebrew letter
meanings, studied for generations among the Orthodox Hebrew people.
10. Messianic Rabbi Zev Porat was born and raised in Israel and speaks

Hebrew as his native language. His father was a renowned rabbi in Israel and the United States. His grandfather and great-grandfather were also renowned rabbis in the land of Israel. Zev attended and completed Yeshiva training and became a certified Sanhedrin rabbi. He gave up that certification when he became a born-again believer in Yeshua. His website is: www.messiahofisraelministries.com.

Rabbi Zev says: "The ancient Hebrew pictographs were having a much larger impact in witnessing to the Jewish people about Yeshua than I had imagined. I politely told [the rabbis who didn't want me to teach them] that I would continue to use the teaching—after all, it is a historical fact of our own language, dating back thousands of years!" See the chapter in this book titled "A Rabbi Speaks" for this quote and others about Hebrew pictograms.

11. Jonathan Chadwick, "Has the 'Missing Link' in the History of the ALPHABET Been Discovered?" *Daily Mail*, 4/14/22, https://www.dailymail.co.uk/sciencetech/article-9470949/Archaeologists-missing-link-early-alphabet.html.

See this image of the archeologically confirmed ancient Semitic languages with attached *letter meanings*...and the evolution of the alphabet. https://i.dailymail.co.uk/1s/2021/04/15/08/37731400-9470949-Detailed_the_process_that_she_thinks_the_Canaanites_used_to_get_-a-61_1618470347913.jpg.

12. Tzvi Freeman, "The Kabbalah [mystical meaning] of Every One of the Letters of the Hebrew Alphabet," https://www.chabad.org/multimedia/video_cdo/aid/829340/jewish/KabAlefBet.htm.

Haaretz is an Israeli newspaper founded in 1918, making it the longest-running newspaper currently in print in Israel. It is now published in both Hebrew and English in the Berliner format. https://en.wikipedia.org/wiki/Haaretz.

173. Michael Handelzalts, "In the Beginning: The Origins of the Hebrew Alphabet," *Haaretz*, 8/4/13, https://www.haaretz.com/jewish/.premium-why-hebrew-should-be-called-jewish-1.5316745.kyeoj.

174. "Hebrew Today is a reputable publication house, specializing in the highly professional and unique fusion of linguistics and journalism. Our products are developed and written by professionals in the fields of education, linguistics, and the Hebrew language.... Many teachers use our

newspapers to teach Hebrew both in classes and in private lessons, because they find that we offer an easy and effective way to learn the Hebrew alphabet and grammar." "Who We Are," HebrewToday.com. Accessed 4/21/22. https://hebrewtoday.com/company-overview.

Also see: https://hebrewtoday.com/content-our-approach-learning-hebrew.

175. "The Hebrew Alphabet—The Letter Aleph," Hebrewtoday. com. Accessed 4/12/22, https://hebrewtoday.com/alphabet/the-letter-alef-%D7%90.

176. Yigal Tzadka, "The Book of Hebrew Letters," HebrewToday. com. Accessed 5/3/22, https://hebrewtoday.com/product/the-book-of-hebrew-letters.

177. "The New Larned History: For Ready Reference Reading and Research," Volume 1, archived by Microsoft Corporation, 2007. Accessed 4/12/22, https://archive.org/details/newlarnedhistory01larnuoft/page/224/mode/2up.

Dr. George Benthien worked for 40 years at the Navy's Spawar Laboratory. He received a PhD in mathematics from Carnegie Mellon University specializing in continuum mechanics. Dr. Benthien was the co-developer of the Chief program for calculating the acoustic radiation or scattering from arbitrary shaped objects. All writings and works of Dr. George Benthien can be found at: https://gbenthien.net/ (Mathematics, Acoustics, Fortran String Utilities, and Science & Faith).

178. Dr. George W. Benthien, "The Hebrew Language and Way of Thinking," January 2013. Accessed 2/23/22, https://gbenthien.net/assets/docs/Hebrew.pdf.

See the original source of Dr. Benthien's attestation: "The New Larned History: For Ready Reference Reading and Research, Volume 1, archived by Microsoft Corporation, 2007, accessed April 12, 2022, https://archive.org/details/newlarnedhistory01larnuoft/page/224/mode/2up.

179. Alexander Poltorak, "History and Customs," Chabad.org. Accessed 4/12/22, https://www.chabad.org/library/article_cdo/aid/310887/jewish/History-and-Customs.htm.

180. "Mezuzah, also spelled Mezuza (Hebrew: "doorpost"), plural Mezuzoth, Mezuzot, Mezuzahs, or Mezuzas, small folded or rolled parchment inscribed by a qualified calligraphist with scriptural verses

(Deuteronomy 6:4–9, 11:13–21) to remind Jews of their obligations toward God. The parchment is placed in a metal, wooden, or glass case so that the word Shaddai ("Almighty") can usually be seen on the back of the parchment. After a special blessing is recited, the mezuzah is firmly fixed to the main doorpost of the home (to the right as one enters). It is a custom with some Jews to kiss the mezuzah as they pass it." Encyclopedia Britannica, "Mezuzah: Judaism." Accessed 4/8/22, https://www.britannica.com/topic/mezuzah.

181. "The Hebrew Alphabet—The Letter Shin (ש)." Accessed 4//8/22, https://hebrewtoday.com/alphabet/the-letter-shin-%D7%A9.

182. Conroy Cole, "Hebrew Numeration." Accessed 3/15/22, https://www.academia.edu/34711733/HEBREW_NUMERATION.

183. Revelation 13:18

1. *Expositor's Commentary*: "[John] invites his readers to count the name or number of the Beast, i.e., to calculate a name whose letters, numerically valued on the…principles of Gematria, would amount to 666… Gematria, which, using Greek and Hebrew letters to denote numbers, could often turn a name into a suggestive cipher." https://biblehub.com/commentaries/revelation/13-18.htm.

2. *Barnes' Notes on the Bible:* "There can be no doubt that the number 666 is the correct reading, though it would seem that this was sometimes expressed in letters, and sometimes written in full." https://biblehub.com/commentaries/revelation/13-18.htm.

184. This chapter and the next two draw heavily from my book, *The Rabbi, the Secret Message and the Identity of Messiah* (Crane, MO: Defender, 2019). See my two books on this very detailed and stunning true story: *The Rabbi Who Found Messiah* (Washington, DC: WND Books, 2014) and *The Rabbi, the Secret Message and the Identity of Messiah*, coauthored by Messianic Rabbi Zev Porat. As of this publication, and to our knowledge, these are the only investigative books released by major publishers that deal with this topic. These books have been distributed all over the world, even into dozens of congregations of China's underground church, as well as the offices of Israel's former prime minister, Benjamin Netanyahu.

185. The condition of the "one year" element follows an Orthodox

denominational tradition of not drawing attention to the deceased in any overt way until at least one year after their passing.

186. The note that Kaduri left is below. For the full story, please see my earlier-referenced book (with Messianic Rabbi Zev Porat as co-author), *The Rabbi, the Secret Message, and the Identity of Messiah*, especially pp. 50–54.

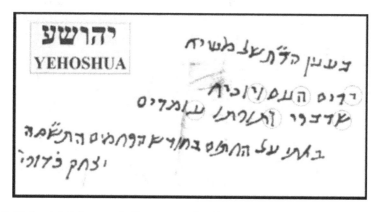

187. "Messiah Mystery Follows Death of Mystical Rabbi," 5/18/07, http://www.wnd.com/2007/05/41669.

188. That original article is no longer available on *Israel Today's* website. However, it was reproduced, word for word, by several other website owners before it was reprinted with the mysterious disappearance of the section titled, "The Rabbi's Followers React." You can see those reproductions at the following websites as of 5/04/18.

a.) Unleavened Bread Ministries, "Rabbi Reveals Name of Messiah," (reprint from *Israel Today's* 4/30/07 article). Accessed 5/04/18, http://www.ubm1.org/?page=rabbireveals.

b.) Rav. Reuven ben Gershom, "Prominent Israeli Rabbi Reveals the Name of the Messiah," Teshuva International, 10/14/08, http://www.rmi-ministries.com/rabbi-reveals-the-messiah.htm.

c.) World Historia, "Rabbi Reveals Name of the Messiah," 10/30/07. https://archive.fo/OYIbV. (This copy/paste of the original article was posted within months of the original's posting—once again proving that the original has since been significantly altered.)

d.) The original web-posted article (at an archived URL): Aviel Schneider, "Rabbi Reveals Name of the Messiah," 4/30/07, https://web.archive.org/

web/20070702085646/http://www.israeltoday.co.il:80/default.aspx?tabid=
128&view=item&idx=1347.

189. "While Christians regard the cross as an inevitable part of human
salvation, for Jews it remains a symbol of centuries of oppression," Giles
Fraser, "Christians Must Understand That for Jews the Cross Is a Symbol
of Oppression," *Guardian*, 4/25/14, https://www.theguardian.com/
commentisfree/2014/apr/25/jews-cross-symbol-of-oppression-christians.

190. Ryan Jones, e-mail messages to author April 2013 and May 29–30,
2013.

191. I have the lengthy email exchange written between the *Israel Today*
representative and me, who has asked to remain anonymous. Since was
so cooperative with me in getting to the bottom of the discrepancies, I
was more than glad to oblige him. I can assure the reader that this *Israel
Today* representative is legitimate and trustworthy, as I have been in
correspondence with him several times since the writing of my first book.
Everything he has told me in the past has proven accurate. I have no reason
to doubt his explanation as represented in this chapter. Following is the
exact response I received from that representative:

"Please note that the definitive publication of this story was in our print
magazine. The iterations that appeared on our website, including that
first appearance, were all just 'republications' of the original article.
Depending on who was in charge of posting the story to the website,
different parts might have been left out, since in the magazine layout some
were in separate 'boxes' and not a single 'story' if my memory serves. The
note regarding the [differing] publication date is likely just a mistake by
whomever was posting to the website, since this would have been different
people in both cases.

"As far as I am aware, there has never been any effort to retract or hide
certain parts of the original story. Our website is very much secondary to
our print magazine, and not all content from the magazine is republished
there in full.

"The website version of any article also appearing in our print magazine is
NOT definitive. The original version in the magazine is the definitive version.

"Whatever appeared in our print magazine regarding this story, including
the original title ('The Rabbi, the Note and the Messiah'), remains *Israel*

Today's official position. What was printed in our magazine is what *Israel Today* had to report and say on the matter. Period. End of story. Our website is very much a promotional platform for the magazine. Sometimes articles are republished online in full, sometimes in part, and often not at all."

192. "See my two books on this very detailed and stunning true story."

193. Tamar Fox, "The Beit Din: The Jewish Court of Law," My Jewish Learning. Accessed 5/24/22, https://www.myjewishlearning.com/article/the-beit-din.

194. We have conducted numerous media interviews together, written books together, jointly assisted in tours of Israel, and preached prophecy conferences and messages in church pulpits and conference centers from Idaho, Texas, New York, Missouri, New Jersey, to Florida.

Zev was born and raised in Israel, coming from a long line of very important Israeli rabbis and powerful Israeli political figures. Hebrew is his native language. Today, he lives with his wife in Tel Aviv, Israel. His amazing life's story and his conversion from Orthodox Judaism to a born again follower of Yeshua is absolutely electrifying, filled with supernatural instances. Read the details of that testimony in *The Rabbi, The Secret Message, and the Identity of Messiah* co-written by Zev and me and in Zev's book, *Unmasking the Chaldean Spirit* (Crane, MO: Defender). Find out more about Zev and his worldwide ministry at www.messiahofisraelministries.com.

195. "Ancient Hebrew Alphabet," (Al-Aleph). Accessed 6/23/28 https://www.studylight.org/lexicons/hebrew/ahl_alphabet.html.

196. See Psalm 22:16–18; Zechariah 12:10; and Isaiah 53:5–6.

197. Gallups and Porat, *Rabbi, the Secret Message, and the Identity of Messiah,*" pp. 45–49.

198. "Redeemer is a synonym for "Savior" and "Jesus." See https://thesaurus.yourdictionary.com/redeemer.

199. See Romans 3:22–25; Titus 2:13–14.

200. Frank Moore Cross, Jr., "Yahweh and the God of the Patriarchs," *Harvard Theological Review*, Vol. 55, No. 4 (Oct., 1962), pp. 225–259. Published by: Cambridge University Press on behalf of the Harvard

Divinity School. https://vdocuments.site/yahweh-and-the-god-of-the-patriarchs.html?page=34.

201. "Ancient Hebrew Alphabet," (Al-Aleph). Accessed 6/23/18, https://www.studylight.org/lexicons/hebrew/ahl_alphabet.html.

202. "The Hebrew Alphabet," Britannica.com. Accessed 5/2/22, https://www.britannica.com/topic/Hebrew-alphabet.

203. See Psalm 22:16–18; Zechariah 12:10; and Isaiah 53:5–6.

204. Michael Handelzalts, "In the Beginning: The Origins of the Hebrew Alphabet," *Haaretz*, 8/04/13, https://www.haaretz.com/jewish/.premium-why-hebrew-should-be-called-jewish-1.5316745.

205. Gallups and Porat, *The Rabbi, the Secret Message*, pp. 45–49.

206. Ibid.

207. Reading the *aleph-tav* in English (left to right) requires the Hebrew letters to be represented as את. However, they are correctly rendered as תא when written in correct Hebrew-styled script, reading right to left.

208. OT 853. "Eth," Biblehub.com, https://biblehub.com/hebrew/853.htm.

209. Depending upon the size of the font used, there are about 1,200 pages of the Old Testament in modern English translations. But the word *eth* is found almost 11,000 times in the Old Testament—being used, on average about ten times for every single page of the Old Testament.

210. Accusative Case: The accusative case is a grammatical case whose main function is to show the direct object of a verb. (Most people will encounter the term when studying a language other than English.) One can find the direct object by finding the verb and asking "what?" (or "whom?"). For example: "The dog ate our turkey." The verb is "ate." Now ask "ate what"? The direct object (accusative case) is "our turkey." See https://www.grammar-monster.com/glossary/accusative_case.htm.

211. O.T. 853. "Eth."

212. Bible Resources. "What are the two Hebrew words, Aleph and Tav existing in Hebrew manuscripts at the beginning of thousands of Scriptures, which are not translated into English language Bible translations?" 7/15/2020, https://bibleresources.info/what-are-the-two-hebrew-words-aleph-and-tav-existing-in-hebrew-

manuscripts-at-the-beginning-of-thousands-of-scriptures-which-are-not-translated-into-english-language-bible-translations-india.

213. A Hebraic Explanation of the word *eth* from *Oxford Jewish Thought—Essays by Rabbi Eli Brackman:* "An extra word in the Bible: finding the mystical in the simple," OxfordChabad.org, 8/27/09, https://www.oxfordchabad.org/templates/blog/post.asp?aid=708481&PostID=14343&p=1.Also see: Harry Goldtmann, *Biblical Word Studies*: "Eth (את) and the three Crosses." Accessed 3/23/22https://goldtmann.wordpress.com/2016/02/11/eth-%D7%90%D6%B5%D7%AA-and-the-three-crosses.

Harry Goldtmann is a chemical engineer with a master's in Lean Six Sigma. A born-again believer and student of Hebrew. https://goldtmann.wordpress.com/author/zachariah28/

"I have learned the use of this word in Hebrew may have had more meaning in the primitive Hebrew language, and that over time as languages improved, the meaning lost its significance. Today, *eth*, is generally used to point out more definitely the object of a verb or preposition. Reading through the scholars on the linguistics of this word, they struggled to define a use. One states, "This word by degrees lost much of its primitive force, so that as set before nouns and pronouns already definite, it scarcely increases the demonstrative power. What I gathered from reading the scholars, basically, this is a Hebrew word that doesn't belong in the Bible today, for its use was in the primitive times… I've been told every word of the Bible is precious and has a purpose. I have also been told how God can take the littlest of things and turn them into something big. Is there a message in this little word, which linguistically no longer applies? Was this a primitive method of placing emphasis on the noun, in today's world, putting a word in BOLD font?"

214. Ibid. Rabbi Eli Brackman: "An extra word in the Bible: finding the mystical in the simple."

From the article: "We will therefore approach this question from an exegetical point of view first followed by a mystical perspective, which ultimately proves most satisfactory in our case."

"This interpretation is found in a Jewish mystical text of 1905 by Rabbi

Sholom Dov Ber of Lubavitch (Sefer Hamamorim 5665 p. 15). Rabbi Sholom Dov Ber analyses the word 'Eth' in the context of love of G-d, whereby he resolves the question posed at the beginning of this essay." "In the simple interpretation of this word it emphasizes a deep mystical meditation that all of existence is nullified before G-d's existence."

215. The sixth letter of the Hebrew alphabet is alternatively pronounced as *vav* or *waw*. See: Nehemiah Gordon. "The Pronunciation of the Hebrew Letter Vav," posted 9/6/16, https://www.youtube.com/watch?v=0td4d2UGP0k&t=179s.

216. "The Hebrew Alphabet—The Letter Vav (ו) In the Hebrew Alphabet." Accessed 5//2/22https://hebrewtoday.com/alphabet/the-letter-vav-%D7%95.

217. O.T. 226. "Oth," Biblehub.com, https://biblehub.com/hebrew/226.htm.

218. This is yet another astounding connection revealed to me by Messianic Rabbi Zev Porat.

219. *Thayer's Greek Lexicon:* "Strongs NT 4592: σημεῖον: σημεῖον, σημείου, τό (σημαίνω (or σῆμα)), from Aeschylus and Herodotus down, Hebrew אות, a sign, mark, token. https://biblehub.com/greek/4592.htm.

220. "What is the biblical significance of the number seven/7?" Accessed 4/8/22, https://www.gotquestions.org/number-7-seven.html.

221. See Colossians 1 and John 1.

222. OT 3319. "Mesos"—The middle: https://biblehub.com/greek/3319.htm.

223. Jonathan Lipnick, "What Is the Holy Of Holies?" Israel Institute of Biblical Studies, 1/10/17 (see the illustration of the Temple interior and the placement of the Menorah). https://blog.israelbiblicalstudies.com/holy-land-studies/what-was-the-holy-of-holies.
Also: The lampstand is described in great detail in Exodus 25:31–39 and 37:17–24.

224. The *aleph-tav* as "and":
There is still another aleph-tav found in Genesis 1:1, besides the one we can clearly see in the middle of the verse. The other av is connected to an additional Hebrew letter. That *letter connection* turns the word into the

Hebrew designation of "and." Only a person intimately familiar with the Hebrew language would see it and understand its profound nature. You can see it in the following illustration.

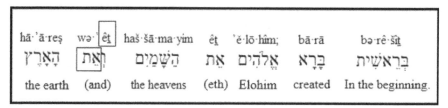

hā·'ā·reṣ	wə·'êṯ	haš·šā·ma·yim	êṯ	'ĕ·lō·hîm;	bā·rā	bə·rê·šîṯ
הָאָרֶץ	וְאֵת	הַשָּׁמַיִם	אֵת	אֱלֹהִים	בָּרָא	בְּרֵאשִׁית
the earth	(and)	the heavens	(eth)	Elohim	created	In the beginning.

Messianic Rabbi Zev Porat explains: "The word *ve'et* is made up of the letter *Vav* joined with the letters *aleph* and *tav*. The designation *ve* means 'and' in the Hebrew language. But to properly use the *ve* in a sentence you *have* to connect the "and" to *something*. It can't just stand in a sentence alone. So, the *ve* is connected to the *et* [the *aleph-tav*] and then it can be used as the word 'and.' Also, since the word 'and' alone can't do anything by itself, once again we see that only through Yeshua [the *aleph/tav*] can the creation of all things come to pass! But this is something that you can only see in the Hebrew language…and there it is, in the very first verse. So, the *et* that is standing alone is the name for Yeshua, but the *et* with the *ve* would read 'and, Yeshua created the Heavens and the Earth.' "However, here is the really remarkable thing about the *ve-et*. As I said, the letter that's connected to the *aleph-tav* to make the word 'and' is the *vav*. And in the ancient Hebrew pictograms, the *vav* represents a nail! Once again we find *a nail*— as in the nail in the hands of Yeshua—that is connected to the *aleph/tav* so that the word 'and' is able to take shape, and properly link the creation event together!"

Note: This information was provided to me for this book, by Zev Porat in his own voice, in a recorded format. Used by permission.

225. See Zev Porat's previously mentioned book, *Unmasking the Chaldean Spirit*, for an in-depth presentation of the place of the crucifixion and the Hebrew/biblical meaning of the word "Golgotha."

226. The soffit forms of the Hebrew alphabet were used as far back as the Paleo-Hebrew, the form of Hebrew that was used to write the Old Testament documents. In Zephaniah 3:8, we find all 27 letters of the entire

Hebrew alphabet (including soffit forms) found in that verse. It is the only verse in the Bible where this phenomenon is found.

Pulpit Commentary: [Zephaniah 3:8 is] "The only verse in the Bible which contains the whole Hebrew alphabet." See Pulpit Commentary entry at: https://biblehub.com/commentaries/zephaniah/3-8.htm.

227. Compound prophecy: See note 62.

228. For example: Psalm 22, a well-known compound prophecy, begins as a prayer and lament of David as he is running from his enemies. Then the scene shifts to David describing, among other startling things, that his hands and feet have been "pierced" and his enemies are gambling for his clothing as he looks down upon them. His mouth has dried up, his bones "stare at him" and are "out of joint."

"Obviously, David is seeing a vision of the crucifixion of Yeshua almost a thousand years into the future. None of these things actually happened to David. This is the psalm from which Jesus quotes the first line, while on the cross, just before His death, "My God, My God, why have you forsaken me"? It is right after this outburst from Yeshua that the centurion cried out, "Surely this man was the Son of God!"

Keil and Delitzsch Biblical Commentary on the Old Testament: "The fulfilment in the nailing of the hands and (at least, the binding fast) of the feet of the Crucified One to the cross is clear. This is not the only passage in which it is predicated that the future Christ shall be murderously pierced; but it is the same in Isaiah 53:5 where He is said to be pierced (מחלל) on account of our sins, and in Zechariah 12:10, where Jahve describes Himself as ἐξεθτνεκκὲ in Him." https://biblehub.com/commentaries/psalms/22-16.htm.

Similarly, Ezekiel 28 and Isaiah 14 begin by being laments or warnings to the king of Tyre and the king of Babylon respectively. Yet each morphs into startling and direct pictures of Satan himself. In that same manner, Psalm 40, as supported by many scholars and especially by Hebrews 10:7, is a compound prophecy that ultimately speaks of Jesus, the one who is to come…and whom David is "seeing" in his prophetic vision state.

229. All of the following commentary entries below are found at: https://biblehub.com/commentaries/psalms/40-7.htm.

1. *Matthew Poole's Commentary:* "These words do most literally and truly belong to Christ…as this phrase is more fully expressed and explained in diverse places of Scripture, and particularly Hebrews 10:5, where this place is explained and applied to Christ. This place manifestly points to Christ, and must necessarily be understood of him, and of him only, concerning whom much is said in the books of Moses, as is evident from Luke 24:27,44 Joh 5:46 Acts 3:22 26:22 28:23."

2. *Gill's Exposition of the Entire Bible:* "[This passage relates to Genesis 3:15]; and seeing the coming of Christ into the world was not only appointed of God, agreed unto by Christ, but was prophesied of, and penned down in the sacred writings; therefore at the appointed time he came, freely and willingly."

3. *Matthew Henry's Concise Commentary:* "In 40:6–10, the psalmist foretells that work of wonder, redemption by our Lord Jesus Christ. The Substance must come, which is Christ, who must bring that glory to God, and that grace to man, which it was impossible the sacrifices should ever do. Observe the setting apart of our Lord Jesus to the work and office of Mediator. In the volume, or roll, of the book it was written of him."

4. *Benson's Commentary:* "And so this place manifestly points to Christ, concerning whom much is said in the books of Moses, as is evident from Luke 24:27; Luke 24:44; John 5:46; Acts 3:22; and Acts 26:22; and Acts 28:23. And this sense being plain and natural, and unforced, and exactly agreeing both with the words, and with the truth of the thing, and with the belief of all Christians, there can be no good reason why we should not acquiesce in it.

230. Psalm 40:7. "Barnes' Notes on the Bible," Biblehub.com, https://biblehub.com/commentaries/psalms/40-7.htm.

231. Psalm 40:7. "Jamieson-Fausset-Brown Bible Commentary," Biblehub.com, https://biblehub.com/commentaries/psalms/40-7.htm.

232. Psalm 40:7. "Guzik's Bible Commentary," Enduring Word, https://enduringword.com/bible-commentary/psalm-40.

233. That which is hidden will be revealed. The following is from an Orthodox Hebrew website explaining the Scroll of Esther and its hidden meaning, validating what Rabbi Porat has just stated:

"The very name of the book we read on Purim hints at this idea: Megillat

Esther, the Scroll of Esther. In Hebrew, the word Esther is related to the word nistar, meaning hidden, and the word megillah is related to the word megillah, meaning to reveal. Thus the Megillah of Esther can be literally translated as the revelation of that which is hidden. Esther's name and essence are one. She focused on what is important and meaningful, even though it might be hidden from the eye.

"Then and now, G-d's Presence is not readily visible. In fact, G-d's Name is not mentioned once throughout the entire megillah. Yet Esther makes her choice. She does not perceive the honor of becoming queen as real. She calls on that which is inner, deeper, and hidden. She prays to the G-d whom she knows is present." See Nicole Landau, "Esther's Choice," Ohr.edu. Accessed 4/12/22, https://ohr.edu/1500.

For verification that God's name *actually is* in the book of Esther—in coded format—see: Dr. Joseph R. Nally, "God is not mentioned in Esther, so why do Christians regard it as scripture?" Third Millennium Ministries. Accessed 4/3/22, https://thirdmill.org/answers/answer.asp?file=40664.

234. The *Aleph-Tav* as "and": Please see note 217.

235. Statement provided in an email and in recordings; used by permission.

236. Efraim Goldstein, "Who's the Subject of Isaiah 53?" Jews for Jesus, 4/20/18, https://jewsforjesus.org/learn/whos-the-subject-of-isaiah-53.

237. Gallups and Porat, *The Rabbi, the Secret Message*, pp. 233–235.

238. Rabbi Tovia Singer, "Who Is God's Suffering Servant? The Rabbinic Interpretation of Isaiah 53," *Outreach Judaism*. Accessed 6/12/18, https://outreachjudaism.org/gods-suffering-servant-isaiah-53.

239. Rabbi Rachmiel Frydland,. "Why I Believe that Yeshua (Jesus) Is the Jewish Messiah," Association of Messianic Congregations. Accessed 5/23/18, http://www.messianicassociation.org/bio-frydland.htm.

240. Rabbi Rachmiel Frydland, "The Rabbis' Dilemma: A Look at Isaiah 53," Jews for Jesus. Accessed 6/12/18, https://jewsforjesus.org/publications/issues/issues-v02-n05/the-rabbis-dilemma-a-look-at-isaiah-53/.

241. Eitan Bar, "Isaiah 53—The Forbidden Chapter," One For Israel. Accessed 6/11/18,https://www.oneforisrael.org/bible-based-teaching-from-israel/inescapable-truth-isaiah-53.

242. Gallups and Porat, *The Rabbi, the Secret Message*," p. 240.

243. For a balanced and scholarly examination of the ELS phenomenon,

and especially its use on Isaiah 53, see this website article: https://www.
angelfire.com/ky/yeshuashmi.

244. Behold The Stone. "The revelation of the divine signature
upon the Holy Bible," Beholdthestone.com. Accessed March
12, 2022, https://beholdthestone.com/mysteries/els-codes/
the-bible-code-of-isaiah-53-jesus-is-my-name.

245. Finding random names, with the letters spaced ridiculously apart in
portions of Scripture that are not related at all to those names, is statistically
useless. One of the most obvious reasons is because we have no idea what
the name might be meant to reveal. For example, "Muhammed is my
name" might be paired with the phrase "I am a false prophet of a false
religion." If that were the case, then finding "Muhammed is my name"
might be worth considering as a significant find. On the other hand, I've
already explained how this dramatically differs from finding *Yeshua Shemi*
in the exact passage that speaks of Yeshua's sacrifice on the cross.

246. Acts 8:34–35.

247. Some have attacked the "reliability" of the ELS skip codes by finding
messages such as, "Jesus is a false messiah," "Jesus is a false prophet" and
"Jesus is a liar." These have also been claimed to have been discovered
embedded in the text of the Old Testament. Again, how do we know
the context of those "finds"? What if those "messages" are meant to read,
"Many will claim that Jesus is a liar, or false prophet?" As a matter of fact,
this is exactly what the Pharisees and Sadducees *did claim* about Yeshua
during His three-year ministry exploits! So, the detractor's claimed "finds"
of this nature, again, prove nothing concerning the reliability of the
legitimately applied ELS codes.

248. This was conveyed to me in a phone conversation in relation to several
emails about this topic. I sent him the same charts that you are seeing in
this book.

249. "Jews demand signs and Greeks look for wisdom, but we preach
Christ crucified: a stumbling block to Jews and foolishness to Gentiles, but
to those whom God has called, both Jews and Greeks, Christ the power
of God and the wisdom of God. For the foolishness of God is wiser
than human wisdom, and the weakness of God is stronger than human
strength," (1 Corinthians 1:22–25).

1. *Cambridge Bible Commentary:* "The Jews (Matthew 12:38; Matthew 16:1; Mark 8:11; Luke 11:16; John 2:18; John 6:30) required external attestations of the power of Christ, and especially that of the subjugation of the world to His kingly authority. The Greeks sought dialectic skill from one who aspired to be their teacher." https://biblehub.com/commentaries/1_corinthians/1-22.htm.

2. *Pulpit Commentary:* "Jews demand signs. This had been their incessant demand during our Lord's ministry; nor would they be content with any sign short of a sign from heaven (Matthew 12:38: 16:1; John 2:18; John 4:48, etc.)....Greeks seek after wisdom. Paul at Athens had found himself surrounded with Stoics and Epicureans, and the same new thing which everyone was looking for mainly took the shape of philosophic novelties (Acts 17:21)." https://biblehub.com/commentaries/1_corinthians/1-22.htm.

250. See a list of eleven verses of Scripture that verify this biblical truth: https://bible.knowing-jesus.com/topics/To-The-Jew-First.

251. See Romans 11 and Ephesians 2, the entire chapters, as vivid examples of this biblical truth.

252. How Did the Bible Get Chapters and Verses? The Bible's chapter divisions that are the most used today were developed by Stephen Langton, an Archbishop of Canterbury, around A.D. 1227. The Wycliffe English Bible of 1382 was the first Bible to use that chapter arrangement. Since the publication of the Wycliffe Bible, practically all Bible translations have followed Langton's chapter divisions. Robert Estienne, also known as Stephanus, was the first to divide the New Testament into standard numbered verses, in 1555. Since that time, beginning with the Geneva Bible, the chapter and verse delineations used by Stephanus have been used in practically all Bible versions.

See: Got Questions. "Who divided the Bible into chapters and verses?" Accessed 6/23/22, https://www.gotquestions.org/divided-Bible-chapters-verses.html.

253. Agape Bible Study, "The Many Names of God."

254. Tetragrammaton: "A Greek word, neuter of *tetragrammatos*, meaning 'having four letters',"; See also Agape Bible Study, "The Many Names of God." Accessed 7/12/18, http://www.agapebiblestudy.com/documents/

The%20Many%20Names%20of%20God.htm.

255. In Hebrew, the phrase "I am" (אֶהְיֶה , *ehyeh*), is linguistically related to God's name, יהוה (YHWH, often represented in English as "Yahweh" or "Jehovah"). Many Hebrew scholars suggest that YHWH means something like "the one who is." In fact, the Septuagint (ancient Greek translations of the OT, widely used by early Jews and Christians) did not translate the second אֶהְיֶה in Exodus 3:14 as ἐγώ εἰμι, but rather as ὁ ὤν, "the one who is." See Gary Manning, Jr., "Does 'I Am' always refer to God in the Gospel of John?" 9/21/15, Biola University, Talbot School of Theology Faculty, https://www.biola.edu/blogs/good-book-blog/2015/does-i-am-always-refer-to-god-in-the-gospel-of-john.

256. See 2 Samuel 6:2, 1 Kings 3:2, and Isaiah 18:7 for examples of where this erroneous idea might have taken root—outside of proper context. Author's Note: It is my opinion that to "not speak" the name of YHWH is a direct violation of the 3rd Commandment…and certainly *not* a way of "keeping" the commandment. The most diabolical of all of God's created beings, Satan, certainly loves the fact that many people around the world (Jews and Christians alike) have been duped into never speaking aloud, or even writing out, the only name in Heaven and on earth that brings Satan's power and exploits into the realm of utter defeat. God's people should have no agreement with Satan in this matter. God's name (YHWH) is to be used and called upon by God's people with a holy reverence.

257. "We Shouldn't Take God's Name in Vain. But What Is It?" Haaretz.com. Accessed 5/2/22, https://www.haaretz.com/archaeology/.premium.MAGAZINE-we-shouldn-t-take-god-s-name-in-vain-but-what-is-it-1.6546806.

258. See Isaiah 12:4, Psalm 105:1, Psalm 68:4, and Psalm 148:13.

259. *Keil and Delitzsch Biblical Commentary on the Old Testament:* "The fruit of the purification is this, that henceforth they call upon [Actually "use"] the name of Jehovah, and serve Him. יי משב ארק, when used of men, always signifies to call solemnly or heartily upon the name of Jehovah. We have here in Old Testament form the thought expressed by the Apostle Paul in Romans 11, namely, that the Gentiles have been made partakers of salvation, that they may incite to emulation the Israelites who have fallen away from the call of divine grace. The words of the prophet treat of

the blessing which will accrue, from the entrance of the Gentiles into the kingdom of God, to the Israelites who have been rejected on account of their guilt, and refer not only to the missionary work of Christians among the Jews in the stricter sense of the term, but to everything that is done, both directly and indirectly, through the rise and spread of Christianity among the nations, for the conversion of the Jews to the Saviour whom they once despised." See: https://biblehub.com/commentaries/zephaniah/3-9.htm.

Author's Notes: The promise to Zephaniah is that there will come a day when YHWH's name will be used properly. It will be spoken, praised, glorified and not "hidden," misused in superstitious ways, or maligned and mingled with the names of other so-called gods. The promise is first for the Jewish people—but also for all the nations. This is, ultimately, so that all might call upon the name of Yeshua—who is YHWH in the flesh!

To "call upon the name of the LORD" is to actually speak His name. It means to proclaim His name—even shout it, or cry out His name. See: Hebrew 7121. "qara" https://biblehub.com/hebrew/7121.htm.

An example of this grammatical use of *qara* can be found in Genesis 2, wherein Adam gives each creature its name - and declares/speaks the names that he gives to them.

"Now the Lord God had formed out of the ground all the wild animals and all the birds in the sky. He brought them to the man to see what he would name them; and whatever the man called [*qara*] each living creature, that was its name." Genesis 2:19.

260. 1. *Pulpit Commentary (Zephaniah 3:8):* "God will allow no rival anywhere (Nahum 1:2). This is the reason of the severity and universality of the judgment. The Masorites note that this ' the only verse in the Bible which contains the whole Hebrew alphabet." See Pulpit Commentary entry at: https://biblehub.com/commentaries/zephaniah/3-8.htm.

2. *Everett's Study Notes on the Holy Scriptures:* "Zephaniah 3:8 has the unique characteristic of containing all twenty-two letters of the Hebrew alphabet, as well as the five final consonant forms. No other verse in the Scriptures repeats this incident." See: https://www.studylight.org/commentaries/eng/ghe/zephaniah-3.html.

3. Author's Note: There are said to be twenty-six known verses in the

entire Old Testament that contain the foundational *twenty-two letters* of the Hebrew alphabet in them. Yet, Zephaniah 3:8 is the only one with all 22 letters plus the 5 soffit forms…the complete biblical alphabet. See: "What verses in the Tanach contain all 22 Hebrew letters?" Answers.com, accessed July 5, 2022, https://www.answers.com/Q/ What_verses_in_the_Tanach_contain_all_22_Hebrew_letters.

261. Judaism 101. "The Name of G-d," (Pronouncing the Name of God). Accessed 7/27/18, http://www.jewfaq.org/name.htm. Also see: Jewish Virtual Library. "Jewish Concepts: The Name of God." Accessed 7/27/18, https://www.jewishvirtuallibrary.org/the-name-of-god.

262. "Tetragrammaton," *New International Dictionary of New Testament Theology* (1984, Volume 2) p. 512.

263. "Tetragrammaton in the New Testament," *Anchor Bible Dictionary*, Volume 6, Ed. David Noel Freedman, (NY: Anchor Bible, 1992).

264. "We Shouldn't Take God's Name in Vain. But What Is It?" Haaretz. com.

265. Hasidic. "The Hasidim, or 'pious ones' in Hebrew, belong to a special movement within Orthodox Judaism, a movement that, at its height in the first half of the nineteenth century, claimed the allegiance of millions in Eastern and Central Europe—perhaps a majority of East European Jews." "Hasidic. A Life Apart," PBS.org. Accessed 4/12/22, https://www.pbs.org/ alifeapart/intro.html.

266. "Chabad.org." Accessed 3/12/22, https://en.wikipedia.org/wiki/ Chabad.org.

267. "About," Hebrew Today. Accessed 4/2/22, https://hebrewtoday.com/ company-overview.

268. *Hebrew Today* also says of the *yod*: "The letter yod is used in the Hebrew expression: יוֹד שֶׁל קוֹצוֹ (kotzo shel yod). Literally translated as the smallest edge of the letter yod. This expression is used to refer to something tiny, insignificant, or inconsequential…. It is interesting to note, that in most sacred literature, the pages are marked with letters, instead of numbers. (There are some books that use both formats.) When they get to the number 15, which would be the letters "ה-י," the printers avoid using this letter combination, since it is also one of the names of the Almighty." https://hebrewtoday.com/alphabet/the-letter-yud-%D7%99.

269. Chabad.org, "The Yod," (The Meaning). Accessed 4/3/22, https://www.chabad.org/library/article_cdo/aid/137082/jewish/Yod.htm.

270. "This Hebrew letter ו (Waw / Vav) is the 6th letter in the Hebrew Aleph-Bet, and is pronounced differently in various dialects of Hebrew. Some dialects (including Modern Hebrew) use the 'v' sound, and then this letter is called 'Vav'. Other dialects use a 'w' sound which makes the name of this Hebrew letter 'Waw'. "Waw or Vav?" Hebrewgospels.com. Accessed 4/2/22 https://www.hebrewgospels.com/video-15-yhwh.

271. "The Letter Vav (ו) In the Hebrew Alphabet." Accessed 3/12/22, Hebrewtoday.com, https://hebrewtoday.com/alphabet/the-letter-vav-%D7%95/.

272. Rabbi Aaron L. Raskin, "Vav: The sixth letter of the Hebrew Alphabet." Accessed 4/23/22 https://www.chabad.org/library/article_cdo/aid/137078/jewish/Vav.htm.

273. "Peg." Accessed 3/24/22 https://thesaurus.yourdictionary.com/peg.

274. Rabbi Aaron L. Raskin, "Heh: The fifth letter of the Hebrew alphabet," Chabad.org, https://www.chabad.org/library/article_cdo/aid/137077/jewish/Heh.htm.

275. Additional meaning of these letters from each of the two Orthodox websites we are examining. Note that even these nuances of definition still fit the exact and overall theme of the greater revelation.
1. Chabad—VAV or WAW: "While the design of the vav looks like a hook, the word vav actually means "hook." A hook is something that holds two things together. It is also a means to connect the spiritual and the physical. https://www.chabad.org/library/article_cdo/aid/137078/jewish/Vav.htm.
2. Hebrew Today—YUD or YOD: "According to the Jewish sages, the yod represents the world to come and completeness." https://hebrewtoday.com/alphabet/the-letter-yud-%D7%99.
3. Hebrew Today—HEH or HEI: "The letter Hei is also often used instead of writing out one of the most common names used for G-d. https://hebrewtoday.com/alphabet/the-letter-hei-%D7%94.

276. Amanda Borschel-Dan, "Archaeologist Claims to Find Oldest Hebrew Text in Israel, Including the Name of God," *Times of Israel*, 3/4/22, https://www.timesofisrael.com/archaeologist-claims-to-find-oldest-hebrew-text-in-israel-including-the-name-of-god. From the article: "Scholars date

tiny 'curse tablet,' found at Mt. Ebal, to 1200 BCE—which would prove Israelites were literate when they entered Holy Land....Archaeologist Dr. Scott Stripling and a team of international scholars held a press conference on Thursday in Houston, Texas, unveiling what he claims is the earliest proto-alphabetic Hebrew text—including the name of God, 'YHWH'—ever discovered in ancient Israel.... 'This is a text you find only every 1,000 years,' Haifa University Prof. Gershon Galil told *The Times of Israel*. Galil helped decipher the hidden internal text of the folded lead tablet based on high-tech scans carried out in Prague at the Academy of Sciences of the Czech Republic.

277. From a popular Orthodox Jewish perspective website. Tracy Rich, "The Name of G-d," jewfaq.com. Accessed 5/5/22, https://www.jewfaq. org/name.htm.

278. Gallups and Porat, *The Rabbi, the Secret Message*, p. 309.

279. The first major written collection of the Jewish oral traditions.

280. See: Mishnah: Yoma 3:8; 4:2; 6:2; Sanhedrin 7:5,8; Babylonian Talmud: Sanhedrin 56b. Also see: Paul Sumner, "Ha-Shem. The Name." Accessed 4/21/22, https://www.hebrew-streams.org/works/hebrew/hashem.html.

281. "Shaddai, ["Almighty"] one of the biblical names of God, also serves here as an acronym for Shomer Daltot Yisrael, 'Guardian of Israel's doors." Many mezuzah cases are also marked with the Hebrew letter ‫ש‬ (*shin*), for Shaddai. Shaddai is most often translated as "God Almighty." See https:// en.wikipedia.org/wiki/Mezuzah.

282. Rabbi Aaron L. Raskin, "Mem. The Thirteenth Letter of the Hebrew Alphabet." Accessed 4/12/22 https://www.chabad.org/library/article_cdo/ aid/137085/jewish/Mem.htm.

283. "The Hebrew Alphabet—The Letter Mem," HebrewToday. com. Accessed 4/12/22, https://hebrewtoday.com/alphabet/ the-letter-mem-%D7%9E.

284. Robert Kugler; Patrick J. Hartin (2009), *An Introduction to the Bible*. (Eerdmans) p. 193.

285. "Ayin," Chabad.org. Accessed 2/12/22, https://www.chabad.org/ library/article_cdo/aid/137088/jewish/Ayen.htm.

286. Ibid. Also see HebrewToday.com: Under the letter Ayin meaning, it says: "However, the word ‫עִיוֵר‬ (i'ver) blind (person) also starts with the

letter ע. This is to teach us that the fact that we can see, doesn't mean that we always understand correctly what we see." https://hebrewtoday.com/alphabet/the-letter-ain-%D7%A2/.

Author's note: This is exactly why this book has been written—to show the Hebrew people and believers all over the world what they have not "seen" but now "see."

287. The Word "pierce" in the three crucifixion passages of the Old Testament:

1. Psalm 22:16–Heb. 3738. *karah*: https://biblehub.com/hebrew/3738.htm.

"To bore or dig"—by implication...*to pierce.* Of the top 27 scholarly English translations, 20 of them use the word "pierce or piercing." Others use "pin, gouge, tear, dug, etc." Young's Literal Version, and the Literal Standard Version use *piercing.* See: https://biblehub.com/psalms/22-16.htm.

2. Isaiah 53: 5–Heb. 2490. *chalal:* https://biblehub.com/hebrew/2490.htm. "To bore, *pierce."* Of the top 27 scholarly English translations, 14 of them use the word "pierce." 13 use "wounded." Young's Literal Version, and the Literal Standard Version use *pierce.* See: https://biblehub.com/isaiah/53-5.htm.

3. Zechariah 12:10 - Heb. 1856. *daqar:* https://biblehub.com/hebrew/1856.htm.

"To *pierce, pierce through."* Of the top 27 scholarly English translations, 23 of them use the word "pierce." The other 4 use the words "thrust, thrust through, stabbed through." Young's Literal Version, and the Literal Standard Version use *pierce.* https://biblehub.com/zechariah/12-10.htm.

288. That verse seems out of place and difficult to understand, even to a number of acclaimed commentaries. I believe one that comes the closest to explaining *how and why* we find that promise in that location and context is Keil and Delitzsch. Their commentary also re-emphasizes the point that our own journey, in the pages of this book, has illustrated all along. Namely, God *does indeed conceal divine secrets* from His people, *until just the right time.* And, He'll conceal those gems and treasures even in the midst of the surface text of His Word!

1. *Keil and Delitzsch Biblical Commentary on the Old Testament:* "The

incarnation of Deity was unquestionably a secret that was not clearly unveiled in the Old Testament, but the veil was not so thick but that some rays could pass through. Such a ray, directed by the spirit of prophecy into the mind of the prophet, was the prediction of Immanuel." https://biblehub.com/commentaries/isaiah/7-14.htm.

2. Also, for a further study on Isaiah 7:14 and its seemingly odd placement in the narrative (yet solved by these scholars)…at the above link, please see especially: Matthew Poole's Commentary, Jamieson-Fausset-Brown Bible Commentary, Barnes' Notes on the Bible, and the Pulpit Commentary. And then, of course, we might wonder how Matthew would have known to open his gospel, and thus the entire New Testament, with this very prophecy! I have no specific biblical proof of it, but I have long conjectured that is one of those things that Jesus revealed to His disciples after His resurrection. It would almost take a divine revealing. Yet Matthew, a mere tax collector, seems so certain of it.

3) *Barnes' Notes on the Bible* addresses this problem: "When we read in the Gospel of Matthew, that Jesus Christ was actually born of a virgin, and that all the circumstances of his birth came to pass that this very prophecy might be fulfilled, it has less the appearance of an unexpected application, than of a conclusion rendered necessary by a series of antecedent facts and reasonings, the last link in a long chain of intimations more or less explicit (referring to such prophecies as Genesis 3:15; Micah 5:2)." https://biblehub.com/commentaries/isaiah/7-14.htm.

289. "Who was the prophet Zechariah in the Bible?" gotquestions.org. Accessed 5/5/22. https://www.gotquestions.org/prophet-Zechariah.html.

290. Of Davidic origin, Zerubbabel is thought to have originally been a Babylonian Jew who returned to Jerusalem at the head of a band of Jewish exiles and became governor of Judaea under the Persians. Influenced by the prophets Haggai and Zechariah, he rebuilt the Temple. The editors of Encyclopaedia Britannica. "Zerubbabel: governor of Judaea," Britannica.com, accessed 7/1/22, https://www.britannica.com/biography/Zerubbabel.

291. Ibid.

292. Bargil Pixner (2010), Rainer Riesner, eds. *Paths of the Messiah.* Translated by Keith Myrick, Miriam Randall. (Ignatius Press), pp. 320–322.

293. The other four references are 2 Chronicles 33:14; Nehemiah 3:26, 11:21; 2 Kings 5:24. (The reference in 2 Kings is often translated as "hill" but the Hebrew is *ophel.*)

294. Opel, OT #6076, "Strong's Concordance," Biblehub.com, http://biblehub.com/hebrew/6076.htm.See also this passage in Micah: "As for you, watchtower of the flock, stronghold of Daughter Zion, the former dominion will be restored to you; kingship will come to Daughter Jerusalem," (Micah 4:8). "Stronghold" is an interpretation of the Hebrew word *ophel.*

295. Compelling Truth. "What Is the Biblical Significance of Zion? What is Zion? What Is Mount Zion?" Accessed 4/12/22, https://www.compellingtruth.org/Zion.html.

296. Zion meaning, "Etymology of the name Zion," Abarim Publications. Accessed 12/12/17, http://www.abarim-publications.com/Meaning/Zion.html#.WjwC69-nHIU.

297. Moriah, "OT: 4179." Accessed 12/14/17, *Biblesoft's New Exhaustive Strong's Numbers and Concordance with Expanded Greek-Hebrew Dictionary.* © 1994, 2003, 2006, Biblesoft, Inc. and International Bible Translators, Inc.

298. Moriah meaning, "Etymology of the name Moriah," Abarim Publications. Accessed 12/12/17, http://www.abarim-publications.com/Meaning/Moriah.html#.WjwG1N-nHIU.

299. There exists a huge body of scholarly evidence that this place called "Golgotha" was located on the Mount of Olives. The Old Testament and the New Testament actually point to this location as the place. This opens up all manner of additional biblical revelations and connections. Following are four examples of scholarly opinions on this matter:

1. Dr. James Tabor: *"The basic case for the Mt. of Olives being the site of Jesus' crucifixion* rests on several interrelated arguments The first, and in my view, the most weighty, is a passage in the New Testament book of Hebrews (13:10–13)." "Locating Golgotha: Archeology," 2/26/16, https://jamestabor.com/locating-golgotha.

Dr. James D. Tabor served as chair (2004–2014) of the Department of Religious Studies at the University of North Carolina, where he has taught since 1989. He is currently professor of ancient Judaism and early Christianity. Previously he held positions at the University of Notre Dame and the College of William and Mary. He received his PhD from the University of Chicago in 1981 in Ancient Mediterranean Religions. https://jamestabor.com/about-dr-tabor/.

2. Dr. Douglas Jacoby: "No need to follow the crowds. There will be little need to 'compete' with the 'tour groups' down the traditional Via Dolorosa and inside the Church of the Holy Sepulcher, since we recognize that they are well over a kilometer from *the true site of the crucifixion, on the Mount of Olives*," "The Red Heifer Sacrifice and the Crucifixion," (1997, Revised 2001), https://www.douglasjacoby.com/the-red-heifer-sacrifice-and-the-crucifixion.

Dr. Douglas Jacoby is a Bible teacher who has served as a minister on church staff for twenty years, in London, Birmingham, Sydney, Stockholm, Philadelphia, Indianapolis, and Washington, DC. He also serves as adjunct professor of theology at Lincoln Christian University and professor of theology in the Rocky Mountain School of Theology and Ministry. With degrees from Drew, Harvard, and Duke, Douglas has written thirty-five books, recorded nearly nine hundred podcasts, and spoken in over one hundred universities, and in over five hundred cities, in 126 nations around the world. Douglas has led twenty-five tours to the biblical world. https://www.douglasjacoby.com/about.

3. Dr. Ernest Martin: "There is no longer any doubt. *Jesus was crucified near the summit of the Mount of Olives about half a mile east of the Temple Mount.* This fact is confirmed in the New Testament in a variety of ways.... In fact...the Book of Hebrews...[was to the early church] sufficient to pinpoint the region where the crucifixion of Jesus took place. "Secrets of Golgotha: The Lost History of Jesus' Crucifixion" (Second Edition), Academy for Scriptural; 2nd edition (6/1/96), pp.14–15. Read the entire book online here: https://www.askelm.com/golgotha/Golgotha%20Chap%2000.pdf.Dr. Ernest Martin,from 1960 to 1972, taught history, theology, and elementary meteorology at the Ambassador College campus in Bricket Wood, England, where he became dean of faculty. He earned his PhD at Ambassador College.

Between 1969 and 1973, Ambassador College entered an alliance with Hebrew University in Israel which had been negotiated by Dr. Martin. This undertaking commenced a five-year archaeological program with students from Ambassador College working on Dr. Benjamin Mazar's excavation near the Western Wall of the Temple Mount. During this period, Martin supervised 450 participating college students during summer months. The partnership was mentioned in a *Time* magazine article. ["Education: Digging for Credit," 9/3/73 via content.time.com.].

Following the eventual closure of the Ambassador College campus in England, Martin became chairman of the Department of Theology at Ambassador College in Pasadena, California, in 1973. Dr. Martin was a dear friend of the famed and deeply conservative theologian, commentary writer, and biblical scholar F. F. Bruce. (See *Secrets of Golgotha: The Lost History of Jesus' Crucifixion* (Second Edition), p. 412).

4. For an outstandingly unique and extremely in-depth study of this topic see (Messianic Rabbi) Zev Porat, *Unmasking the Chaldean Spirit* (Crane, MO: Defender 2022).

300. Zechariah 9:9; Matthew 21:5.

301. Katrin Weigmann, "The Code, the Text and the Language of God," National Library of Medicine, February 2004, https://www.ncbi.nlm.nih.gov/pmc/articles/PMC1298980.

302. Cold Spring Harbor Laboratory. "The Human Genome Project." Accessed 4/2/22.

"When the Human Genome Project was officially launched back in 1990, it was envisioned as an international effort that would span 15 years with a price tag of $3 billion—$1 for each base of the genetic code." https://www.cshl.edu/archives/guide-to-hgp/.

303. National Human Genome Research Institute: Genome.gov. Accessed 3/22/22, https://www.genome.gov/human-genome-project.

304. Elizabeth Landau, "DNA Project Interprets 'Book of Life'," CNN, 9/5/12, https://www.cnn.com/2012/09/05/health/encode-human-genome/index.html.

305. "June 2000 White House Event," (Remarks Made by the President, Prime Minister Tony Blair of England (via satellite), Dr. Francis Collins, Director of the National Human Genome Research Institute, and Dr. Craig Venter, President and Chief Scientific Officer, Celera Genomics

Corporation, on the Completion of the First Survey of the Entire Human Genome Project), Genome.gov. Accessed 4/23/22 https://www.genome.gov/10001356/june-2000-white-house-event.

306. In the "depths of the earth" is a Hebrew expression for something along the lines of: "In an unseen place that is impossible to plumb the deepest and completest depths."

Barnes' Notes on the Bible: "Wrought in a place as dark, as obscure, and as much beyond the power of human observation as though it had been done low down beneath the ground where no eye of man can penetrate," https://biblehub.com/commentaries/psalms/139-15.htm.

307. Brookhaven National Laboratory, "Researchers Find Surprising Similarities between Genetic and Computer Codes," Phys.org, 3/29/13, https://phys.org/news/2013-03-similarities-genetic-codes.html.

1. "Computational biologist Sergei Maslov of Brookhaven National Laboratory worked with graduate student Tin Yau Pang from Stony Brook University to compare the frequency with which components 'survive' in two complex systems: bacterial genomes and operating systems on Linux computers. Their work is published in the Proceedings of the National Academy of Sciences."

2. Also see Robert R. Service, "DNA Could Store All of the World's Data in One Room: New algorithm delivers the highest-ever density for large-scale data storage," Science.org, 3/2/17, https://www.science.org/content/article/dna-could-store-all-worlds-data-one-room.

"Humanity has a data storage problem: More data were created in the past 2 years than in all of preceding history. And that torrent of information may soon outstrip the ability of hard drives to capture it. Now, researchers report that they've come up with a new way to encode digital data in DNA to create the highest-density large-scale data storage scheme ever invented. Capable of storing 215 petabytes (215 million gigabytes) in a single gram of DNA, the system could, in principle, store every bit of datum ever recorded by humans in a container about the size and weight of a couple of pickup trucks."

3. Also see USA. (Video). "Scientists Found Proof of GOD in DNA Code—Evidence of God—The God Code—God DNA," Uploaded

11/28/19 https://www.youtube.com/watch?v=XuUR7v7hkOQ.

308. A number of scientists do not believe evolution is scientifically accurate or plausible:

1. "A Scientific Dissent from Darwinism," dissentfromdarwin.org. Accessed 4.23.22, https://dissentfromdarwin.org/.

2. The List, "A Scientific Dissent from Darwinism." Accessed 4/23/22. To see the signed list of each scientist (update 20210) see: https://www.discovery.org/m/securepdfs/2021/07/Scientific-Dissent-from-Darwinism-List-07152021.pdf.

309. "A Scientific Dissent from Darwinism," (Scientists), dissentfromdarwin.org. Accessed 4/23/22, https://dissentfromdarwin.org/scientists.

310. Ibid.

311. Ibid.

312. "Googleplexian: 1 with 100 zeroes behind it. The largest "named" number, as of this writing. "American Heritage® Dictionary of the English Language, Fifth Edition. © 2016 by Houghton Mifflin Harcourt. Published by Houghton Mifflin Harcourt All rights reserved. https://www.thefreedictionary.com/Googolplexian.

313. Prof. Israel Rubinstein. Functional Nanomaterials. Complete Publications. Curriculum Vitae. Accessed 4/16/22, https://www.weizmann.ac.il/materials/Rubinstein/israel-rubinsten-cv-publications.

314. Erica Winter. YouTube Video. "Israeli scientist, Dr [Israel] Rubinstein, finds God's name, YHWH, in our DNA," YouTube.com, 6/23/21, https://www.youtube.com/watch?v=ZnXVLa_EqWE.

Also available for viewing here: Carl Gallups, "Did God Really Leave His Signature On Our DNA?" *Pastor Carl Gallups Explains,* 1/27/22, https://www.youtube.com/watch?v=SB_6Vi1LqHQ and here: http://www.carlgallups.com/godsigneddna.html.

315. Di-sulfide bonds in DNA:

1. "Cross-Linking in DNA," 7/12/21. Accessed 2/12/22, https://chem.libretexts.org/Ancillary_Materials/Exemplars_and_Case_Studies/Exemplars/Biology/Cross-Linking_in_DNA."Disulfide bonds can play an important role in stabilizing the tertiary structure of proteins, lowering the

entropy of the three-dimensional structure." [Translation: Sometimes there are sulfuric "bridges' that hold the DNA together to keep it from collapsing in on itself, just like Dr. Rubinstein said.]

2. "Disulfide bonds in ER protein folding and homeostasis." Accessed 2/22/22, https://www.ncbi.nlm.nih.gov/pmc/articles/PMC3078216. "Disulfide bonds can stabilize a protein by reducing the entropy of the unfolded state."

3. M. J. Feige; J. Buchner J, "The Role of Disulfide Bonds in Protein Folding and Stability," In: Luis Moroder, Johannes Buchner, editors, *Oxidative Folding of Peptides and Proteins* (2010).

316. Carl Gallups, "More Info about This Video," Carlgallups.com. Accessed 4/3/22, http://www.carlgallups.com/godsigneddna.html.

317. Rubinstein, *Functional Nanomaterials*. Complete Publications. Curriculum Vitae.

318. This phenomenon might remind many of the well-known biological phenomenon of the Laminin protein molecule…appearing in the shape of a cross!

Laminins are a family of glycoproteins of the extracellular matrix of all animals. The proteins of Laminin intersect to form a distinctly cross-like structure that bind to other cell membrane and extracellular matrix molecules. Laminins vitally contribute to cell attachment and promotion of tissue survival.

See: M. A. Haralson; John R. Hassell (1995). Extracellular matrix: a practical approach. Ithaca, N.Y.: IRL Press.

Also see: "A Simplified Laminin Nomenclature," Sciencedirect.com, Matrix Biology

Volume 24, Issue 5, August 2005, Pages 326-332, https://www. sciencedirect.com/science/article/pii/S0945053X0500065X?via%3Dihub. Also see: Holly Colognato,Peter D. Yurchenco. "Form and function: The laminin family of heterotrimers," American Association for Anatomy, 5/24/00, https://anatomypubs.onlinelibrary.wiley.com/doi/10.1002/ (SICI)1097-0177(200006)218:2%3C213::AID-DVDY1%3E3.0.CO;2-R.

319. John 13:27–29.

320. John 14.

321. Translated means: "Peace be unto you! Bless the Name of the Lord!"

322. For this section I have admittedly taken liberties with the narrative. The Scriptures do not disclose all the exact and marvelous mysteries Jesus unveiled to His disciples. We are simply assured that He did indeed disclose one revelation after another. The ones I chose to put in Jesus' mouth are all backed by scriptural and scientific truths that we now know to be true. And most are backed by the Scriptures that Matthew, Peter, and John would later record in the surface text of the New Testament. Others were recorded by the Apostle Paul, years later, who also claimed to have been at the feet of the resurrected Jesus to receive the many revelations he wrote about. Many of the things I've written are undeniably possibile lessons that Jesus could have actually taught over the forty days He was among the disciples. The others may be open to debate, but yet again, there are elements of deep biblical truth in them. I urge you to simply enjoy the narrative and feel His presence, as though you were among the disciples that night.

323. Job 9:8.

324. Isaiah 52:13–5; Isaiah 53.

325. Psalm 22:16–18.

326. Psalm 22:6–8.

327. Zechariah 12:10.

328. 1 Corinthians 15:3–8.

329. John 21.

330. 1 John 5:11; Acts 4:12; John 14:6.

331. Numbers 6:7, "Pulpit Commentary," Biblehub.com, https://biblehub.com/commentaries/numbers/6-27.htm.
Henry Donald Maurice Spence-Jones was the vicar and rural dean of St. Pancras, London and the principal of Gloucester Theological College. He authored the entire *Pulpit Commentary* collection still widely used by biblical scholars today. Doctor of Divinity from Cambridge University. "Pulpit Commentary." Accessed 4/2/22, https://en.wikipedia.org/wiki/Pulpit_Commentary.

332. 2 Peter 1:4.

333. Romans 8:29; 2 Corinthians 3:18.

334. Ada Yardeni (1997), *The Book of Hebrew Script* (Jerusalem: Carta: 13.15.17.)

335. Jonathan P. Siegel, "The Evolution of Two Hebrew Scripts," *Biblical Archaeology Review 5:3*, May/June 1979, https://www.baslibrary.org/biblical-archaeology-review/5/3/4. "Paleo-Hebrew or Phoenician script was used before Aramaic script was introduced by Jews returning from Babylonia."